THE MIGHTY

VOLUME **ONE**

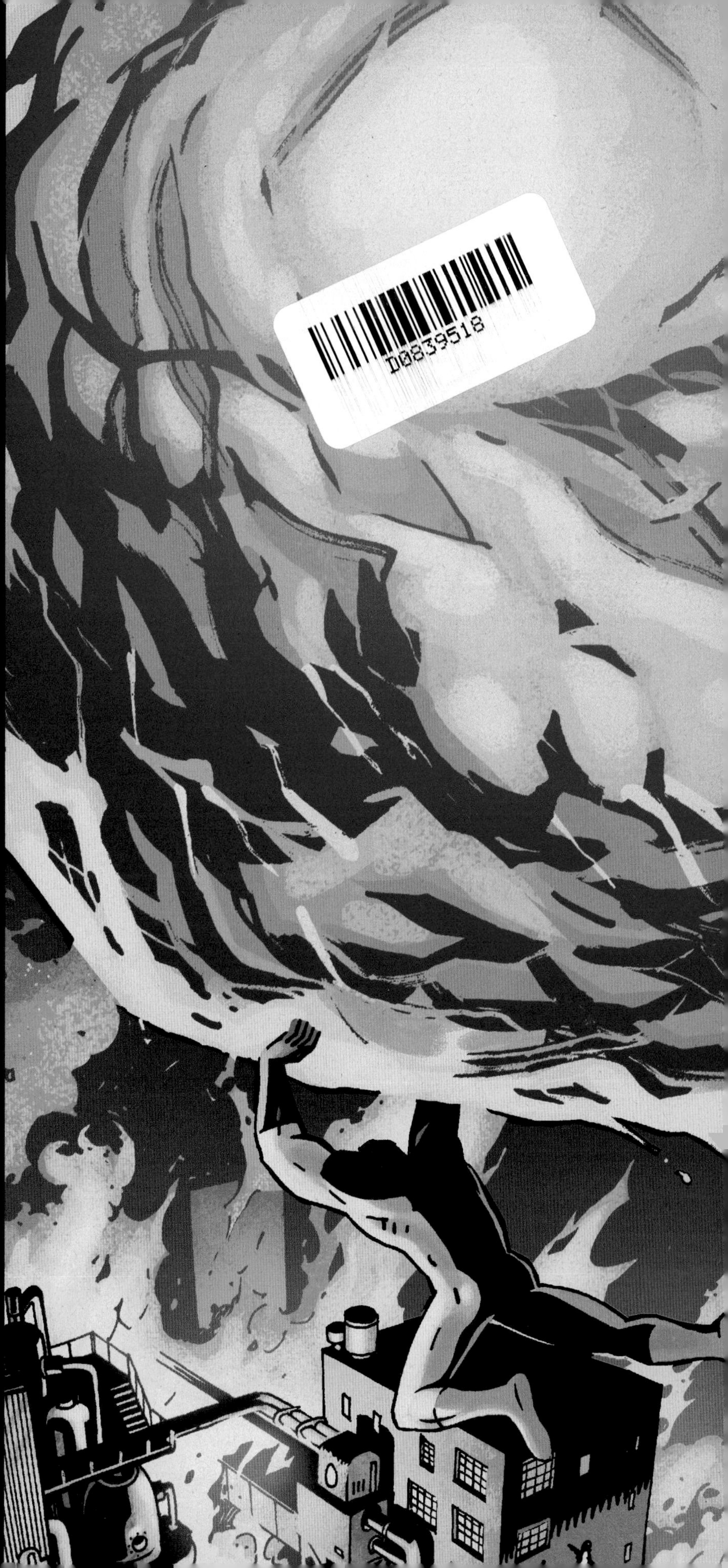

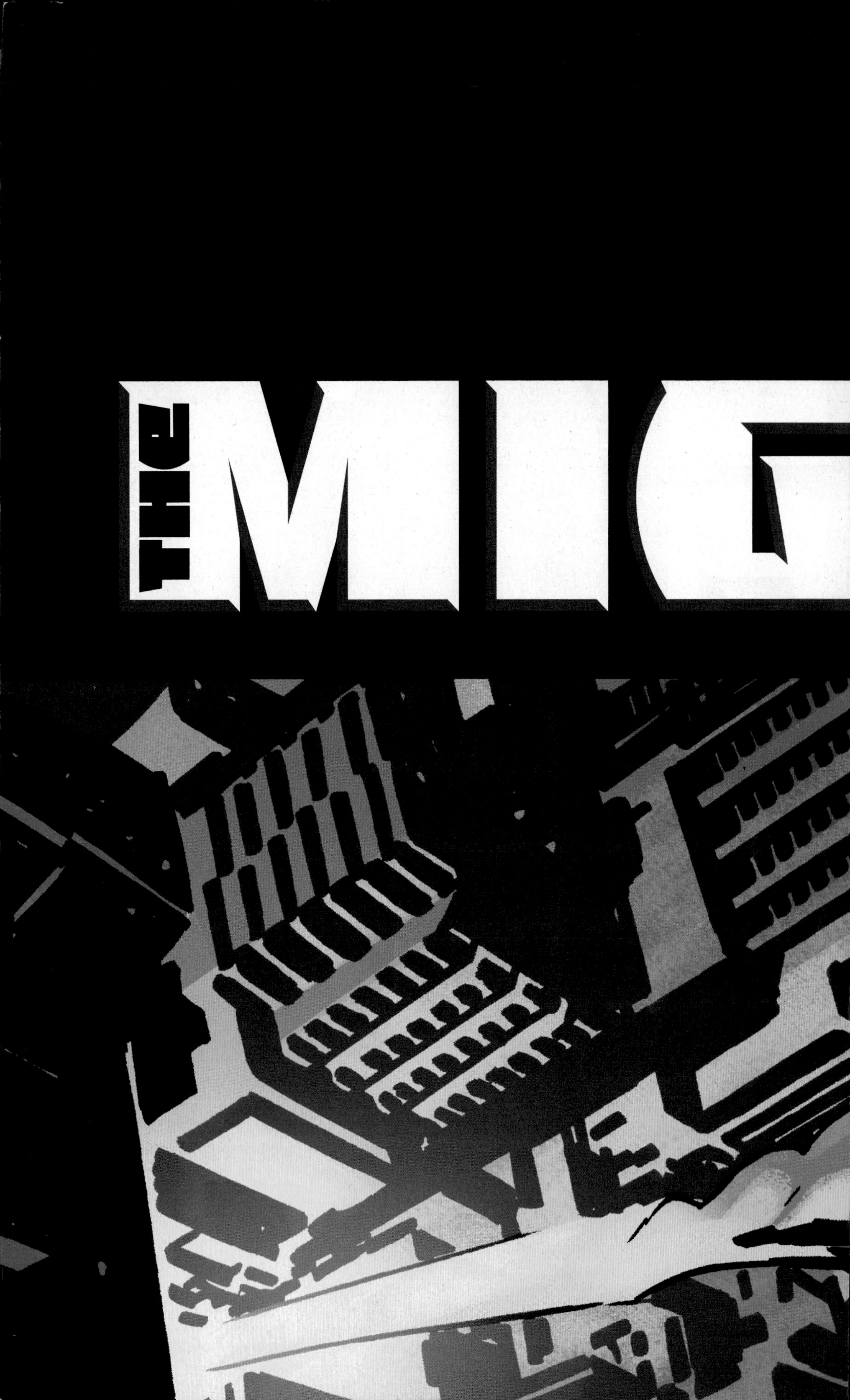
THE MIG

Peter J. Tomasi and **Keith Champagne** Writers

Peter Snejbjerg (Chapters 1-4) **Chris Samnee** (Chapters 5-6) Artists

John Kalisz Colorist

Rob Leigh Letterer

Dave Johnson Original Series Covers

HTY

THE MIGHTY created by **Peter J. Tomasi**, **Keith Champagne** and **Peter Snejbjerg**

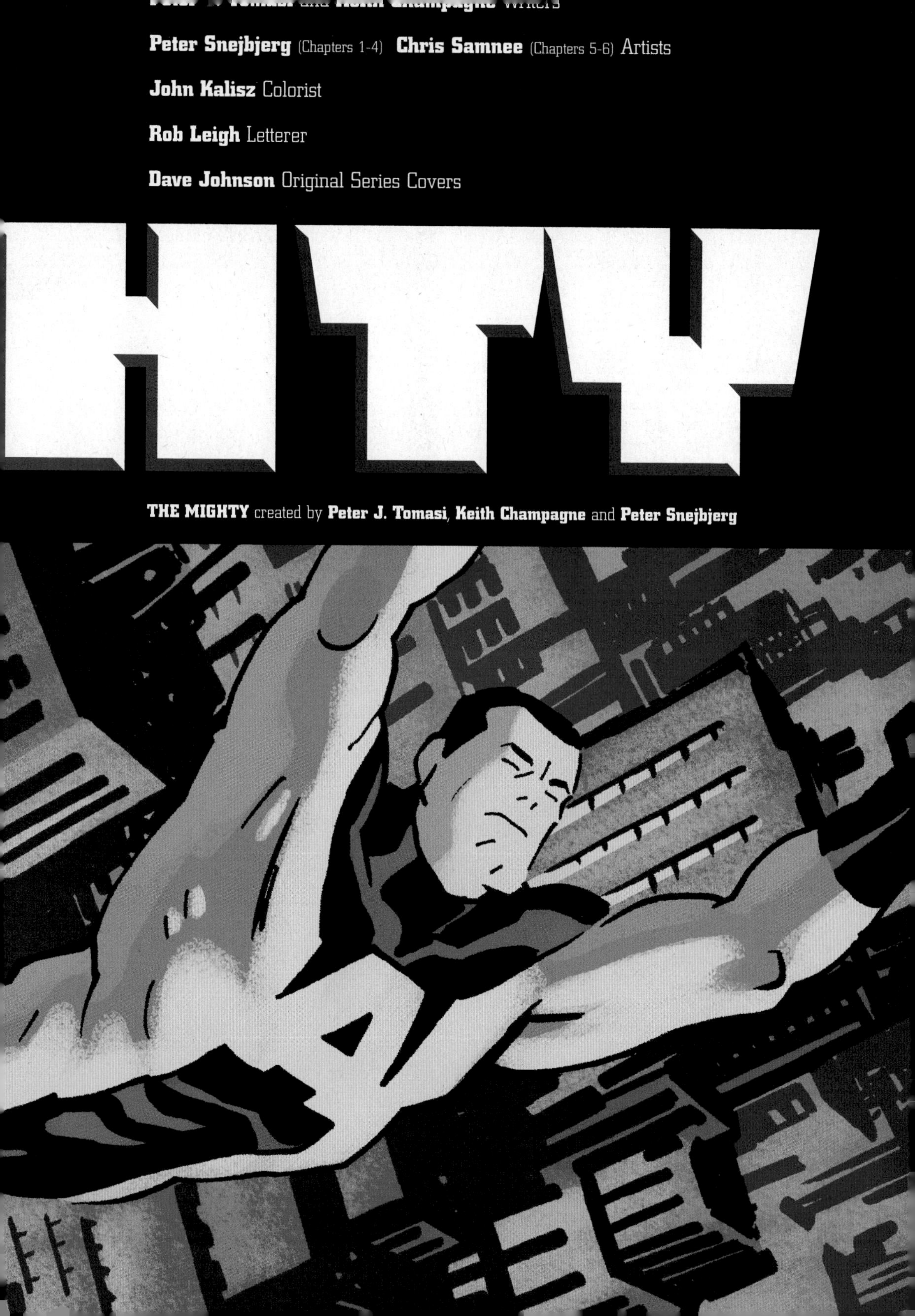

Dan DiDio SVP – Executive Editor
Joey Cavalieri Editor – Original Series
Chris Conroy Assistant Editor – Original Series
Georg Brewer VP – Design & DC Direct Creative
Bob Harras Group Editor – Collected Editions
Scott Nybakken Editor
Robbin Brosterman Design Director – Books

DC COMICS
Paul Levitz President & Publisher
Richard Bruning SVP-Creative Director
Patrick Caldon EVP – Finance & Operations
Amy Genkins SVP – Business & Legal Affairs
Jim Lee Editorial Director – WildStorm
Gregory Noveck SVP – Creative Affairs
Steve Rotterdam SVP – Sales & Marketing
Cheryl Rubin SVP – Brand Management

Cover art by **Dave Johnson**

THE MIGHTY VOLUME ONE
Published by DC Comics.

DC Comics, 1700 Broadway, New York, NY 10019
A Warner Bros. Entertainment Company
Printed by World Color Press, Inc.,
St-Romuald, QC, Canada 11/25/09
First Printing. ISBN: 978-1-4012-2511-7

SUSTAINABLE FORESTRY INITIATIVE
Certified Fiber Sourcing
www.sfiprogram.org

Fiber used in this product line meets the sourcing requirements of the SFI program. www.sfiprogram.org PWC-SFICOC-260

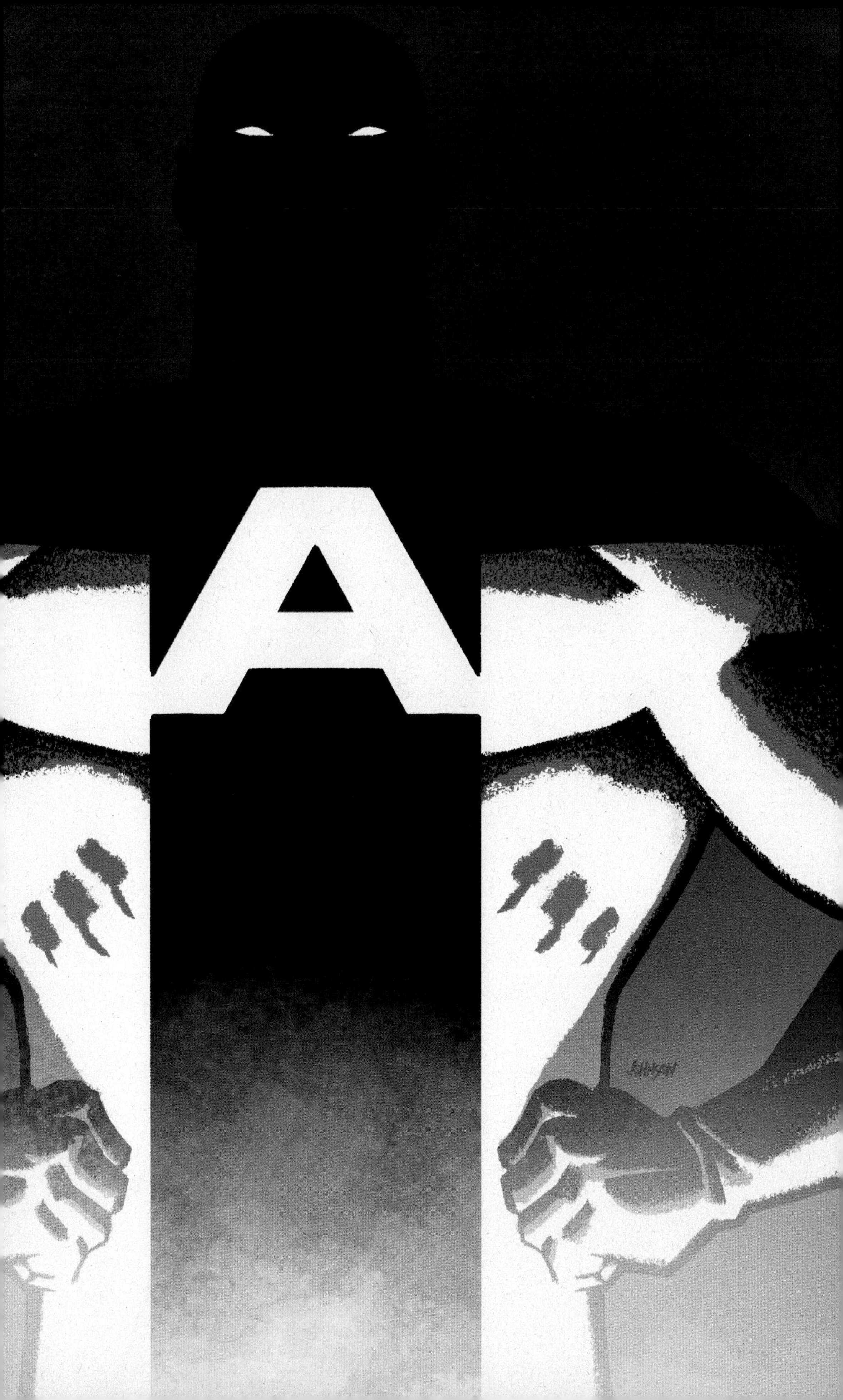
JOHNSON

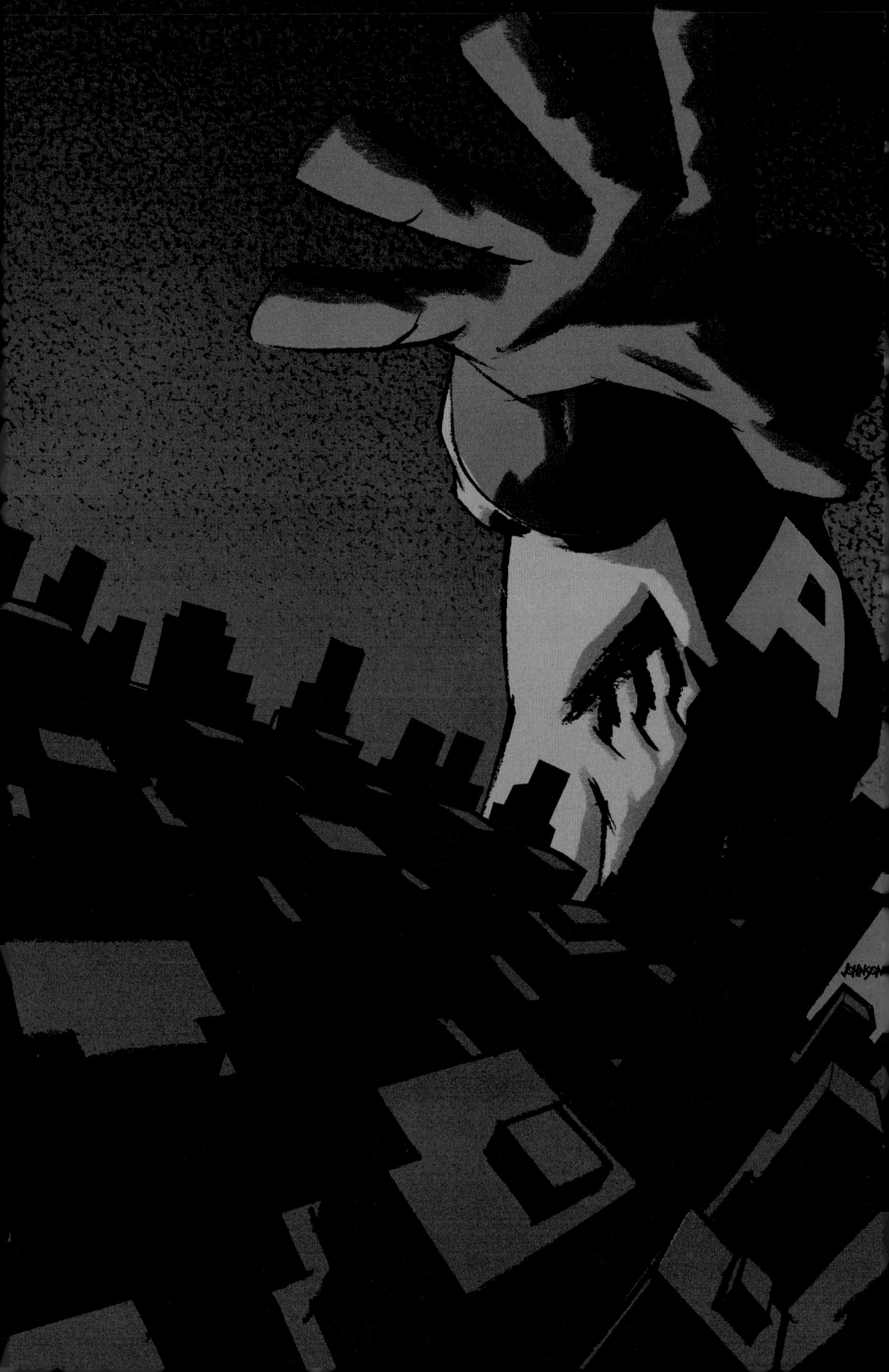
JOHNSON

DECEMBER 17th, 1952.

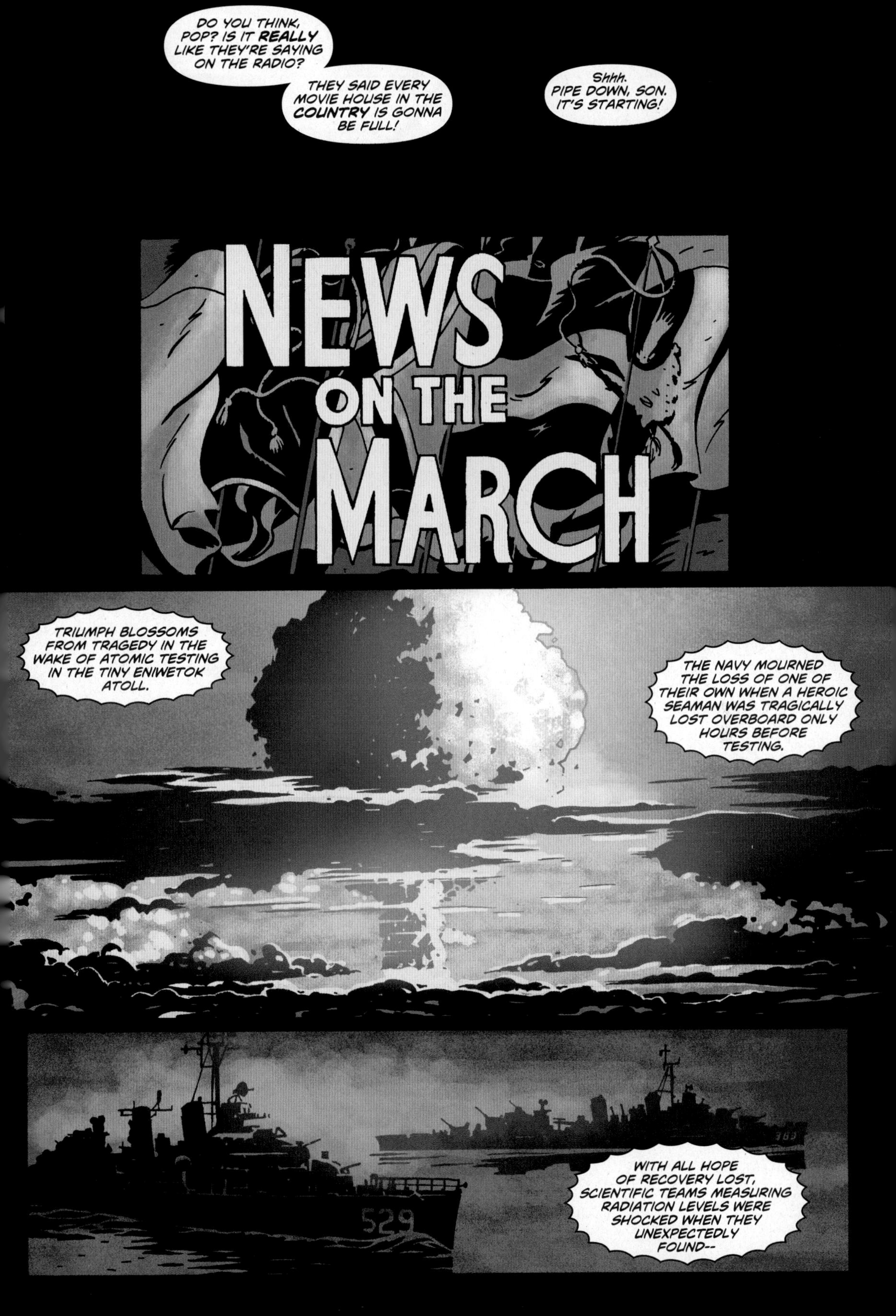
DO YOU THINK, POP? IS IT REALLY LIKE THEY'RE SAYING ON THE RADIO?
THEY SAID EVERY MOVIE HOUSE IN THE COUNTRY IS GONNA BE FULL!
Shhh. PIPE DOWN, SON. IT'S STARTING!
NEWS ON THE MARCH
TRIUMPH BLOSSOMS FROM TRAGEDY IN THE WAKE OF ATOMIC TESTING IN THE TINY ENIWETOK ATOLL.
THE NAVY MOURNED THE LOSS OF ONE OF THEIR OWN WHEN A HEROIC SEAMAN WAS TRAGICALLY LOST OVERBOARD ONLY HOURS BEFORE TESTING.
529
WITH ALL HOPE OF RECOVERY LOST, SCIENTIFIC TEAMS MEASURING RADIATION LEVELS WERE SHOCKED WHEN THEY UNEXPECTEDLY FOUND--

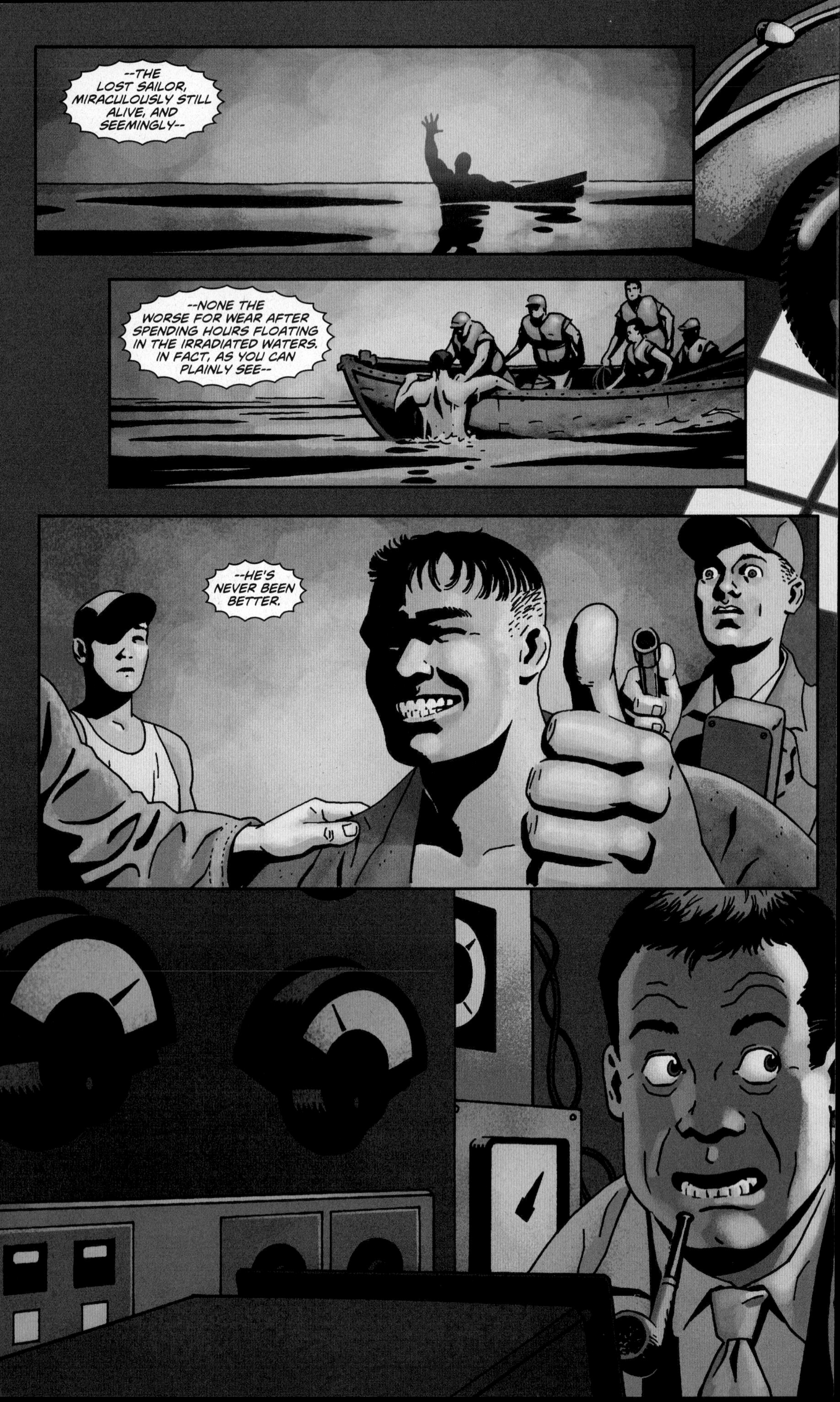
--THE LOST SAILOR, MIRACULOUSLY STILL ALIVE, AND SEEMINGLY--
--NONE THE WORSE FOR WEAR AFTER SPENDING HOURS FLOATING IN THE IRRADIATED WATERS. IN FACT, AS YOU CAN PLAINLY SEE--
--HE'S NEVER BEEN BETTER.

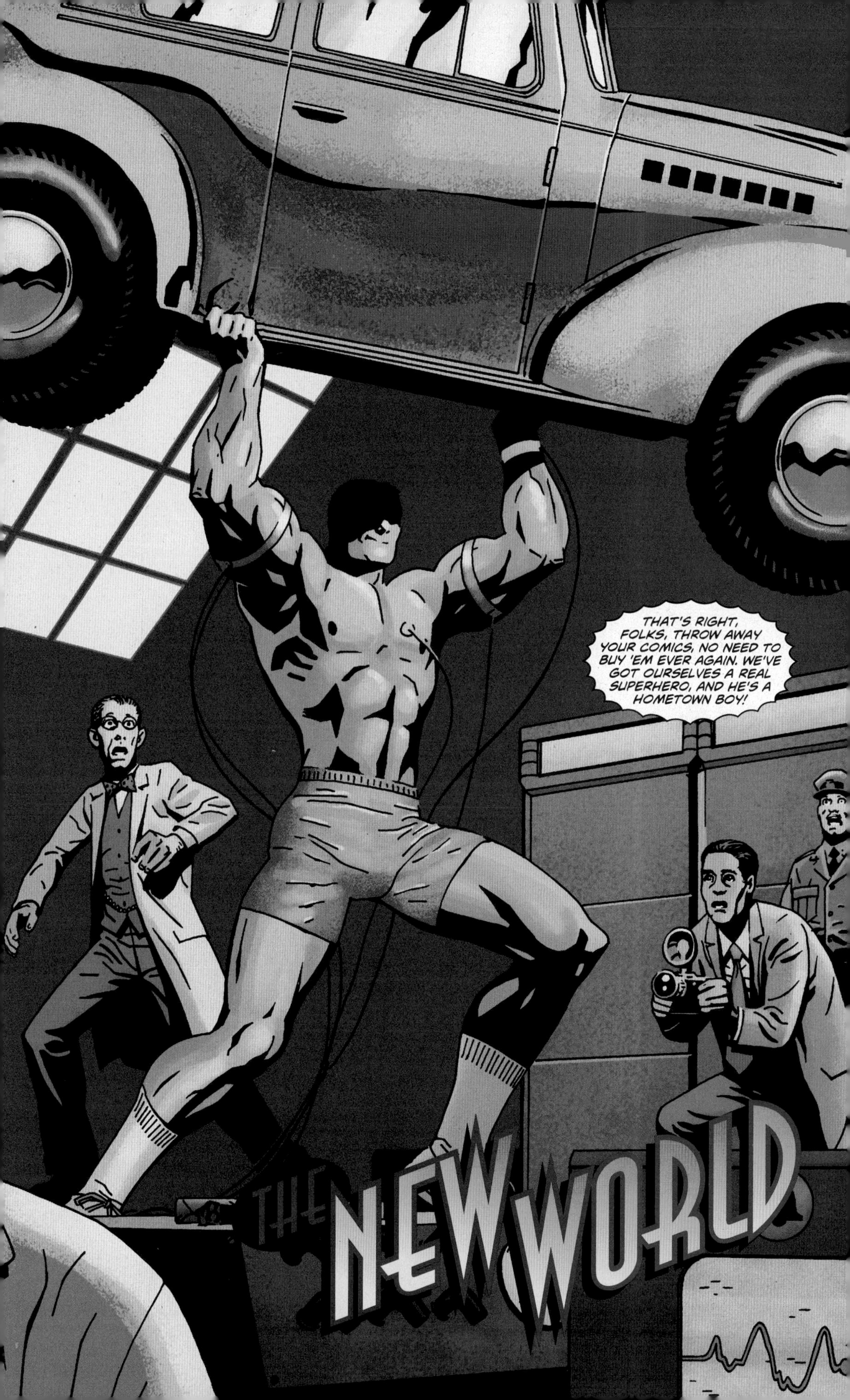
THAT'S RIGHT, FOLKS, THROW AWAY YOUR COMICS, NO NEED TO BUY 'EM EVER AGAIN. WE'VE GOT OURSELVES A REAL SUPERHERO, AND HE'S A HOMETOWN BOY!
THE NEW WORLD

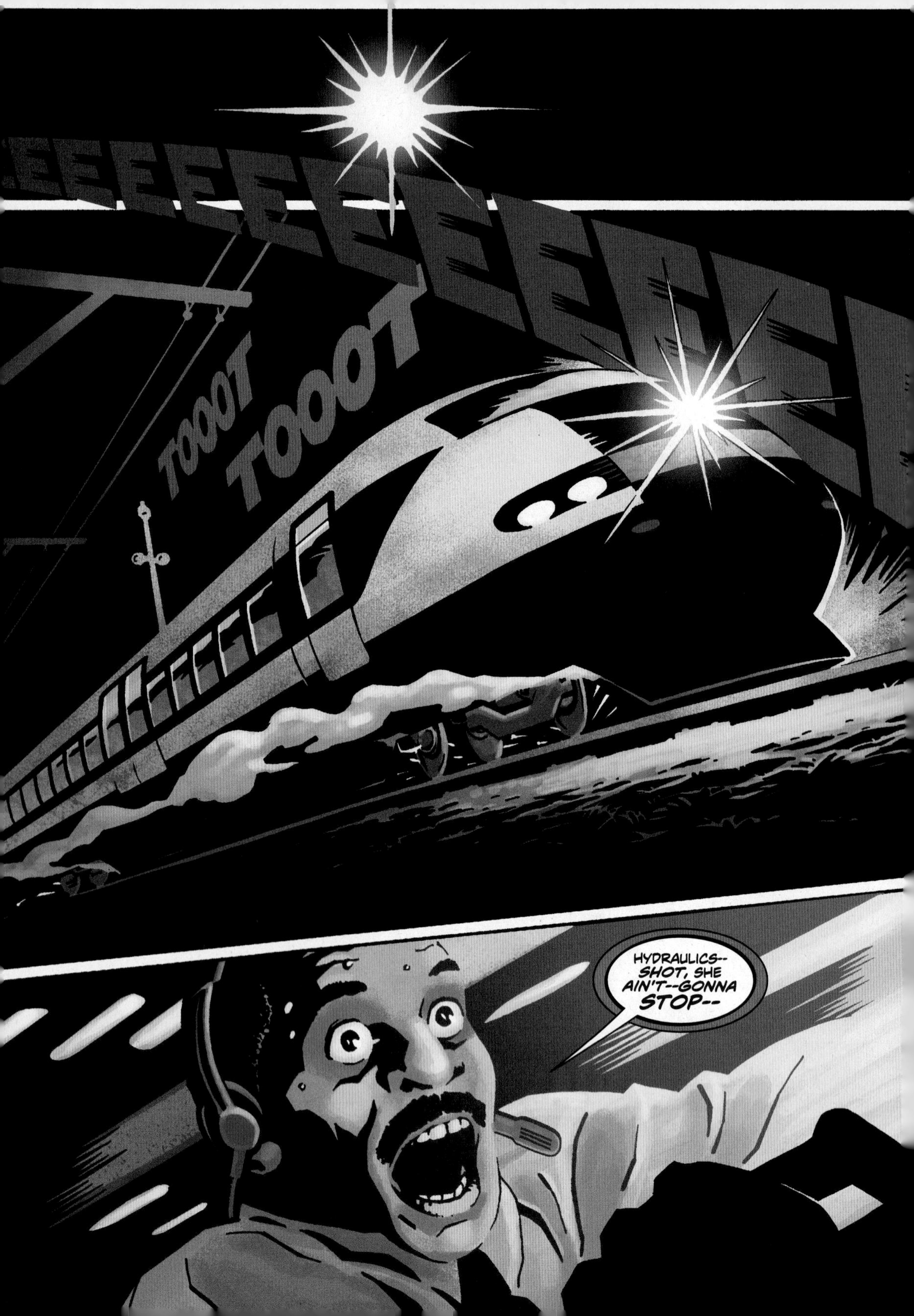
EEEEEEEEEEE
TOOOT
TOOOT
HYDRAULICS--SHOT, SHE AIN'T--GONNA STOP--

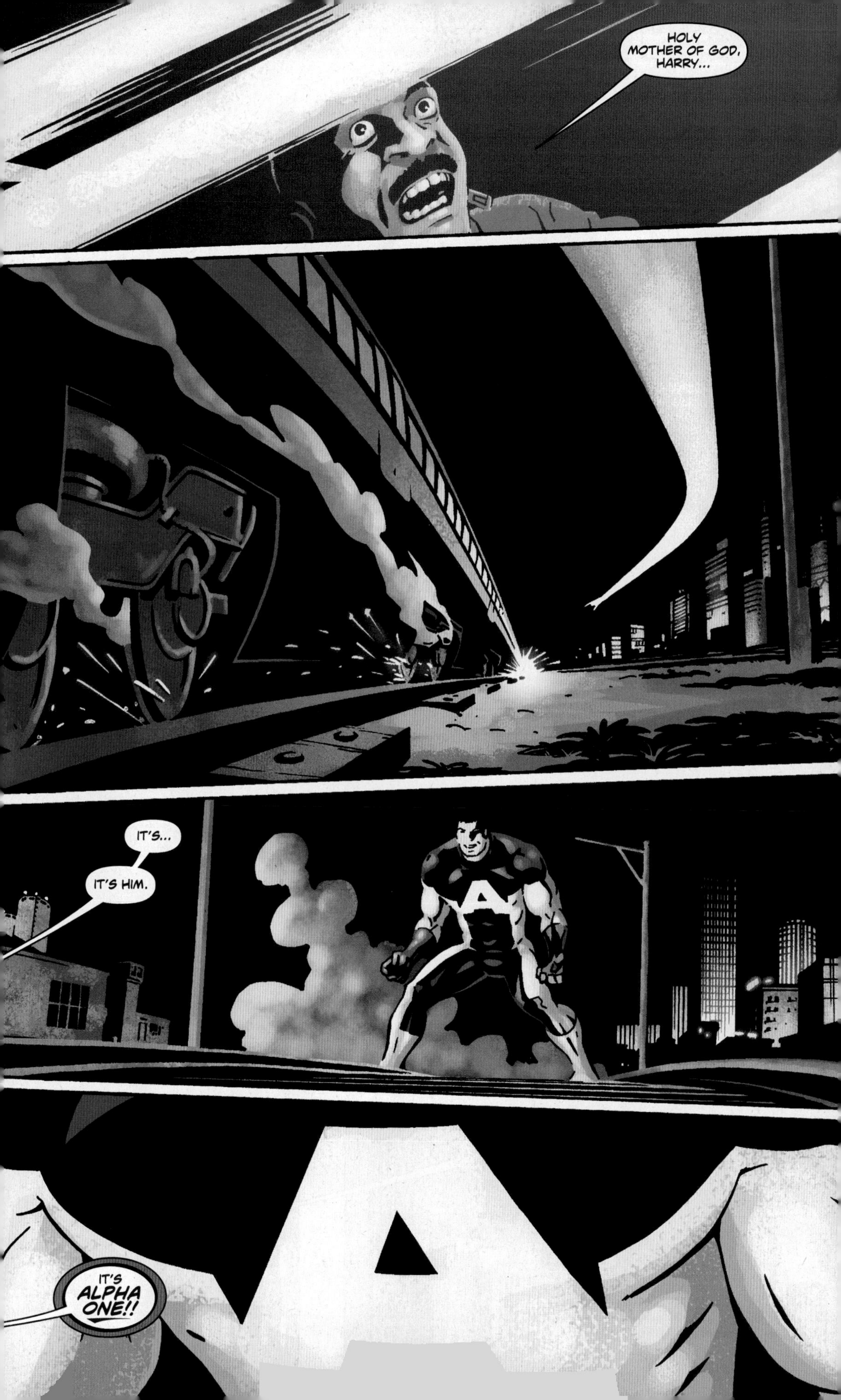
HOLY MOTHER OF GOD, HARRY...
IT'S...
IT'S HIM.
IT'S ALPHA ONE!!

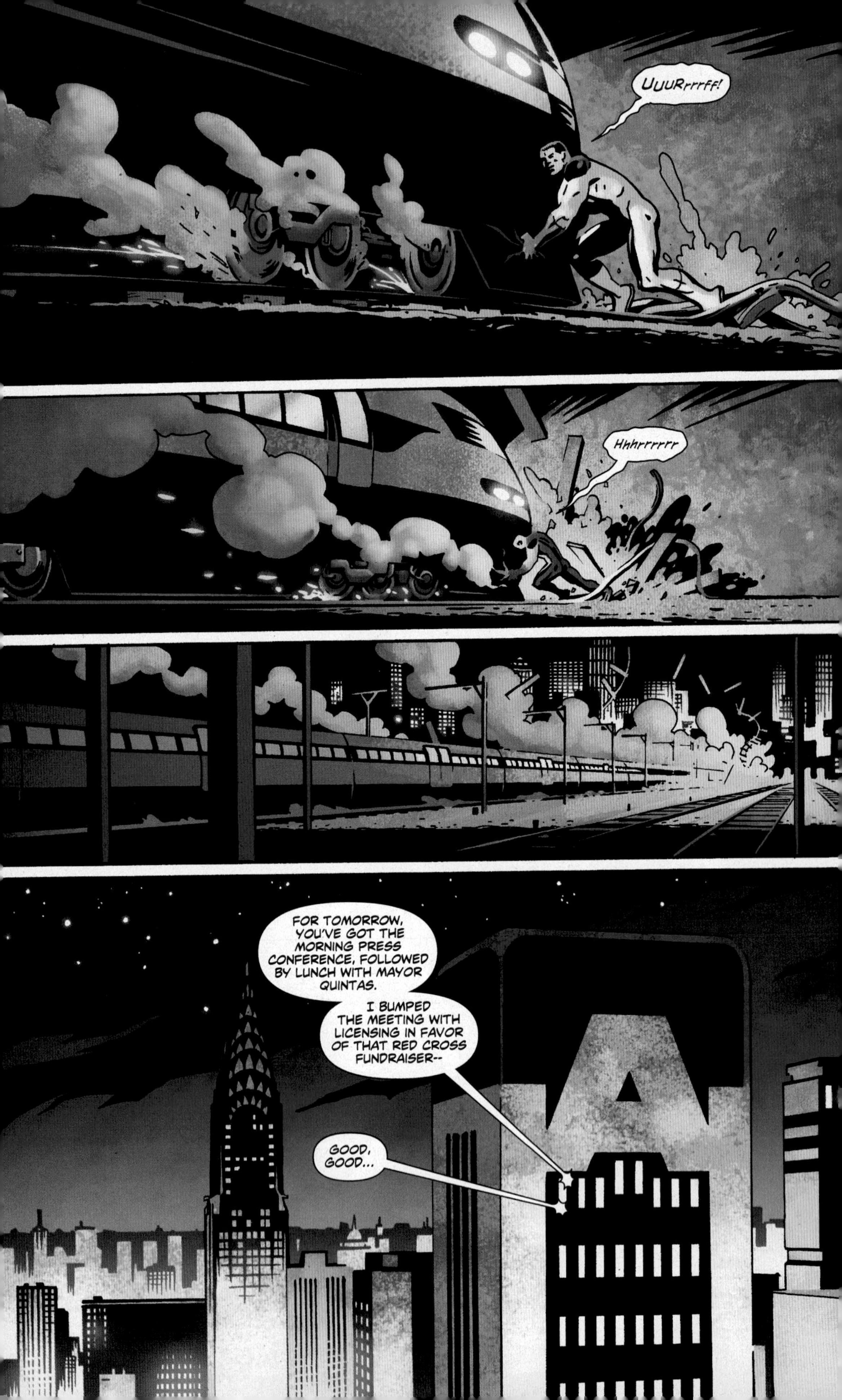
UUURrrrff!
Hhhrrrrrr
FOR TOMORROW, YOU'VE GOT THE MORNING PRESS CONFERENCE, FOLLOWED BY LUNCH WITH MAYOR QUINTAS.
I BUMPED THE MEETING WITH LICENSING IN FAVOR OF THAT RED CROSS FUNDRAISER--
GOOD, GOOD...

ONE MORE THING, MON CAPITAINE.

MR. SPIELBERG REQUESTED THAT YOU SIT NEXT TO HIM AT HIS PREMIERE TOMORROW NIGHT.

AGAIN? FINE, *LANA*, BUT PLEASE...

...NO SALT ON MY POPCORN THIS TIME.

UNDERSTOOD. I'LL PUT IT ON YOUR MILK DUDS INSTEAD.

EXCUSE ME, *CAPTAIN SHAW*?

IF YOU WOULDN'T MIND SITTING DOWN, THE FEED IS *LIVE*.

SAM IS COMING BACK FROM COMMERCIAL AT T-MINUS FIVE, FOUR, THREE, TWO...

DON'T FORGET ONE. IT'S THE LONELIEST NUMBER, AFTER ALL.

JOINING US NOW, LIVE VIA SATELLITE, IS CAPTAIN MICHAEL SHAW, HEAD OF *SECTION OMEGA*.

CAPTAIN, YOU HEAD THE FIRST AND *ONLY* INDEPENDENTLY FUNDED, *NATIONWIDE POLICE FORCE* DEDICATED EXCLUSIVELY TO *ALPHA ONE*.

TELL ME, CAPTAIN, WHO *FUNDS* SECTION OMEGA?

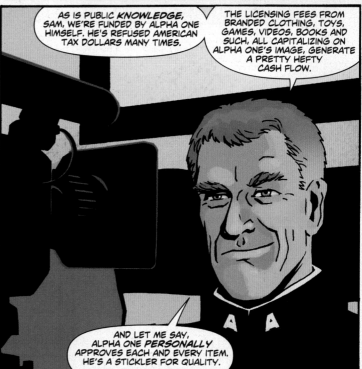

AS IS PUBLIC *KNOWLEDGE*, SAM, WE'RE FUNDED BY ALPHA ONE HIMSELF. HE'S REFUSED AMERICAN TAX DOLLARS MANY TIMES.

THE LICENSING FEES FROM BRANDED CLOTHING, TOYS, GAMES, VIDEOS, BOOKS AND SUCH, ALL CAPITALIZING ON ALPHA ONE'S IMAGE, GENERATE A PRETTY HEFTY CASH FLOW.

AND LET ME SAY, ALPHA ONE *PERSONALLY* APPROVES EACH AND EVERY ITEM. HE'S A STICKLER FOR QUALITY.

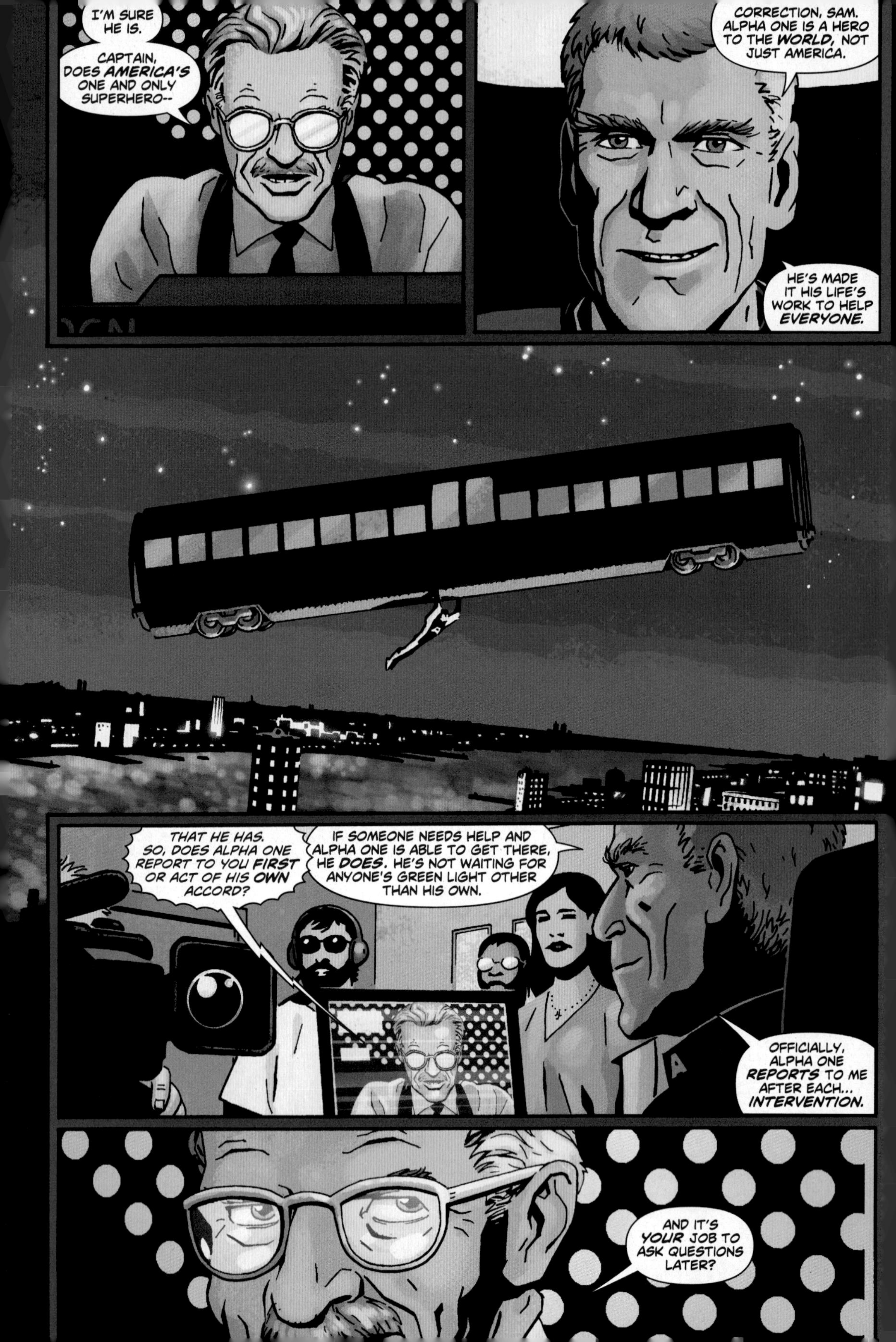
I'M SURE HE IS.
CAPTAIN, DOES AMERICA'S ONE AND ONLY SUPERHERO--
CORRECTION, SAM. ALPHA ONE IS A HERO TO THE WORLD, NOT JUST AMERICA.
HE'S MADE IT HIS LIFE'S WORK TO HELP EVERYONE.
THAT HE HAS. SO, DOES ALPHA ONE REPORT TO YOU FIRST OR ACT OF HIS OWN ACCORD?
IF SOMEONE NEEDS HELP AND ALPHA ONE IS ABLE TO GET THERE, HE DOES. HE'S NOT WAITING FOR ANYONE'S GREEN LIGHT OTHER THAN HIS OWN.
OFFICIALLY, ALPHA ONE REPORTS TO ME AFTER EACH... INTERVENTION.
AND IT'S YOUR JOB TO ASK QUESTIONS LATER?

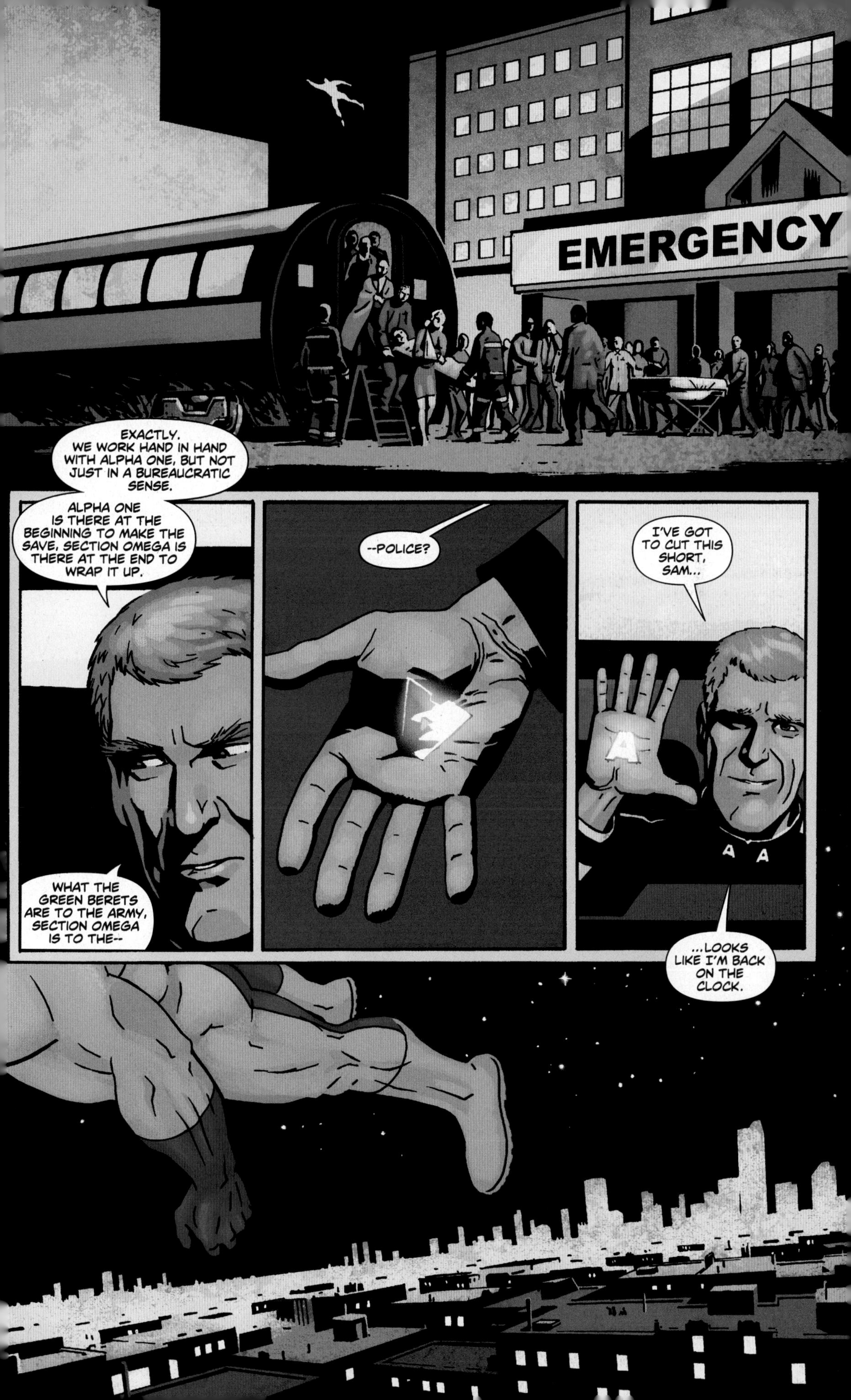
EMERGENCY
EXACTLY. WE WORK HAND IN HAND WITH ALPHA ONE, BUT NOT JUST IN A BUREAUCRATIC SENSE.
ALPHA ONE IS THERE AT THE BEGINNING TO MAKE THE SAVE, SECTION OMEGA IS THERE AT THE END TO WRAP IT UP.
WHAT THE GREEN BERETS ARE TO THE ARMY, SECTION OMEGA IS TO THE--
--POLICE?
I'VE GOT TO CUT THIS SHORT, SAM...
...LOOKS LIKE I'M BACK ON THE CLOCK.

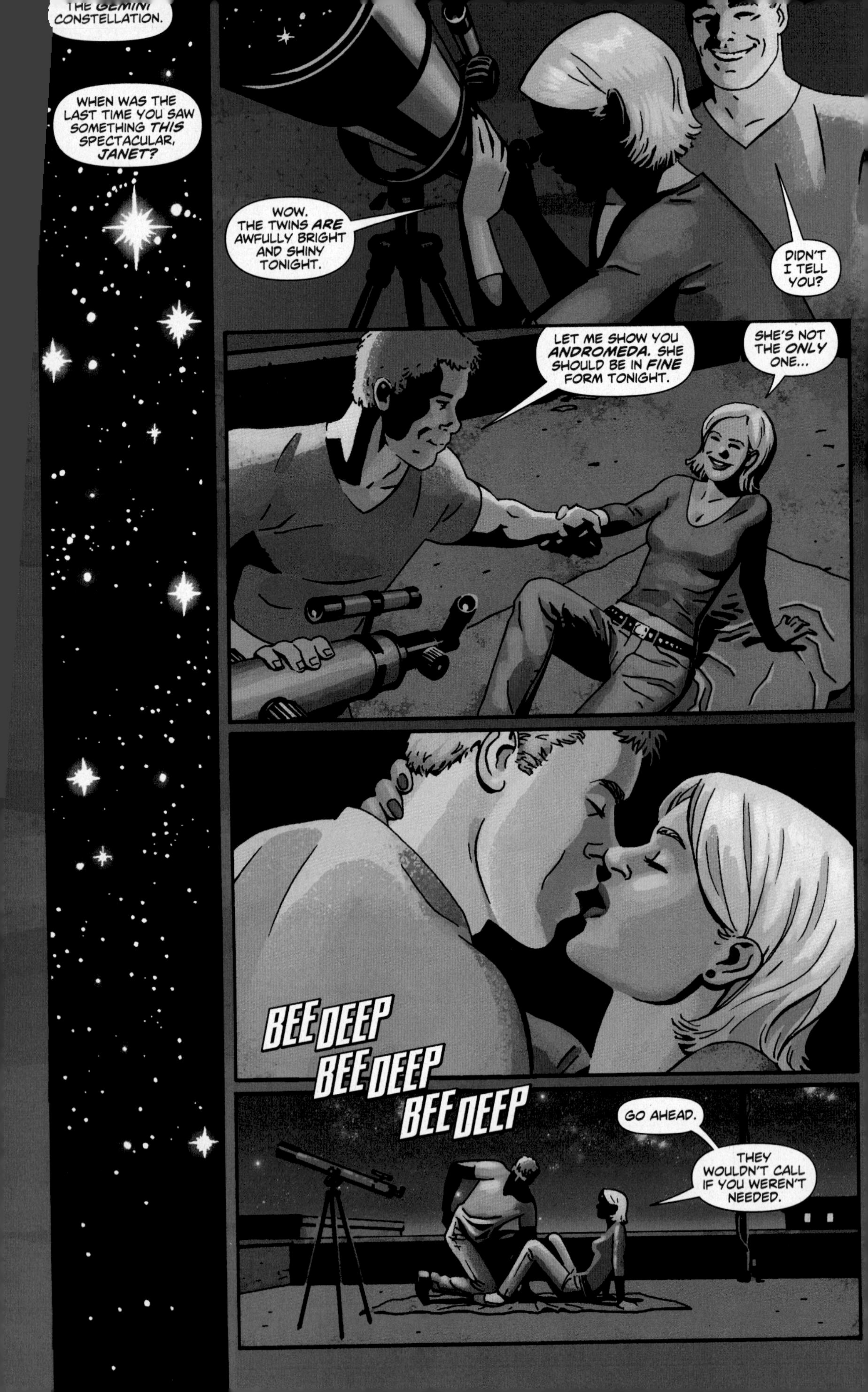
THE GEMINI CONSTELLATION.
WHEN WAS THE LAST TIME YOU SAW SOMETHING THIS SPECTACULAR, JANET?
WOW. THE TWINS ARE AWFULLY BRIGHT AND SHINY TONIGHT.
DIDN'T I TELL YOU?
LET ME SHOW YOU ANDROMEDA. SHE SHOULD BE IN FINE FORM TONIGHT.
SHE'S NOT THE ONLY ONE...
BEE DEEP
BEE DEEP
BEE DEEP
GO AHEAD.
THEY WOULDN'T CALL IF YOU WEREN'T NEEDED.

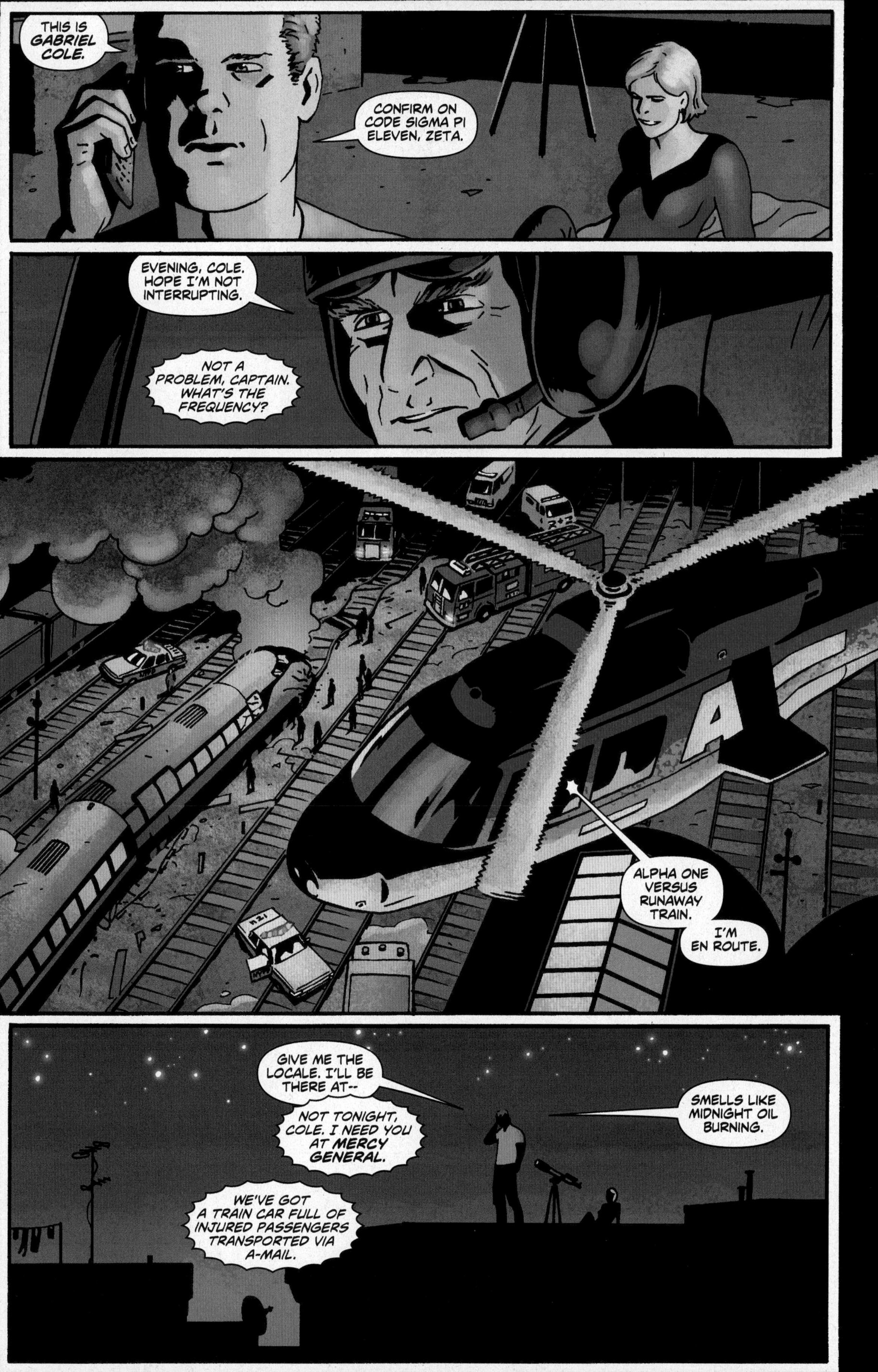
THIS IS GABRIEL COLE.
CONFIRM ON CODE SIGMA PI ELEVEN, ZETA.
EVENING, COLE. HOPE I'M NOT INTERRUPTING.
NOT A PROBLEM, CAPTAIN. WHAT'S THE FREQUENCY?
ALPHA ONE VERSUS RUNAWAY TRAIN.
I'M EN ROUTE.
GIVE ME THE LOCALE. I'LL BE THERE AT--
NOT TONIGHT, COLE. I NEED YOU AT MERCY GENERAL.
WE'VE GOT A TRAIN CAR FULL OF INJURED PASSENGERS TRANSPORTED VIA A-MAIL.
SMELLS LIKE MIDNIGHT OIL BURNING.

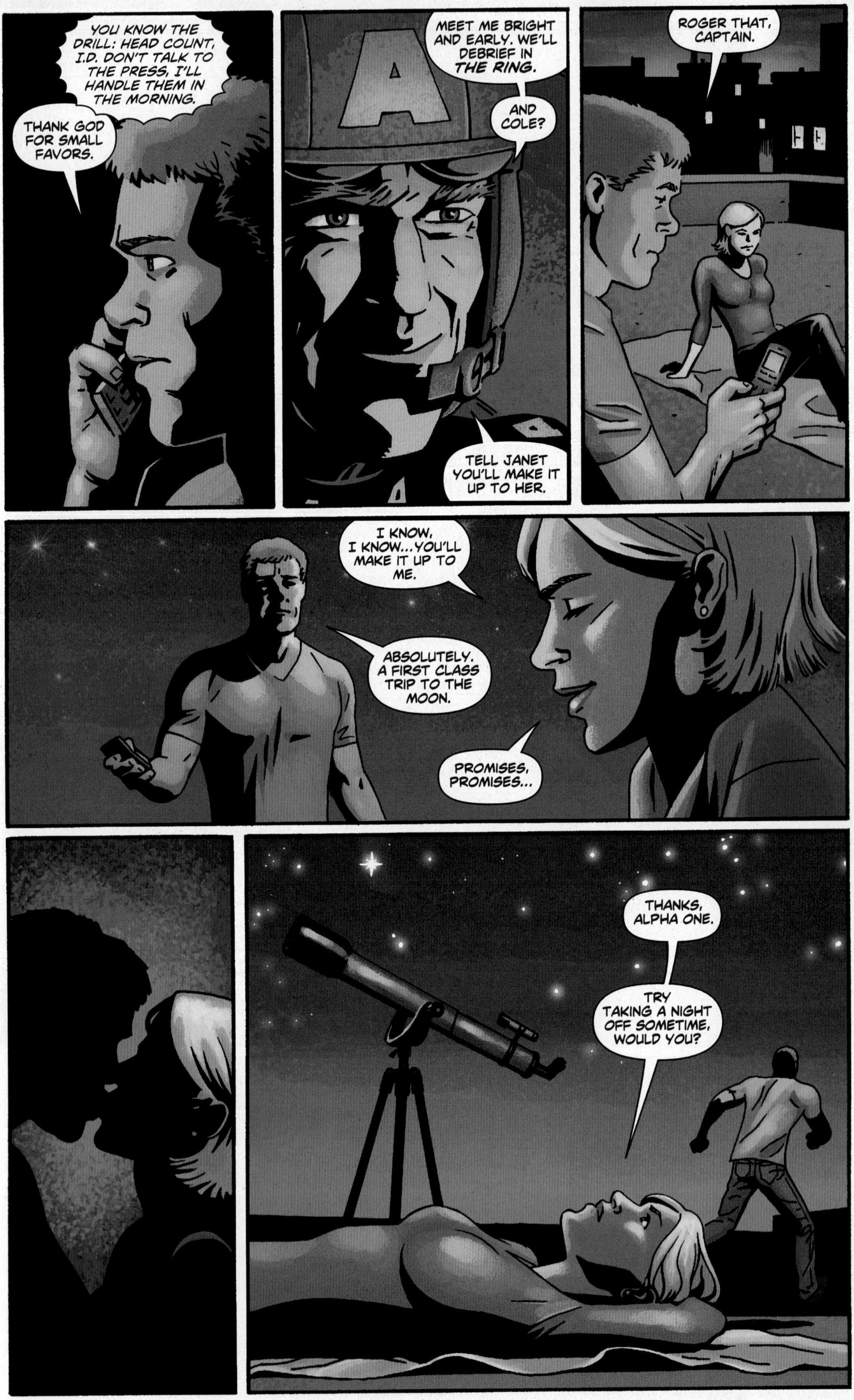
YOU KNOW THE DRILL: HEAD COUNT, I.D. DON'T TALK TO THE PRESS, I'LL HANDLE THEM IN THE MORNING.
THANK GOD FOR SMALL FAVORS.
MEET ME BRIGHT AND EARLY. WE'LL DEBRIEF IN THE RING.
AND COLE?
TELL JANET YOU'LL MAKE IT UP TO HER.
ROGER THAT, CAPTAIN.
I KNOW, I KNOW...YOU'LL MAKE IT UP TO ME.
ABSOLUTELY. A FIRST CLASS TRIP TO THE MOON.
PROMISES, PROMISES...
THANKS, ALPHA ONE.
TRY TAKING A NIGHT OFF SOMETIME, WOULD YOU?

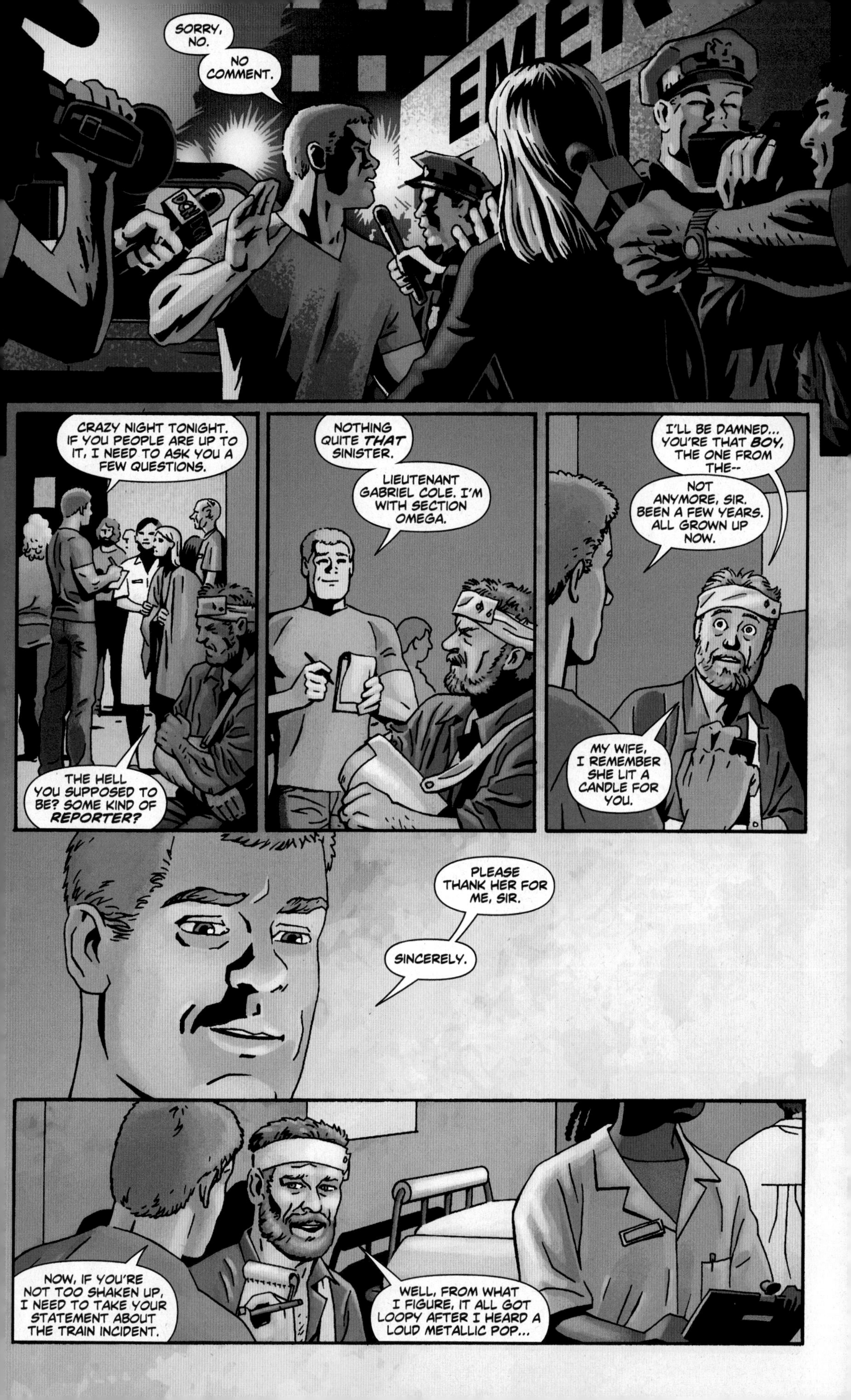
SORRY, NO.
NO COMMENT.
CRAZY NIGHT TONIGHT. IF YOU PEOPLE ARE UP TO IT, I NEED TO ASK YOU A FEW QUESTIONS.
THE HELL YOU SUPPOSED TO BE? SOME KIND OF *REPORTER*?
NOTHING QUITE *THAT* SINISTER.
LIEUTENANT GABRIEL COLE. I'M WITH SECTION OMEGA.
I'LL BE DAMNED... YOU'RE THAT *BOY*, THE ONE FROM THE--
NOT ANYMORE, SIR. BEEN A FEW YEARS. ALL GROWN UP NOW.
MY WIFE, I REMEMBER SHE LIT A CANDLE FOR YOU.
PLEASE THANK HER FOR ME, SIR.
SINCERELY.
NOW, IF YOU'RE NOT TOO SHAKEN UP, I NEED TO TAKE YOUR STATEMENT ABOUT THE TRAIN INCIDENT.
WELL, FROM WHAT I FIGURE, IT ALL GOT LOOPY AFTER I HEARD A LOUD METALLIC POP...

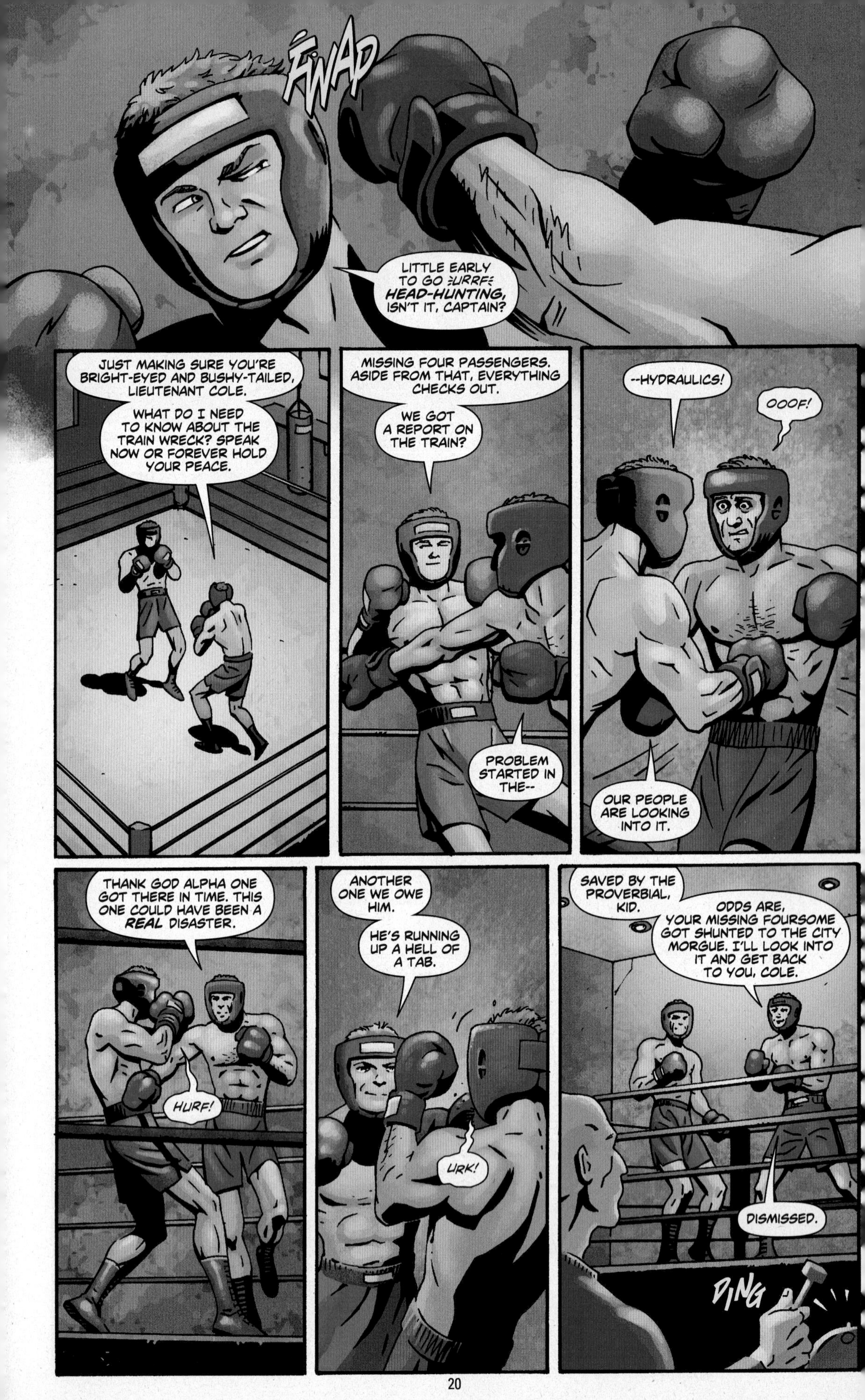
FWAP
LITTLE EARLY TO GO =URRF= HEAD-HUNTING, ISN'T IT, CAPTAIN?
JUST MAKING SURE YOU'RE BRIGHT-EYED AND BUSHY-TAILED, LIEUTENANT COLE.
WHAT DO I NEED TO KNOW ABOUT THE TRAIN WRECK? SPEAK NOW OR FOREVER HOLD YOUR PEACE.
MISSING FOUR PASSENGERS. ASIDE FROM THAT, EVERYTHING CHECKS OUT.
WE GOT A REPORT ON THE TRAIN?
PROBLEM STARTED IN THE--
--HYDRAULICS!
OOOF!
OUR PEOPLE ARE LOOKING INTO IT.
THANK GOD ALPHA ONE GOT THERE IN TIME. THIS ONE COULD HAVE BEEN A REAL DISASTER.
HURF!
ANOTHER ONE WE OWE HIM.
HE'S RUNNING UP A HELL OF A TAB.
URK!
SAVED BY THE PROVERBIAL, KID.
ODDS ARE, YOUR MISSING FOURSOME GOT SHUNTED TO THE CITY MORGUE. I'LL LOOK INTO IT AND GET BACK TO YOU, COLE.
DISMISSED.
DING

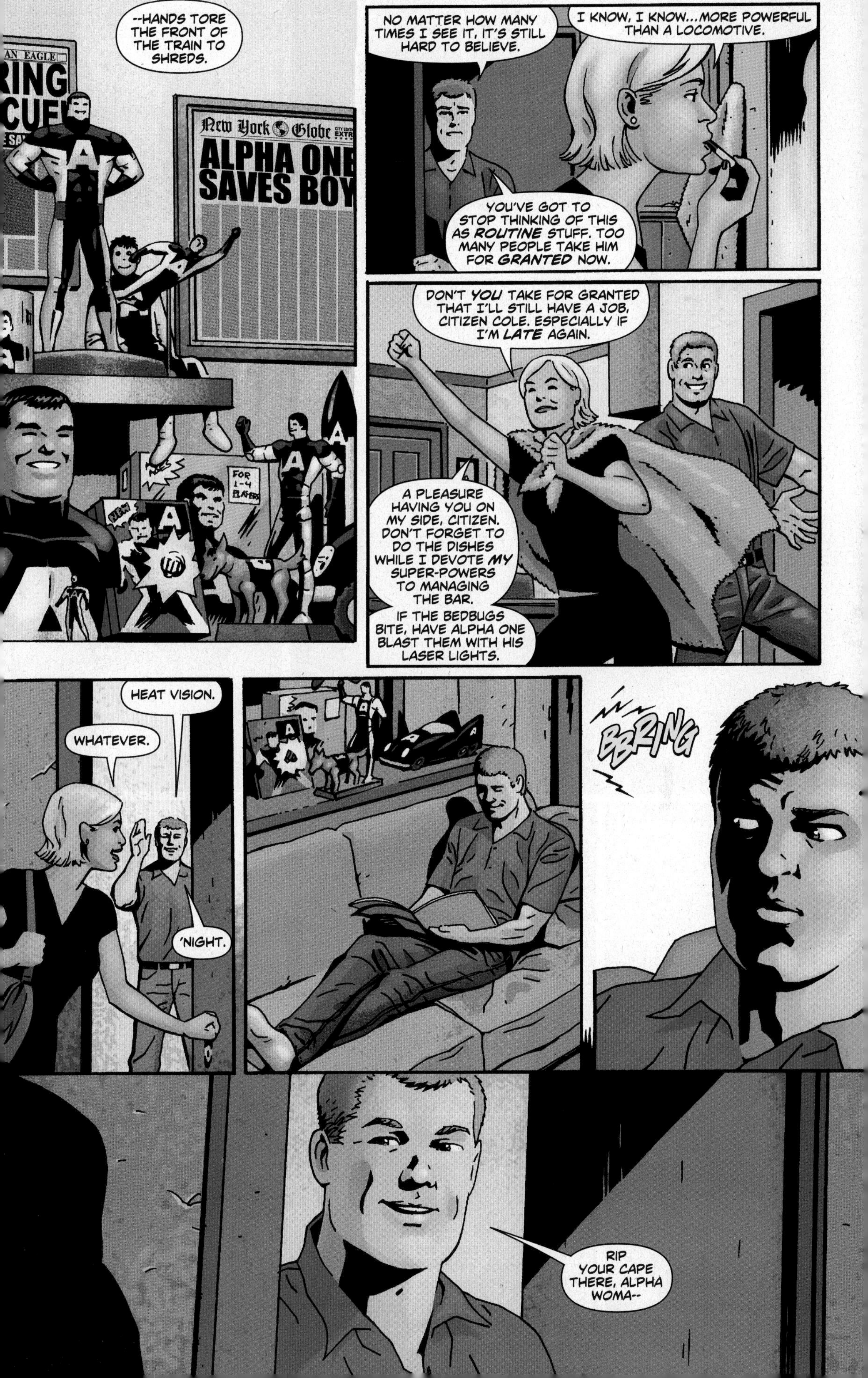

--HANDS TORE THE FRONT OF THE TRAIN TO SHREDS.
New York Globe
FOR 1-4 PLAYERS
NO MATTER HOW MANY TIMES I SEE IT, IT'S STILL HARD TO BELIEVE.
I KNOW, I KNOW... MORE POWERFUL THAN A LOCOMOTIVE.
YOU'VE GOT TO STOP THINKING OF THIS AS ROUTINE STUFF. TOO MANY PEOPLE TAKE HIM FOR GRANTED NOW.
DON'T YOU TAKE FOR GRANTED THAT I'LL STILL HAVE A JOB, CITIZEN COLE. ESPECIALLY IF I'M LATE AGAIN.
A PLEASURE HAVING YOU ON MY SIDE, CITIZEN. DON'T FORGET TO DO THE DISHES WHILE I DEVOTE MY SUPER-POWERS TO MANAGING THE BAR.
IF THE BEDBUGS BITE, HAVE ALPHA ONE BLAST THEM WITH HIS LASER LIGHTS.
HEAT VISION.
WHATEVER.
'NIGHT.
BBRING
RIP YOUR CAPE THERE, ALPHA WOMA--

CAPTAIN!!

MY GOD, WHAT--?

hhhhhhh

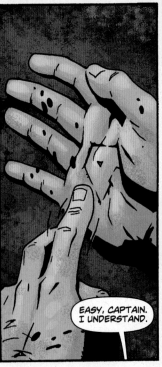

EASY, CAPTAIN. I UNDERSTAND.

TRY TO RELAX. SAVE YOUR STRENGTH.

I'M ACTIVATING THE SIGNAL.

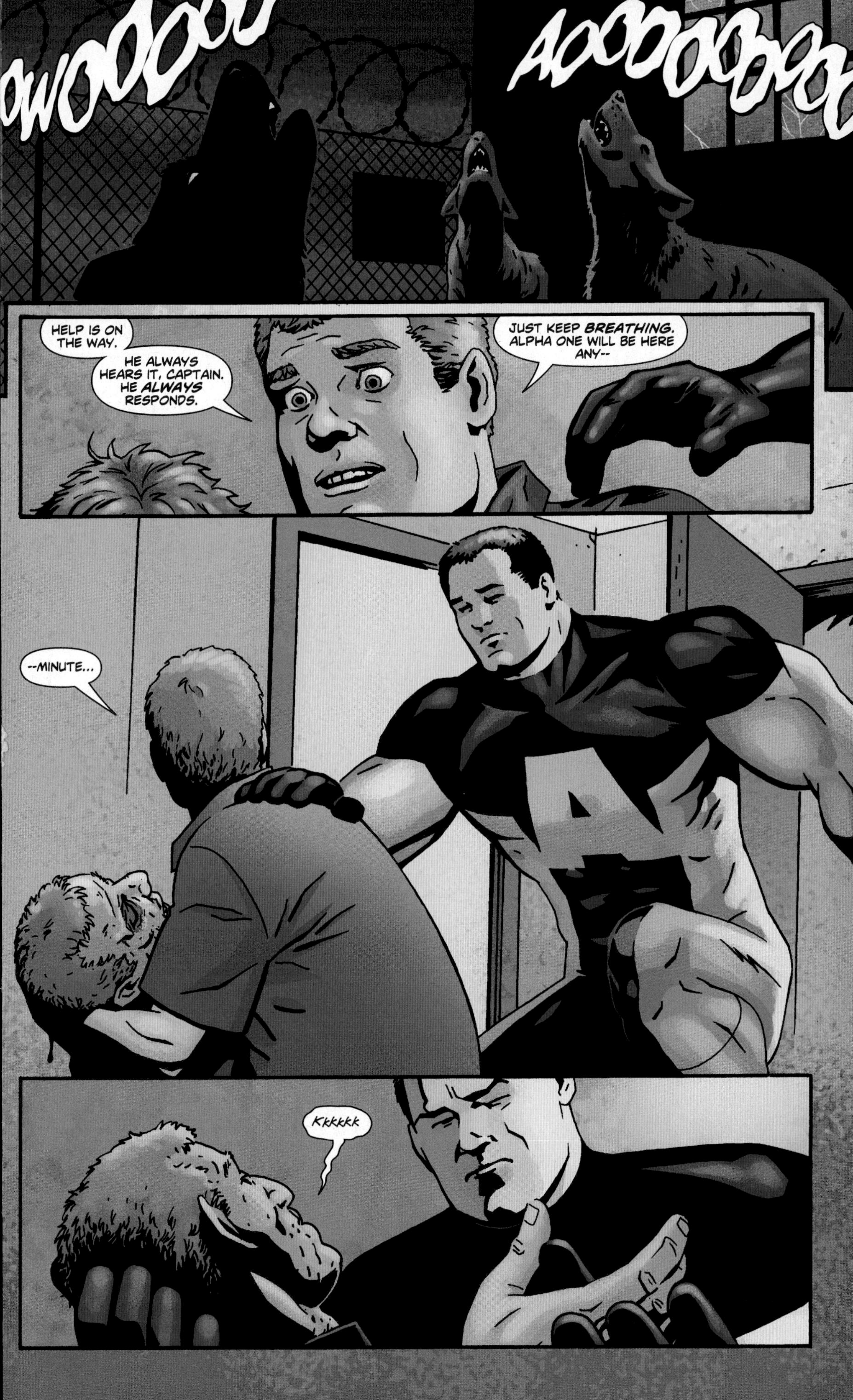
OWOOOOO
AOOOOOOOO
HELP IS ON THE WAY.
HE ALWAYS HEARS IT, CAPTAIN. HE ALWAYS RESPONDS.
JUST KEEP BREATHING. ALPHA ONE WILL BE HERE ANY--
--MINUTE...
Kkkkkk

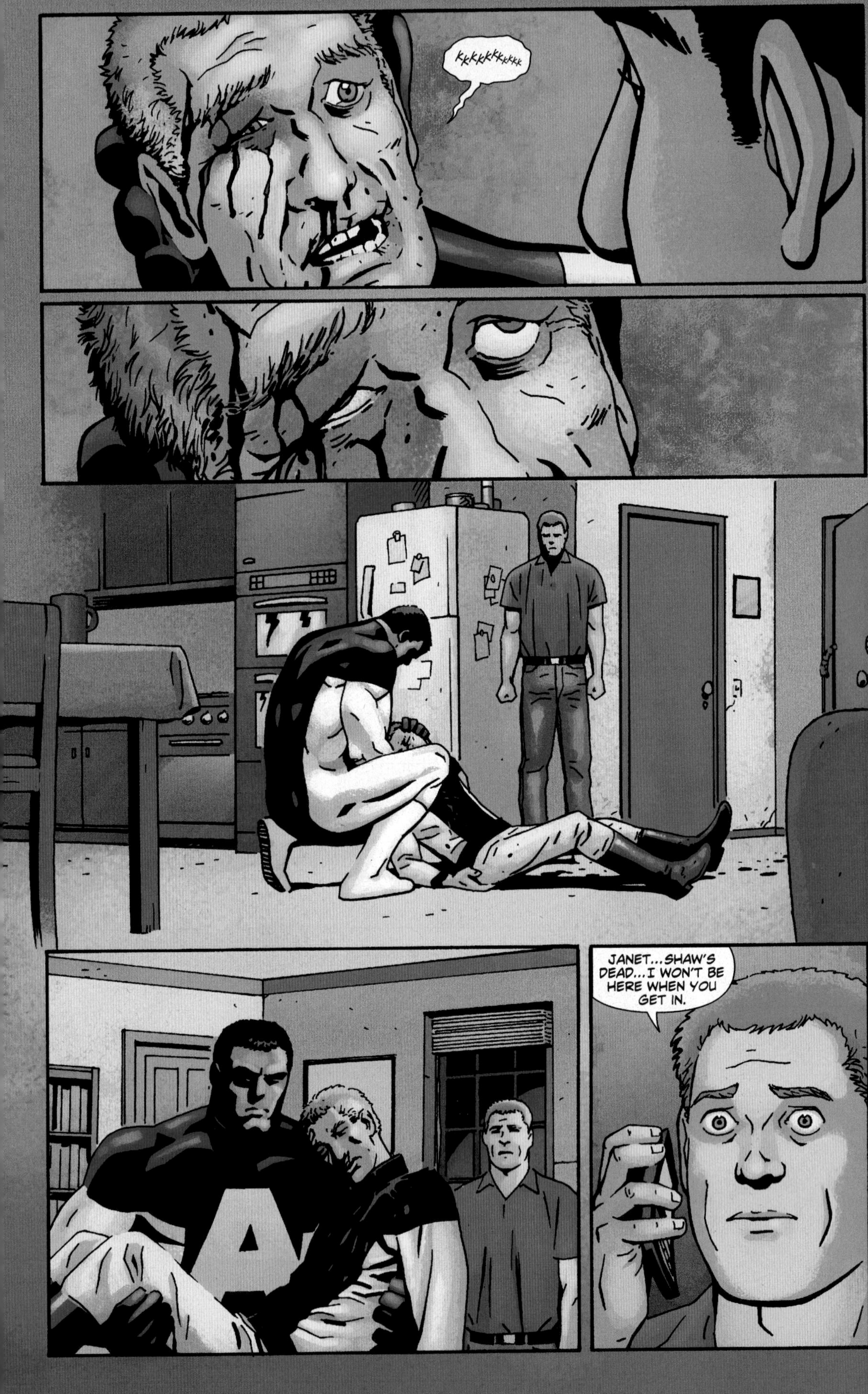
KKKKKKKKKK
JANET...SHAW'S DEAD...I WON'T BE HERE WHEN YOU GET IN.

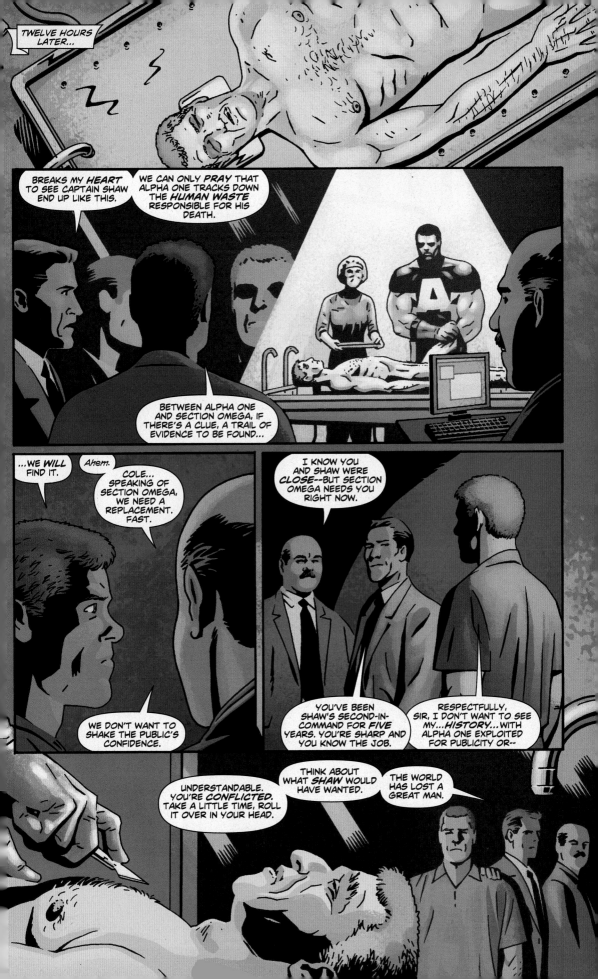

TWELVE HOURS LATER...

BREAKS MY *HEART* TO SEE CAPTAIN SHAW END UP LIKE THIS.

WE CAN ONLY *PRAY* THAT ALPHA ONE TRACKS DOWN THE *HUMAN WASTE* RESPONSIBLE FOR HIS DEATH.

BETWEEN ALPHA ONE AND SECTION OMEGA, IF THERE'S A CLUE, A TRAIL OF EVIDENCE TO BE FOUND...

...WE *WILL* FIND IT.

Ahem. COLE... SPEAKING OF SECTION OMEGA, WE NEED A REPLACEMENT. FAST.

WE DON'T WANT TO SHAKE THE PUBLIC'S CONFIDENCE.

I KNOW YOU AND SHAW WERE *CLOSE*--BUT SECTION OMEGA NEEDS YOU RIGHT NOW.

YOU'VE BEEN SHAW'S SECOND-IN-COMMAND FOR *FIVE* YEARS. YOU'RE SHARP AND YOU KNOW THE JOB.

RESPECTFULLY, SIR, I DON'T WANT TO SEE MY...*HISTORY*...WITH ALPHA ONE EXPLOITED FOR PUBLICITY OR--

UNDERSTANDABLE. YOU'RE *CONFLICTED*. TAKE A LITTLE TIME, ROLL IT OVER IN YOUR HEAD.

THINK ABOUT WHAT *SHAW* WOULD HAVE WANTED.

THE WORLD HAS LOST A GREAT MAN.

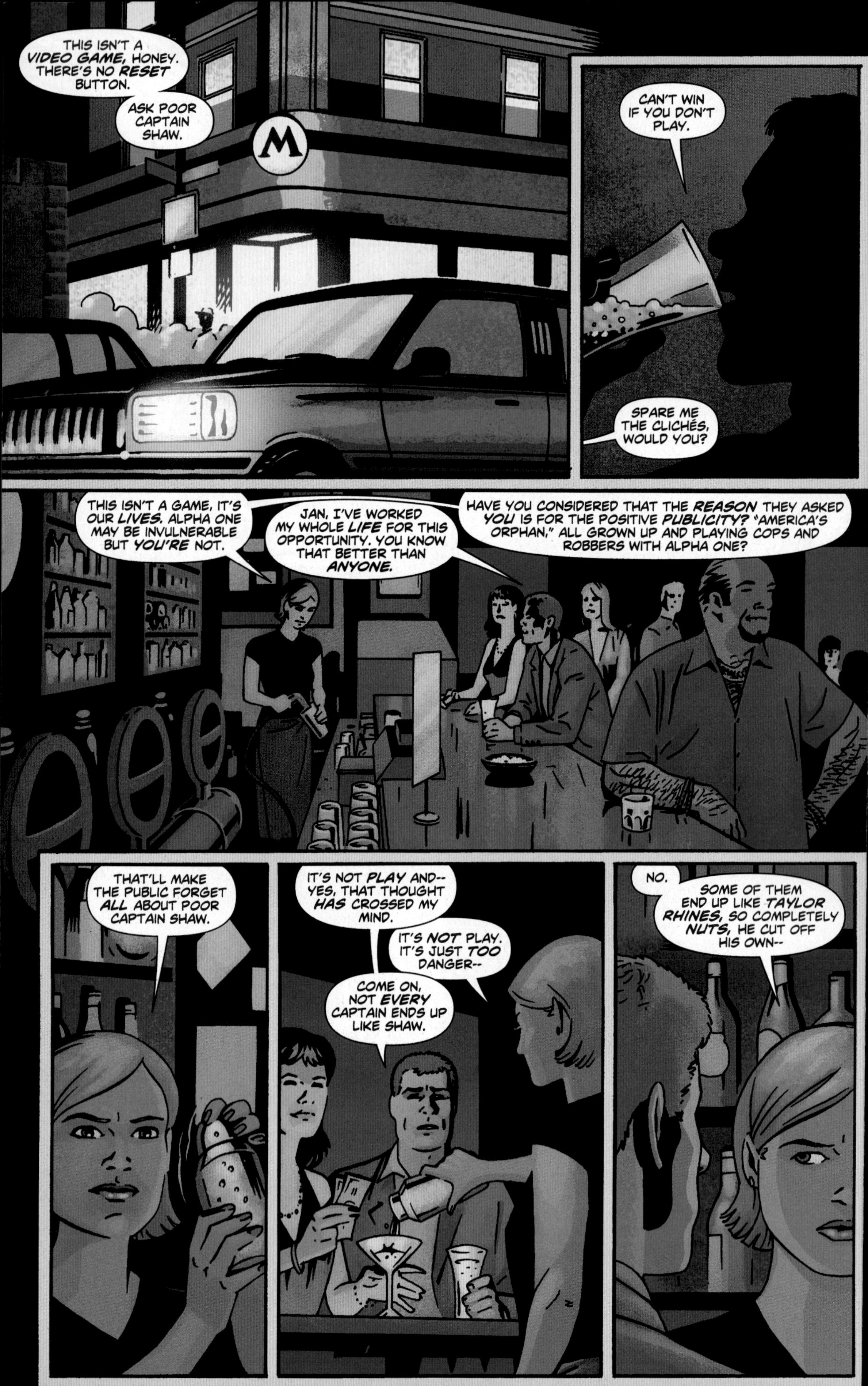
THIS ISN'T A VIDEO GAME, HONEY. THERE'S NO RESET BUTTON.
ASK POOR CAPTAIN SHAW.
CAN'T WIN IF YOU DON'T PLAY.
SPARE ME THE CLICHÉS, WOULD YOU?
THIS ISN'T A GAME, IT'S OUR LIVES. ALPHA ONE MAY BE INVULNERABLE BUT YOU'RE NOT.
JAN, I'VE WORKED MY WHOLE LIFE FOR THIS OPPORTUNITY. YOU KNOW THAT BETTER THAN ANYONE.
HAVE YOU CONSIDERED THAT THE REASON THEY ASKED YOU IS FOR THE POSITIVE PUBLICITY? "AMERICA'S ORPHAN," ALL GROWN UP AND PLAYING COPS AND ROBBERS WITH ALPHA ONE?
THAT'LL MAKE THE PUBLIC FORGET ALL ABOUT POOR CAPTAIN SHAW.
IT'S NOT PLAY AND-- YES, THAT THOUGHT HAS CROSSED MY MIND.
IT'S NOT PLAY. IT'S JUST TOO DANGER--
COME ON, NOT EVERY CAPTAIN ENDS UP LIKE SHAW.
NO.
SOME OF THEM END UP LIKE TAYLOR RHINES, SO COMPLETELY NUTS, HE CUT OFF HIS OWN--

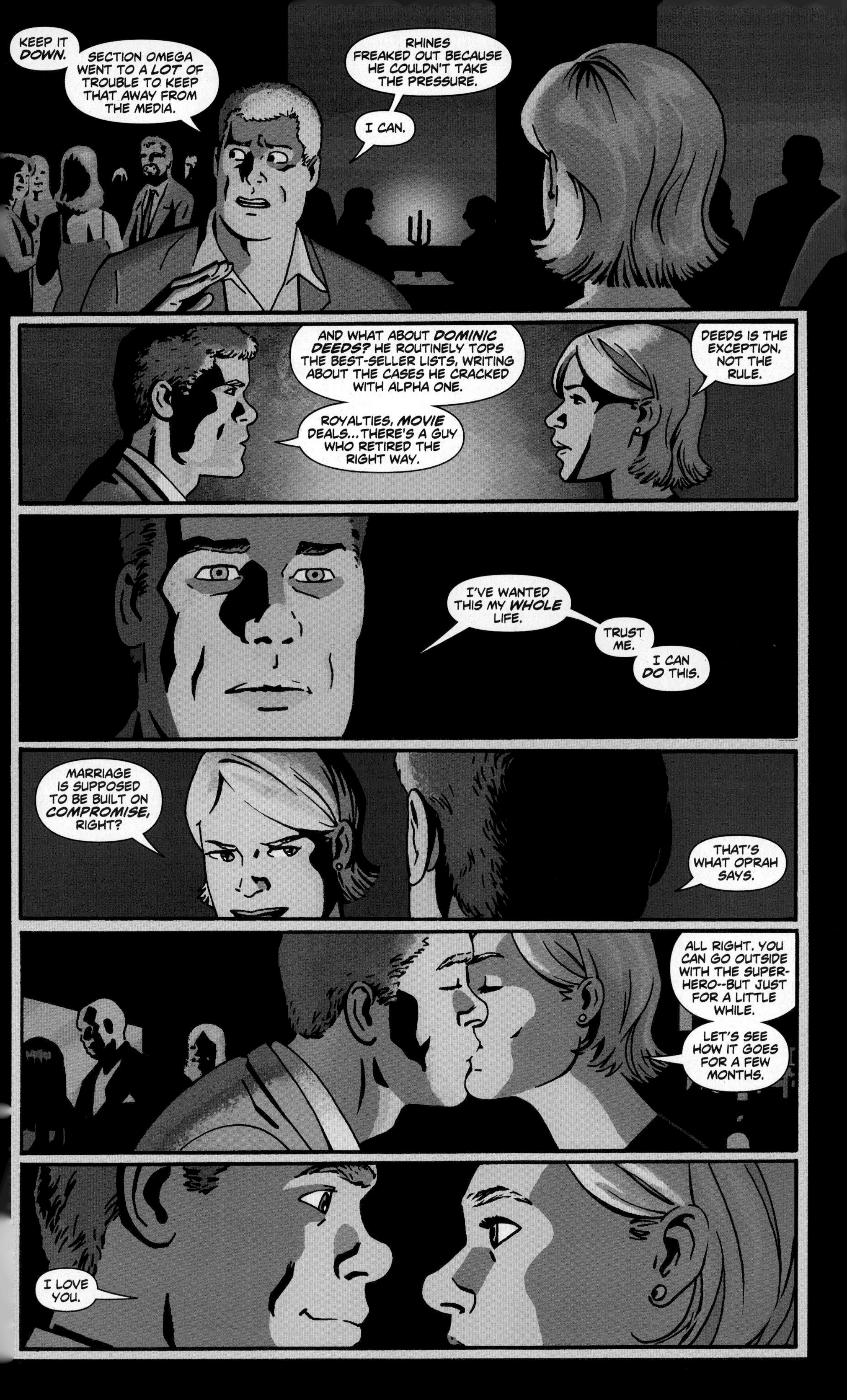
KEEP IT DOWN.
SECTION OMEGA WENT TO A LOT OF TROUBLE TO KEEP THAT AWAY FROM THE MEDIA.
RHINES FREAKED OUT BECAUSE HE COULDN'T TAKE THE PRESSURE.
I CAN.
AND WHAT ABOUT DOMINIC DEEDS? HE ROUTINELY TOPS THE BEST-SELLER LISTS, WRITING ABOUT THE CASES HE CRACKED WITH ALPHA ONE.
ROYALTIES, MOVIE DEALS...THERE'S A GUY WHO RETIRED THE RIGHT WAY.
DEEDS IS THE EXCEPTION, NOT THE RULE.
I'VE WANTED THIS MY WHOLE LIFE.
TRUST ME.
I CAN DO THIS.
MARRIAGE IS SUPPOSED TO BE BUILT ON COMPROMISE, RIGHT?
THAT'S WHAT OPRAH SAYS.
ALL RIGHT. YOU CAN GO OUTSIDE WITH THE SUPER-HERO--BUT JUST FOR A LITTLE WHILE.
LET'S SEE HOW IT GOES FOR A FEW MONTHS.
I LOVE YOU.

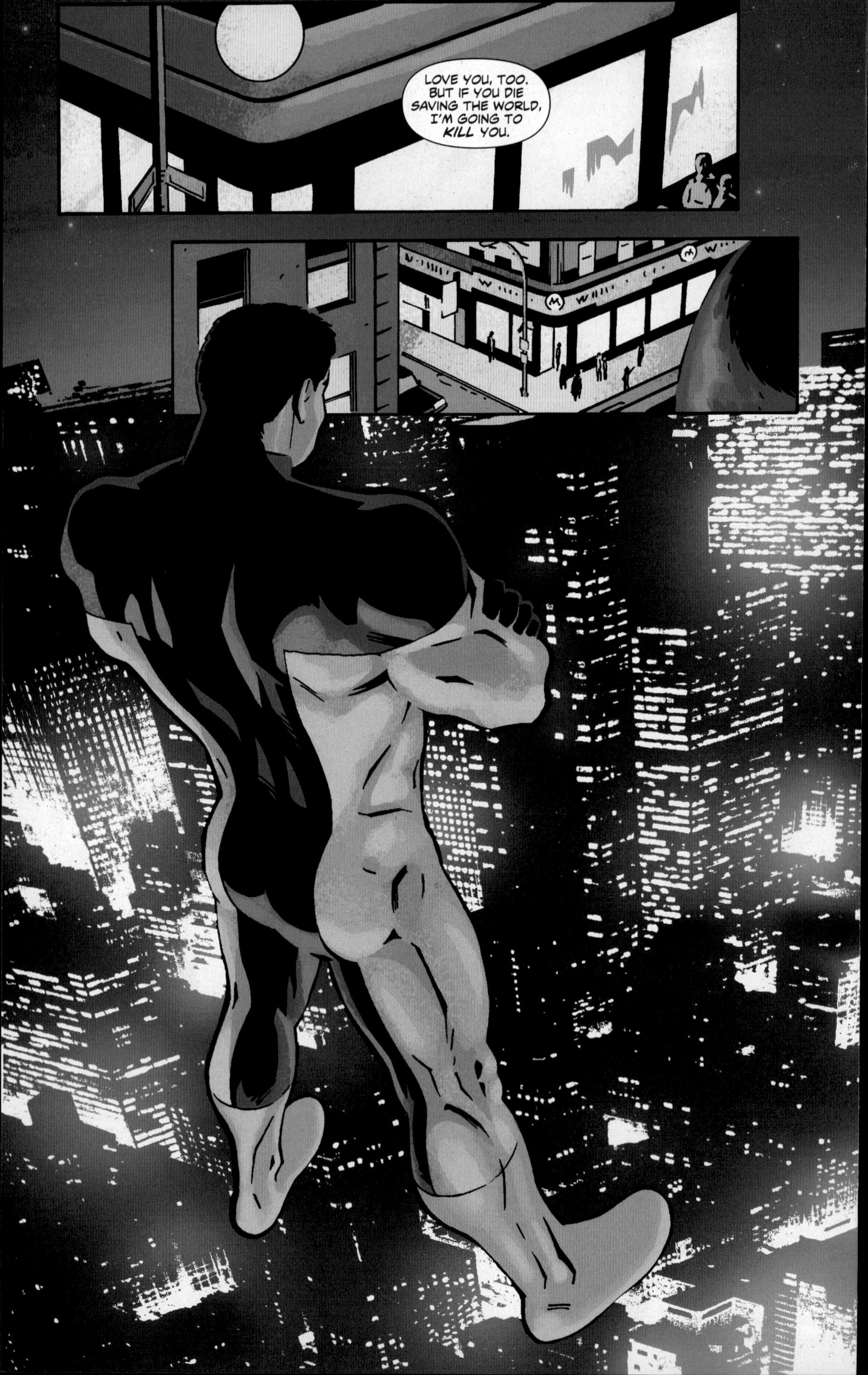
LOVE YOU, TOO. BUT IF YOU DIE SAVING THE WORLD, I'M GOING TO KILL YOU.

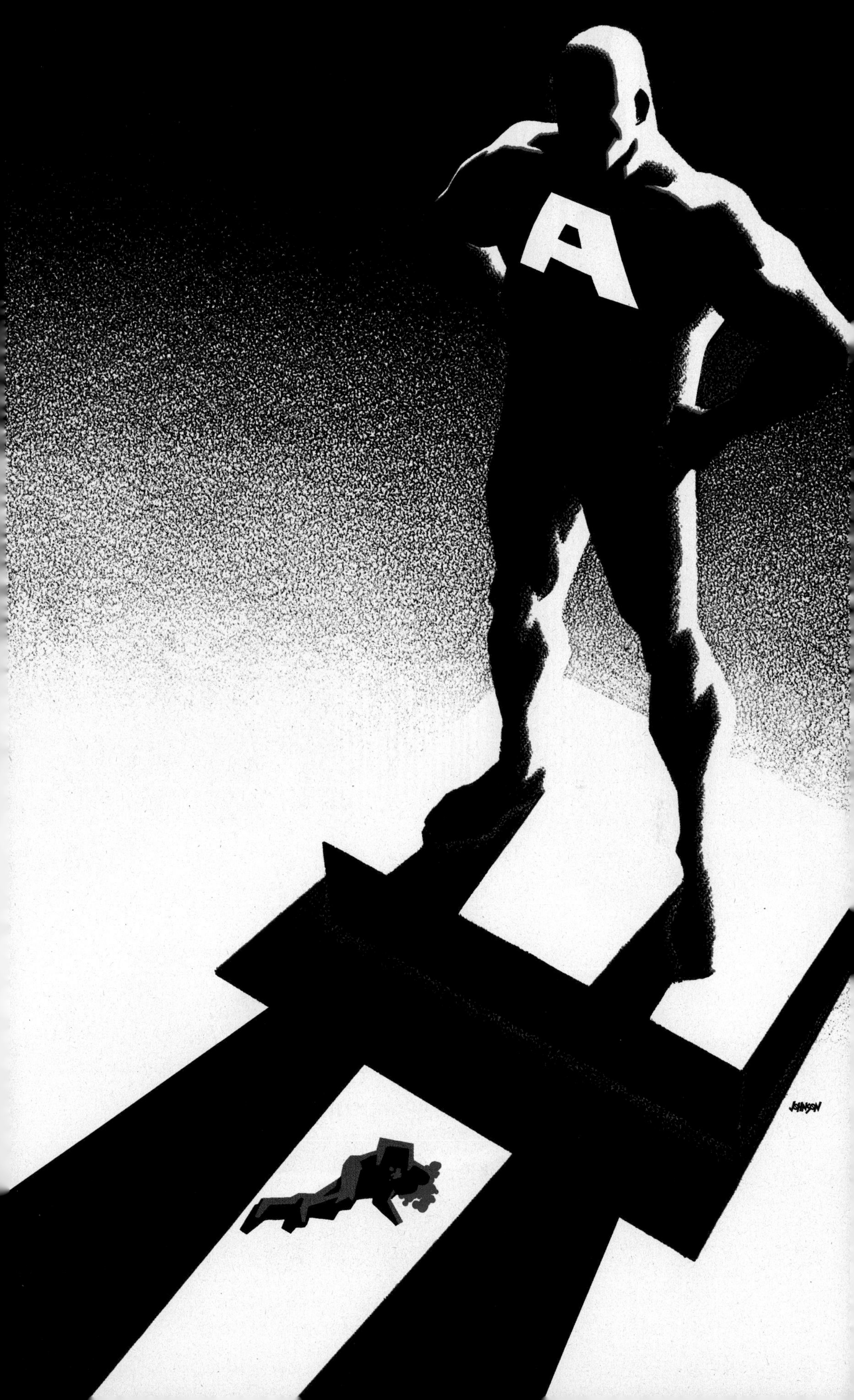
JOHNSON

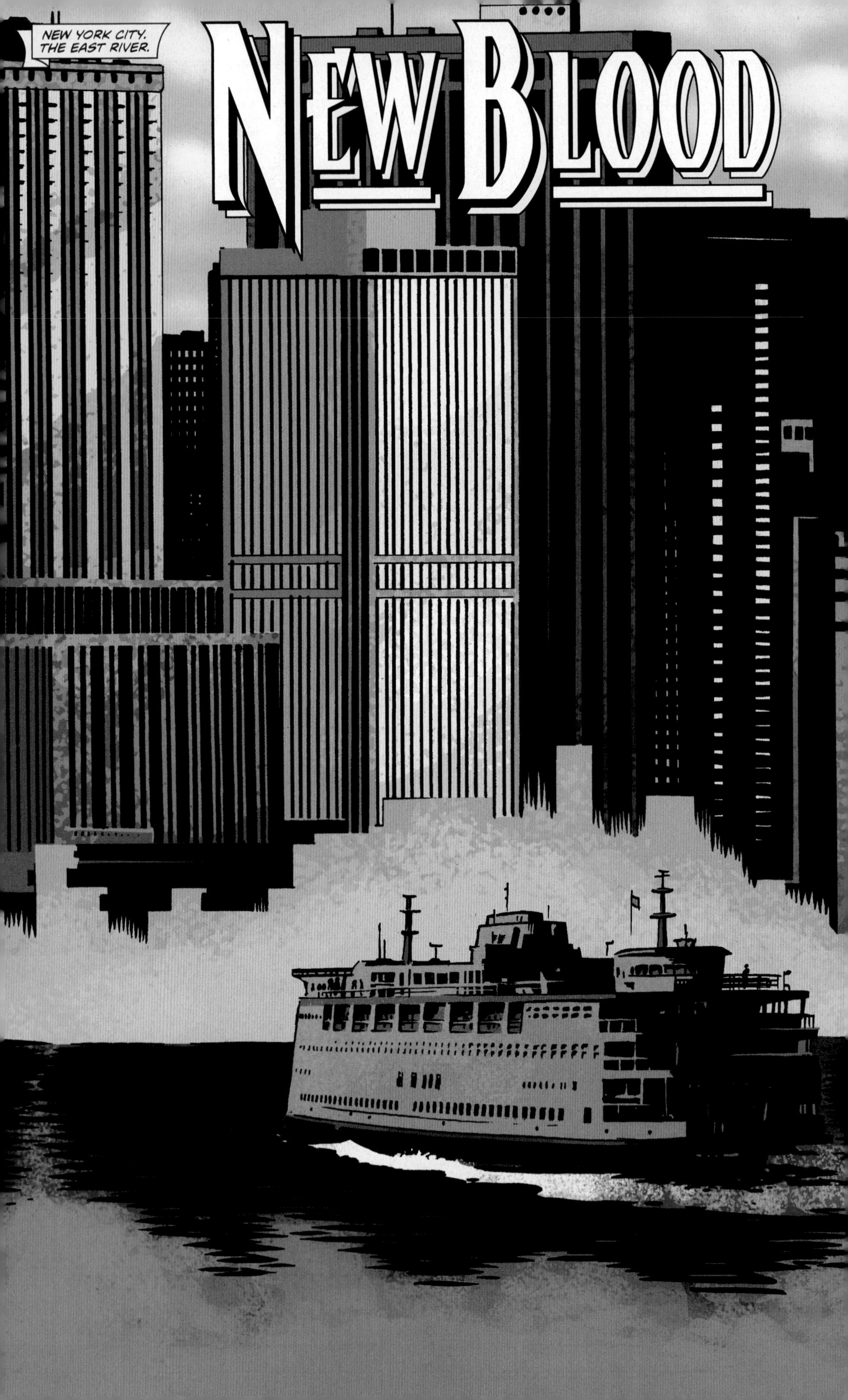
NEW YORK CITY.
THE EAST RIVER.
NEW BLOOD

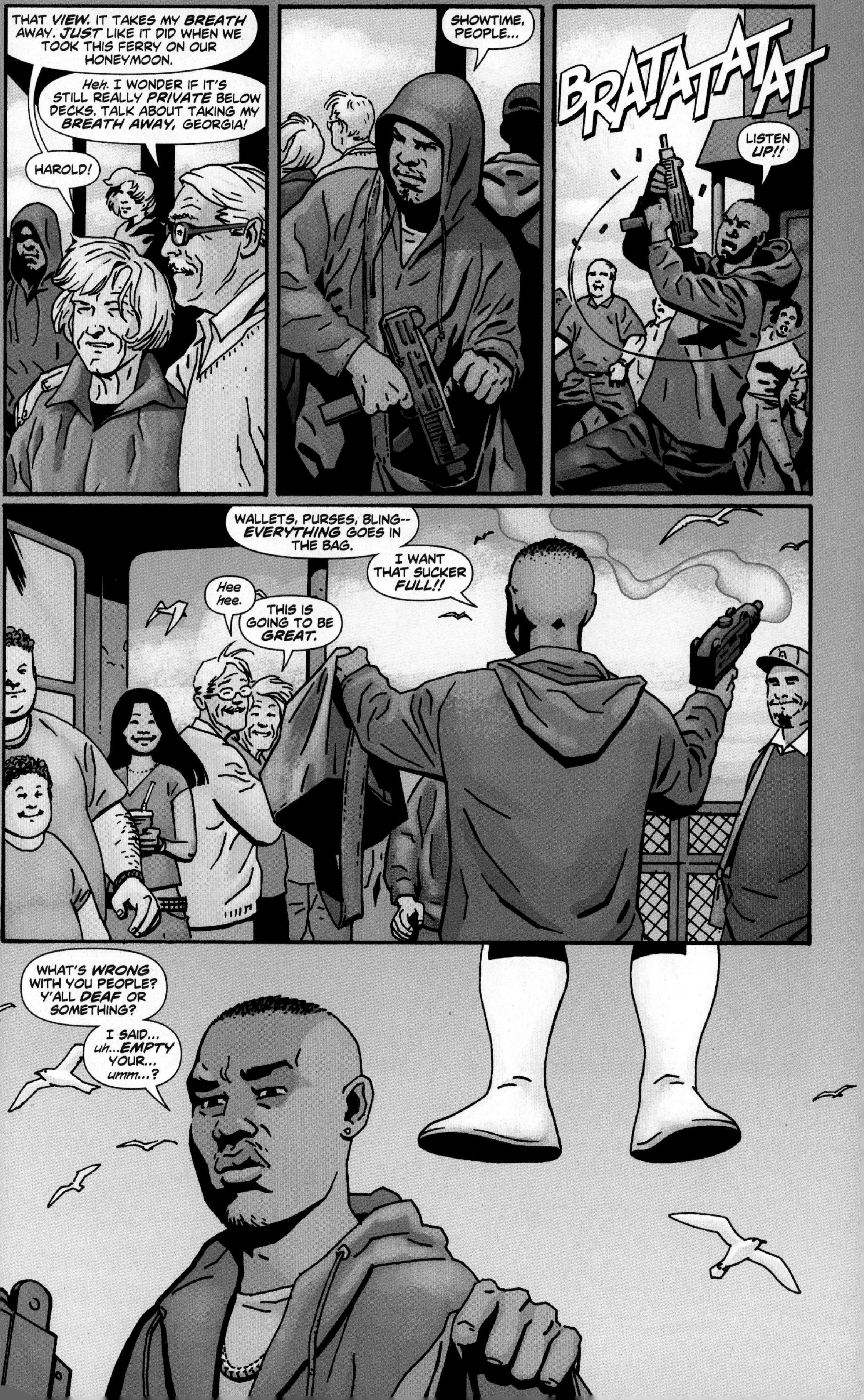
THAT VIEW. IT TAKES MY BREATH AWAY. JUST LIKE IT DID WHEN WE TOOK THIS FERRY ON OUR HONEYMOON.
Heh. I WONDER IF IT'S STILL REALLY PRIVATE BELOW DECKS. TALK ABOUT TAKING MY BREATH AWAY, GEORGIA!
HAROLD!
SHOWTIME, PEOPLE...
BRATATATAT
LISTEN UP!!
WALLETS, PURSES, BLING-- EVERYTHING GOES IN THE BAG.
I WANT THAT SUCKER FULL!!
Hee hee.
THIS IS GOING TO BE GREAT.
WHAT'S WRONG WITH YOU PEOPLE? Y'ALL DEAF OR SOMETHING?
I SAID... uh...EMPTY YOUR... umm...?

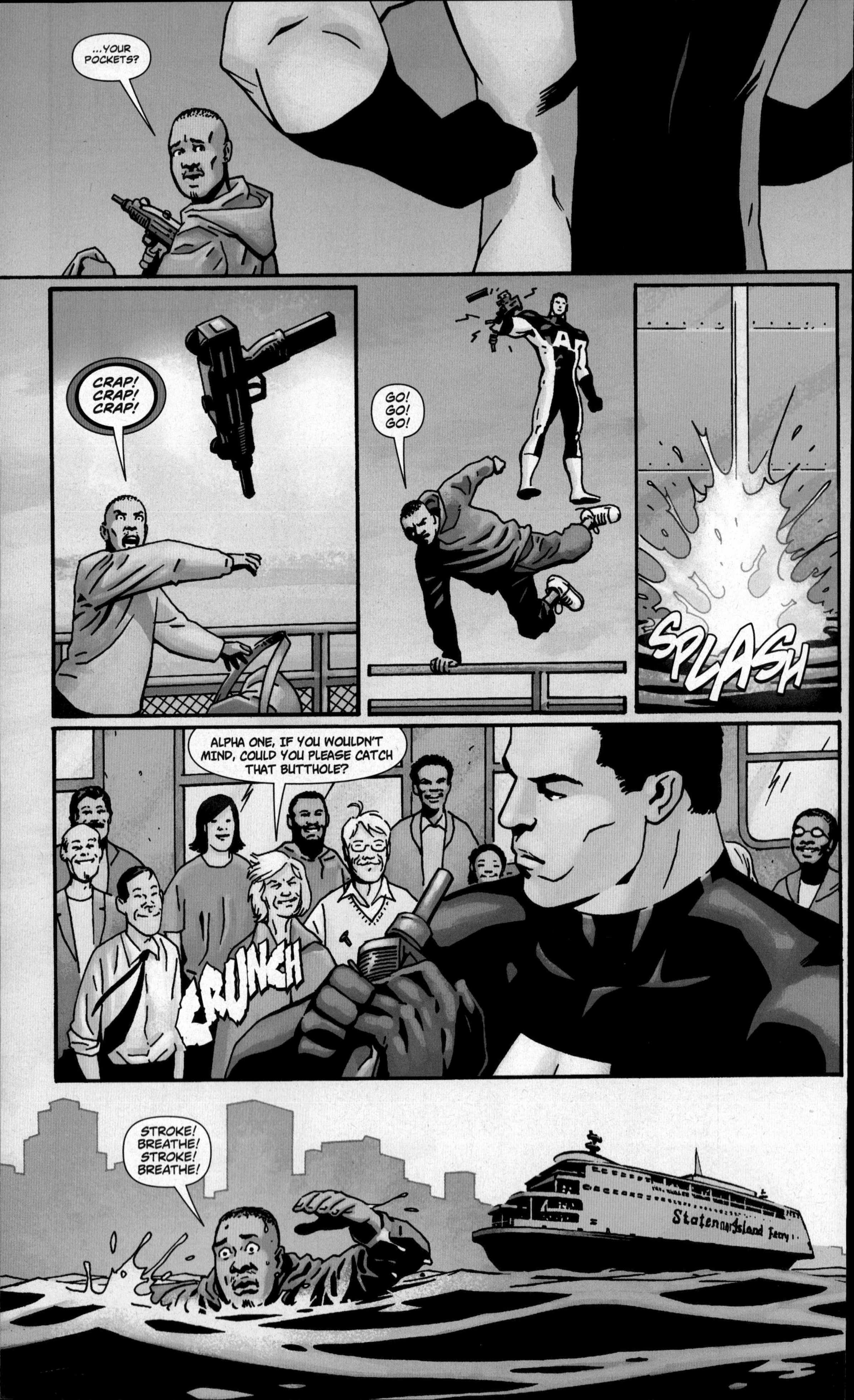
...YOUR POCKETS?
CRAP! CRAP! CRAP!
GO! GO! GO!
SPLASH
ALPHA ONE, IF YOU WOULDN'T MIND, COULD YOU PLEASE CATCH THAT BUTTHOLE?
CRUNCH
STROKE! BREATHE! STROKE! BREATHE!
Staten Island Ferry

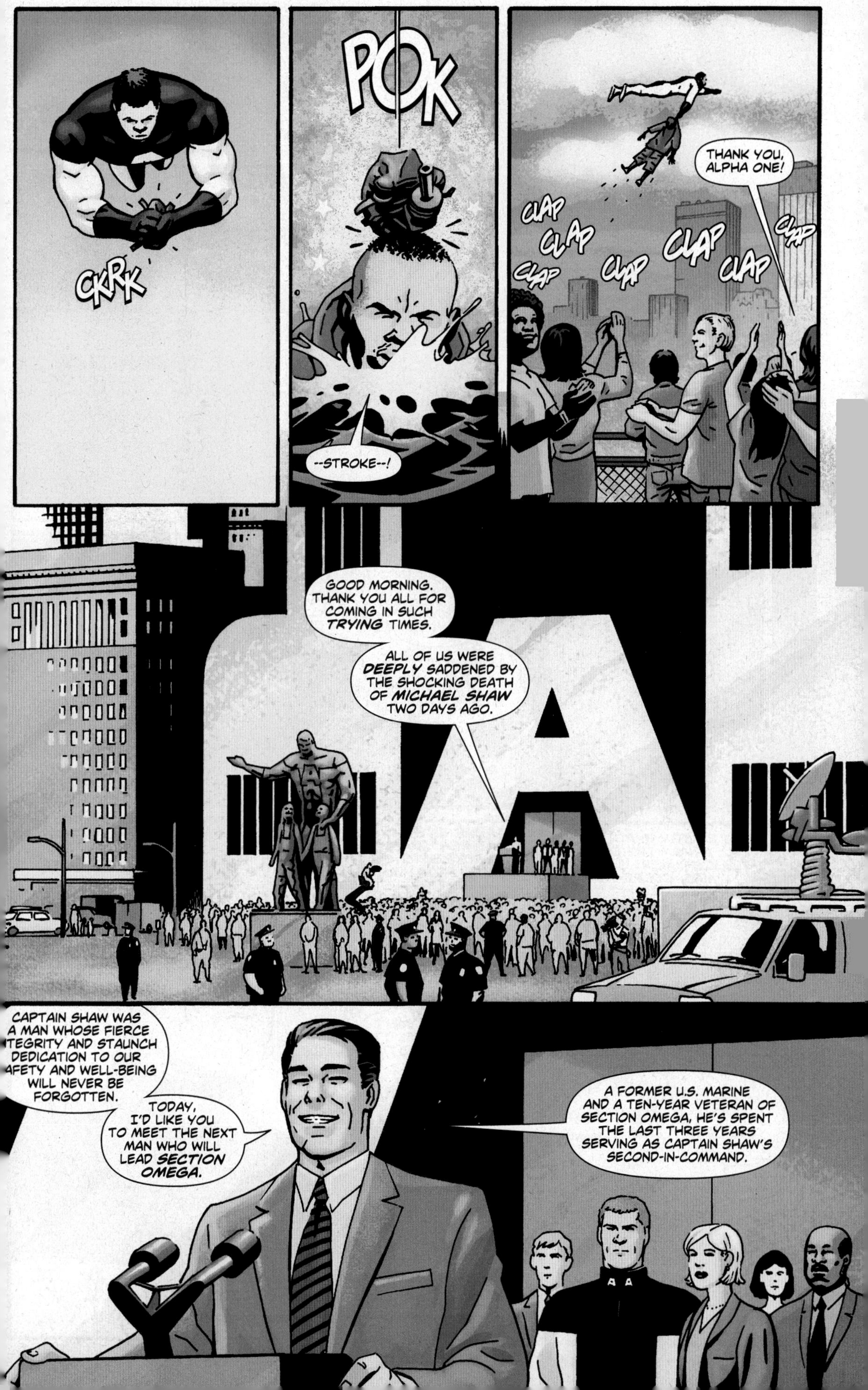
CKRK
POK
--STROKE--!
THANK YOU, ALPHA ONE!
CLAP
CLAP
CLAP
CLAP
CLAP
CLAP
CLAP
GOOD MORNING. THANK YOU ALL FOR COMING IN SUCH TRYING TIMES.
ALL OF US WERE DEEPLY SADDENED BY THE SHOCKING DEATH OF MICHAEL SHAW TWO DAYS AGO.
CAPTAIN SHAW WAS A MAN WHOSE FIERCE TEGRITY AND STAUNCH DEDICATION TO OUR AFETY AND WELL-BEING WILL NEVER BE FORGOTTEN.
TODAY, I'D LIKE YOU TO MEET THE NEXT MAN WHO WILL LEAD SECTION OMEGA.
A FORMER U.S. MARINE AND A TEN-YEAR VETERAN OF SECTION OMEGA, HE'S SPENT THE LAST THREE YEARS SERVING AS CAPTAIN SHAW'S SECOND-IN-COMMAND.

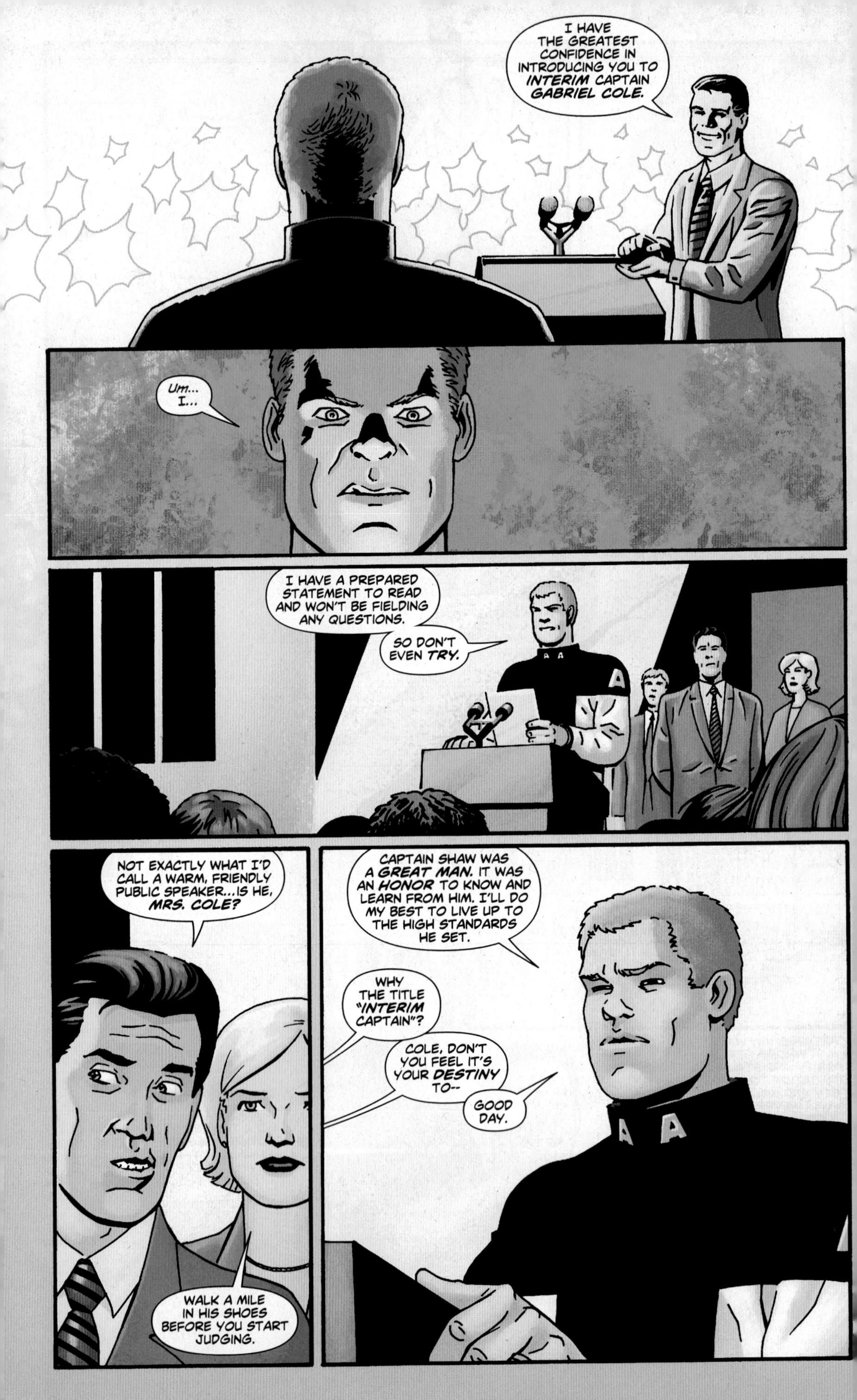
I HAVE THE GREATEST CONFIDENCE IN INTRODUCING YOU TO INTERIM CAPTAIN GABRIEL COLE.
Um... I...
I HAVE A PREPARED STATEMENT TO READ AND WON'T BE FIELDING ANY QUESTIONS.
SO DON'T EVEN TRY.
NOT EXACTLY WHAT I'D CALL A WARM, FRIENDLY PUBLIC SPEAKER...IS HE, MRS. COLE?
WALK A MILE IN HIS SHOES BEFORE YOU START JUDGING.
CAPTAIN SHAW WAS A GREAT MAN. IT WAS AN HONOR TO KNOW AND LEARN FROM HIM. I'LL DO MY BEST TO LIVE UP TO THE HIGH STANDARDS HE SET.
WHY THE TITLE "INTERIM CAPTAIN"?
COLE, DON'T YOU FEEL IT'S YOUR DESTINY TO--
GOOD DAY.

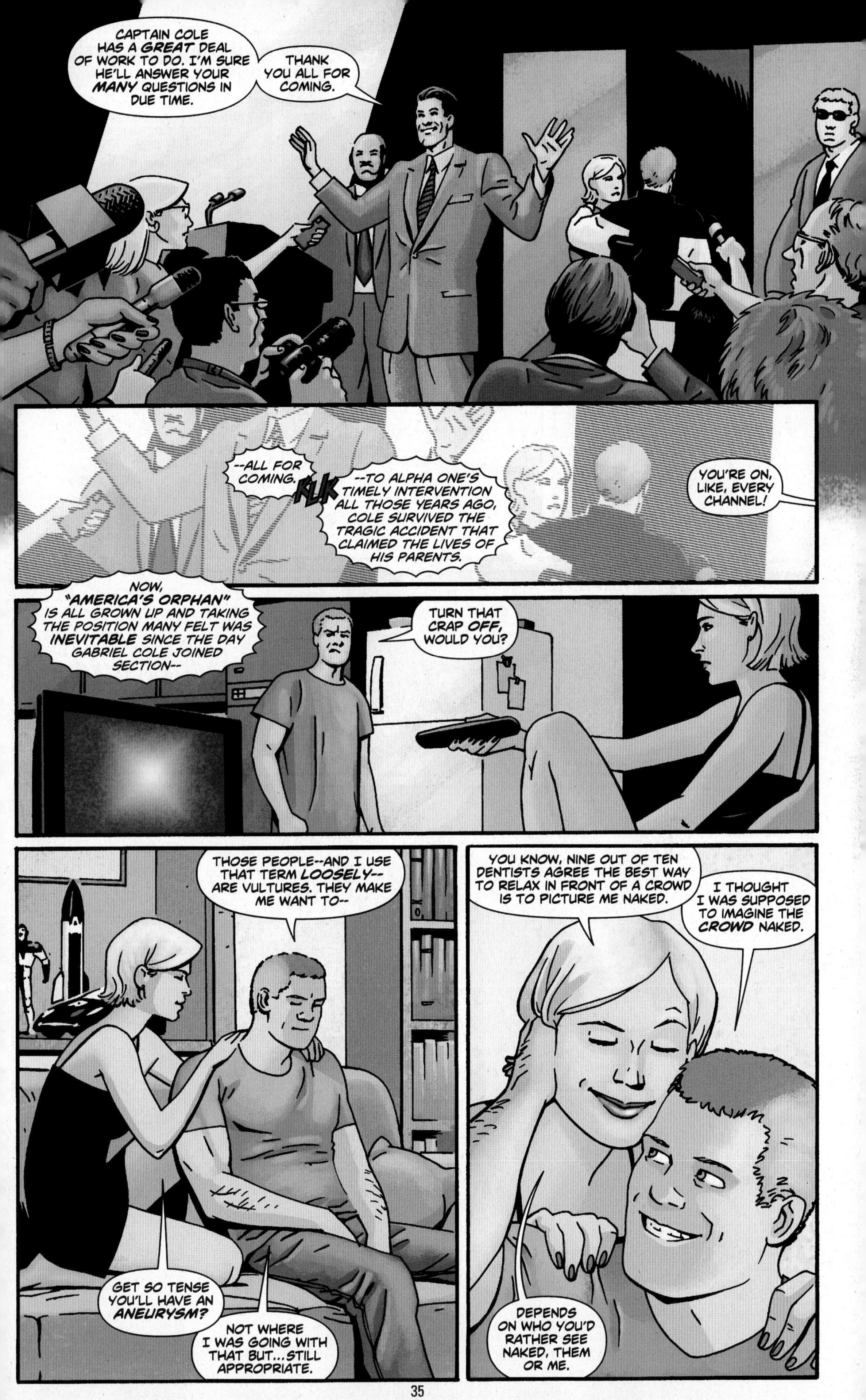
CAPTAIN COLE HAS A GREAT DEAL OF WORK TO DO. I'M SURE HE'LL ANSWER YOUR MANY QUESTIONS IN DUE TIME.
THANK YOU ALL FOR COMING.
--ALL FOR COMING.
KLIK
--TO ALPHA ONE'S TIMELY INTERVENTION ALL THOSE YEARS AGO, COLE SURVIVED THE TRAGIC ACCIDENT THAT CLAIMED THE LIVES OF HIS PARENTS.
YOU'RE ON, LIKE, EVERY CHANNEL!
NOW, "AMERICA'S ORPHAN" IS ALL GROWN UP AND TAKING THE POSITION MANY FELT WAS INEVITABLE SINCE THE DAY GABRIEL COLE JOINED SECTION--
TURN THAT CRAP OFF, WOULD YOU?
THOSE PEOPLE--AND I USE THAT TERM LOOSELY--ARE VULTURES. THEY MAKE ME WANT TO--
GET SO TENSE YOU'LL HAVE AN ANEURYSM?
NOT WHERE I WAS GOING WITH THAT BUT...STILL APPROPRIATE.
YOU KNOW, NINE OUT OF TEN DENTISTS AGREE THE BEST WAY TO RELAX IN FRONT OF A CROWD IS TO PICTURE ME NAKED.
I THOUGHT I WAS SUPPOSED TO IMAGINE THE CROWD NAKED.
DEPENDS ON WHO YOU'D RATHER SEE NAKED, THEM OR ME.

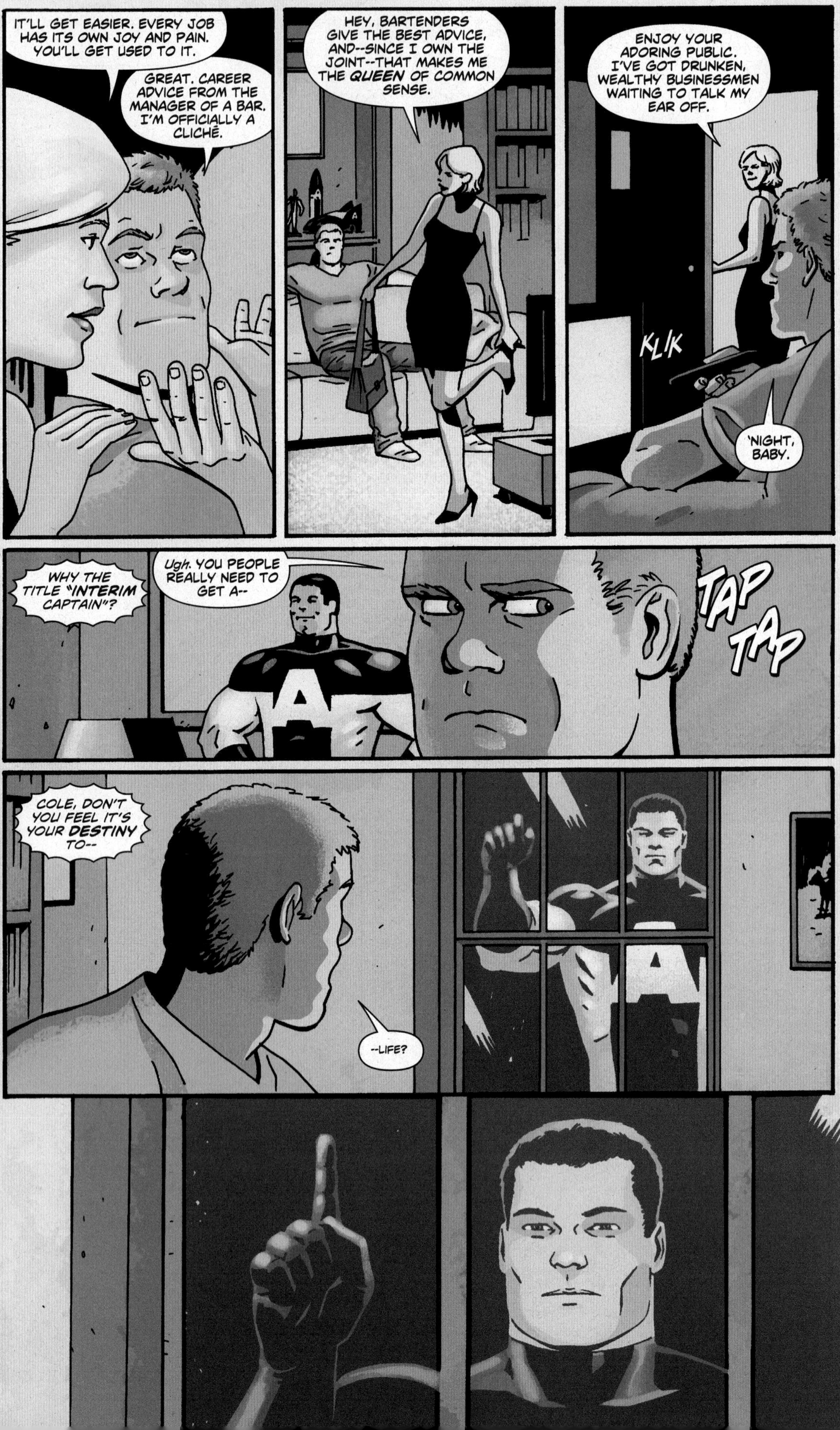
IT'LL GET EASIER. EVERY JOB HAS ITS OWN JOY AND PAIN. YOU'LL GET USED TO IT.
GREAT. CAREER ADVICE FROM THE MANAGER OF A BAR. I'M OFFICIALLY A CLICHÉ.
HEY, BARTENDERS GIVE THE BEST ADVICE, AND--SINCE I OWN THE JOINT--THAT MAKES ME THE QUEEN OF COMMON SENSE.
ENJOY YOUR ADORING PUBLIC. I'VE GOT DRUNKEN, WEALTHY BUSINESSMEN WAITING TO TALK MY EAR OFF.
KLIK
'NIGHT, BABY.
WHY THE TITLE "INTERIM CAPTAIN"?
Ugh. YOU PEOPLE REALLY NEED TO GET A--
TAP TAP
COLE, DON'T YOU FEEL IT'S YOUR DESTINY TO--
--LIFE?

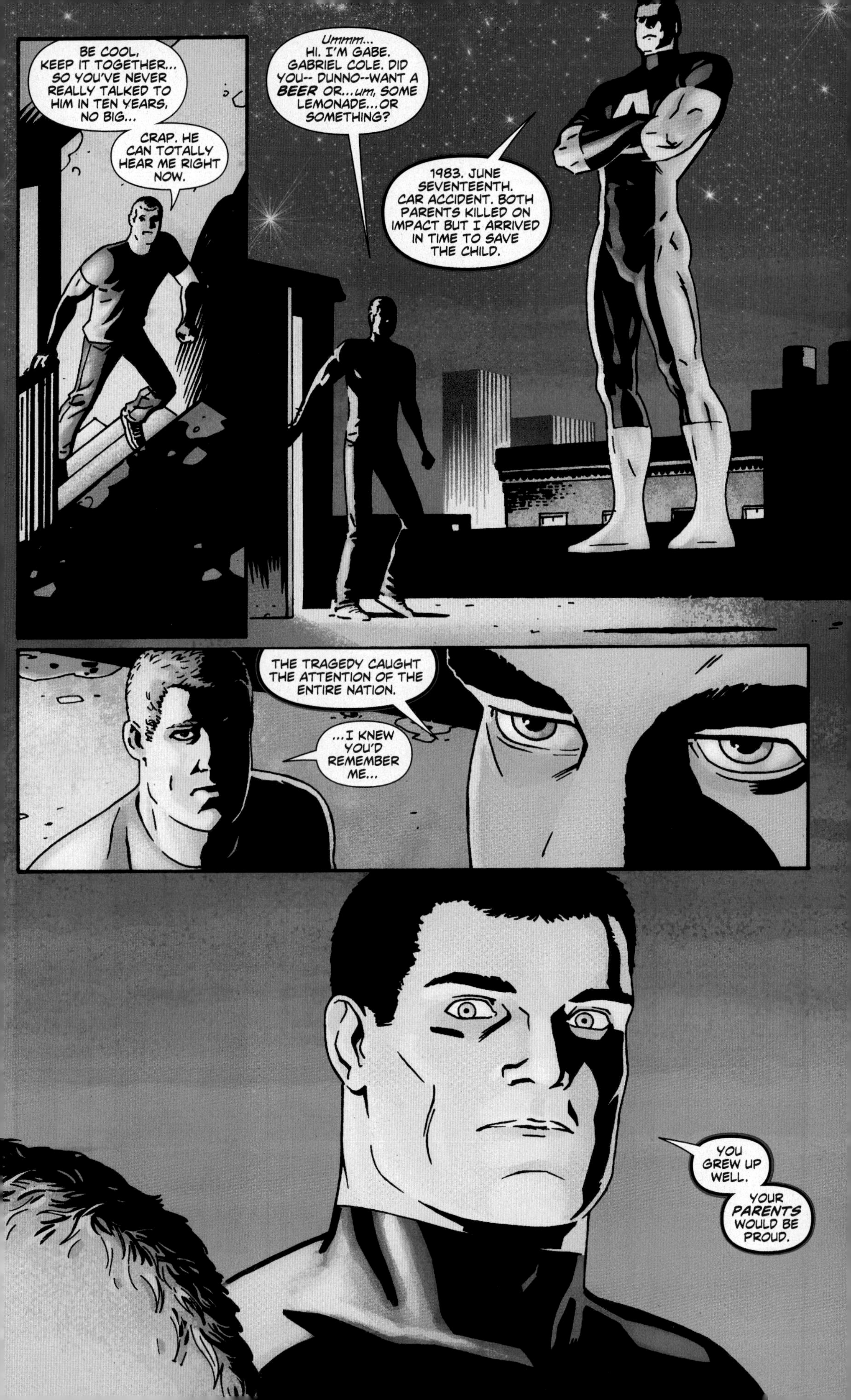
BE COOL, KEEP IT TOGETHER... SO YOU'VE NEVER REALLY TALKED TO HIM IN TEN YEARS, NO BIG...
CRAP. HE CAN TOTALLY HEAR ME RIGHT NOW.
Ummm... HI. I'M GABE. GABRIEL COLE. DID YOU-- DUNNO--WANT A BEER OR...um, SOME LEMONADE...OR SOMETHING?
1983. JUNE SEVENTEENTH. CAR ACCIDENT. BOTH PARENTS KILLED ON IMPACT BUT I ARRIVED IN TIME TO SAVE THE CHILD.
THE TRAGEDY CAUGHT THE ATTENTION OF THE ENTIRE NATION.
...I KNEW YOU'D REMEMBER ME...
YOU GREW UP WELL.
YOUR PARENTS WOULD BE PROUD.

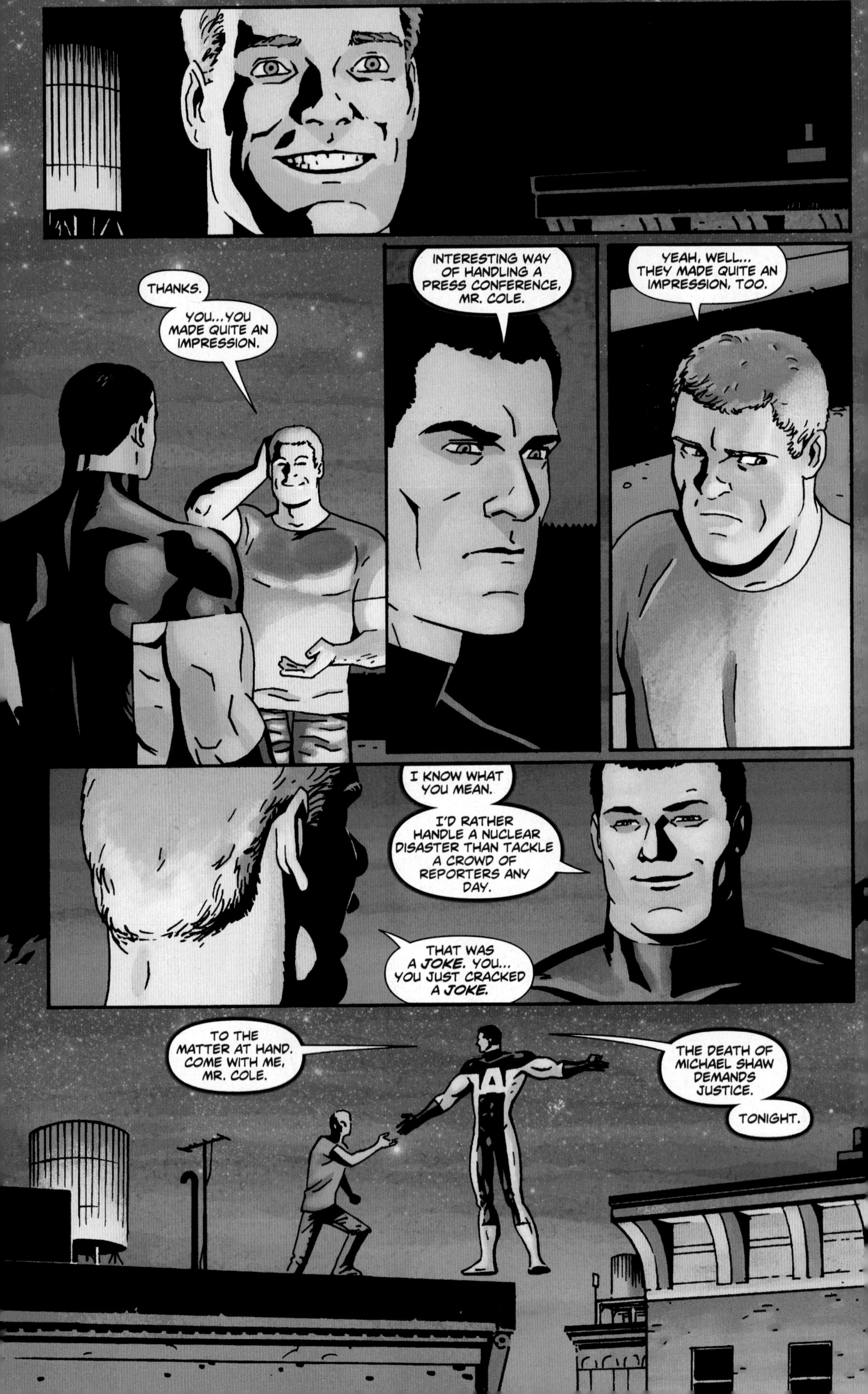
THANKS.
YOU...YOU MADE QUITE AN IMPRESSION.
INTERESTING WAY OF HANDLING A PRESS CONFERENCE, MR. COLE.
YEAH, WELL... THEY MADE QUITE AN IMPRESSION, TOO.
I KNOW WHAT YOU MEAN.
I'D RATHER HANDLE A NUCLEAR DISASTER THAN TACKLE A CROWD OF REPORTERS ANY DAY.
THAT WAS A ***JOKE***. YOU... YOU JUST CRACKED A ***JOKE***.
TO THE MATTER AT HAND. COME WITH ME, MR. COLE.
THE DEATH OF MICHAEL SHAW DEMANDS JUSTICE.
TONIGHT.

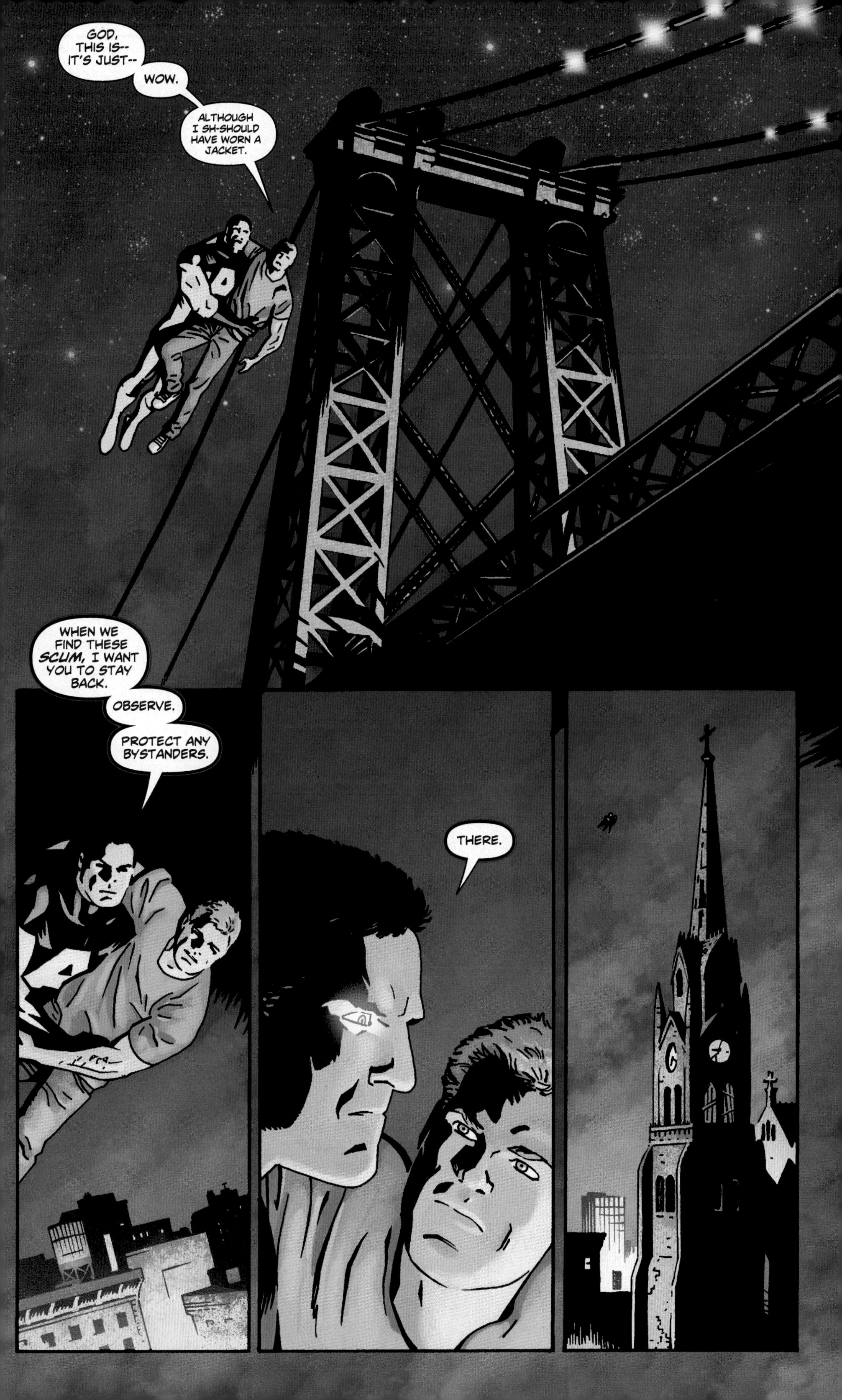
GOD, THIS IS-- IT'S JUST--
WOW.
ALTHOUGH I SH-SHOULD HAVE WORN A JACKET.
WHEN WE FIND THESE *SCUM*, I WANT YOU TO STAY BACK.
OBSERVE.
PROTECT ANY BYSTANDERS.
THERE.

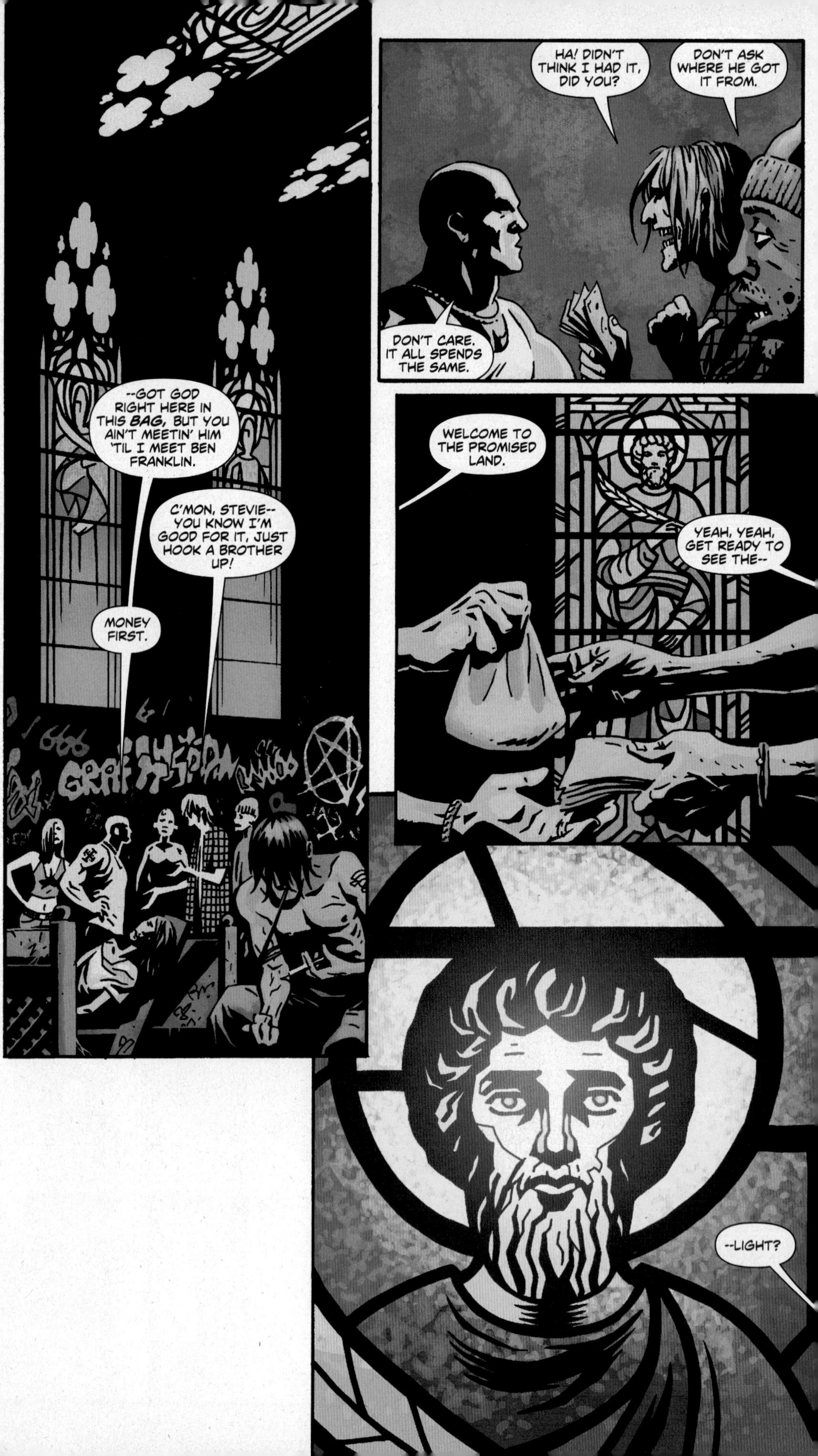
--GOT GOD RIGHT HERE IN THIS BAG, BUT YOU AIN'T MEETIN' HIM 'TIL I MEET BEN FRANKLIN.
C'MON, STEVIE-- YOU KNOW I'M GOOD FOR IT, JUST HOOK A BROTHER UP!
MONEY FIRST.
HA! DIDN'T THINK I HAD IT, DID YOU?
DON'T ASK WHERE HE GOT IT FROM.
DON'T CARE. IT ALL SPENDS THE SAME.
WELCOME TO THE PROMISED LAND.
YEAH, YEAH, GET READY TO SEE THE--
--LIGHT?

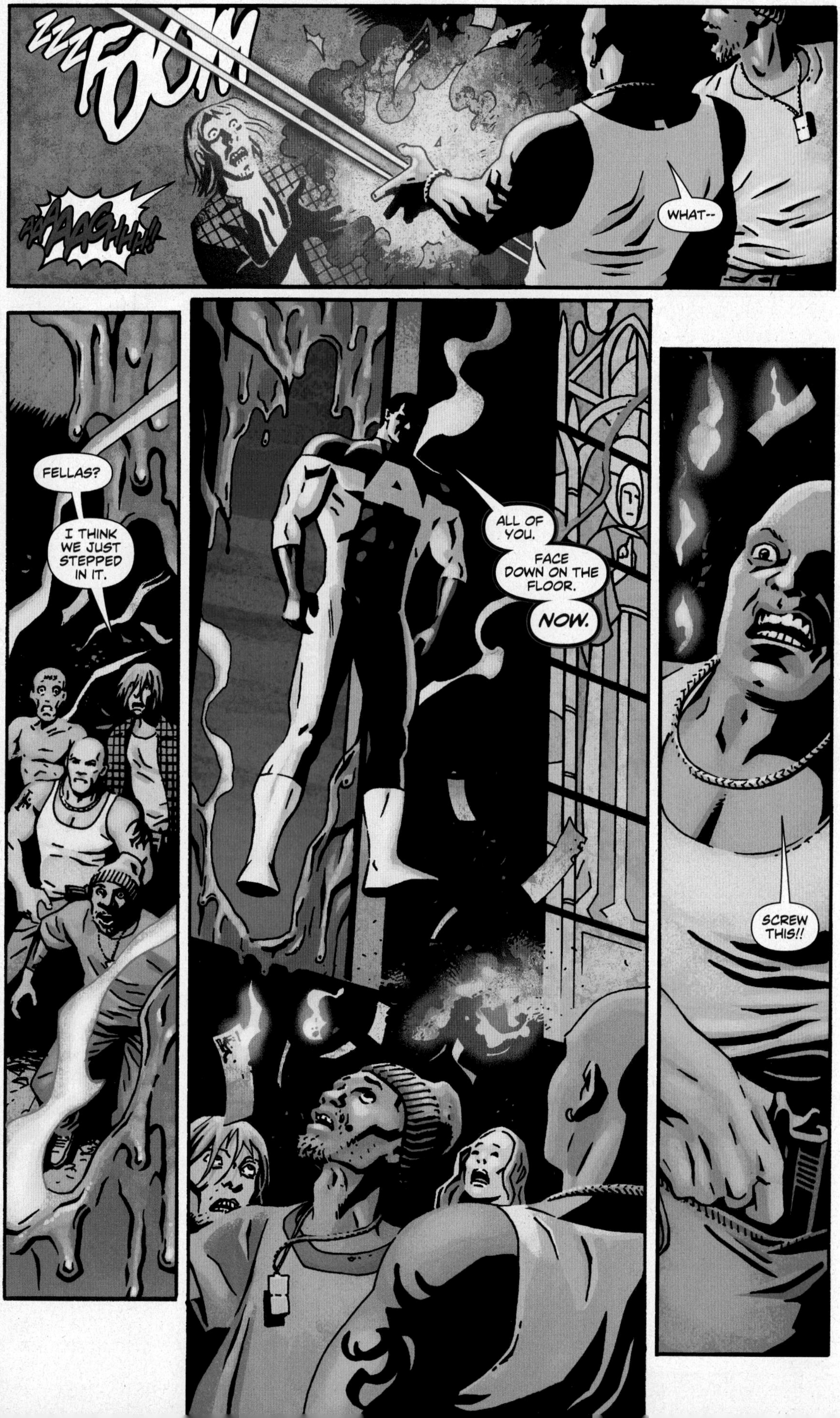
ZZZFOOM
AAAAAGHHH!!
WHAT--
FELLAS?
I THINK WE JUST STEPPED IN IT.
ALL OF YOU.
FACE DOWN ON THE FLOOR.
NOW.
SCREW THIS!!

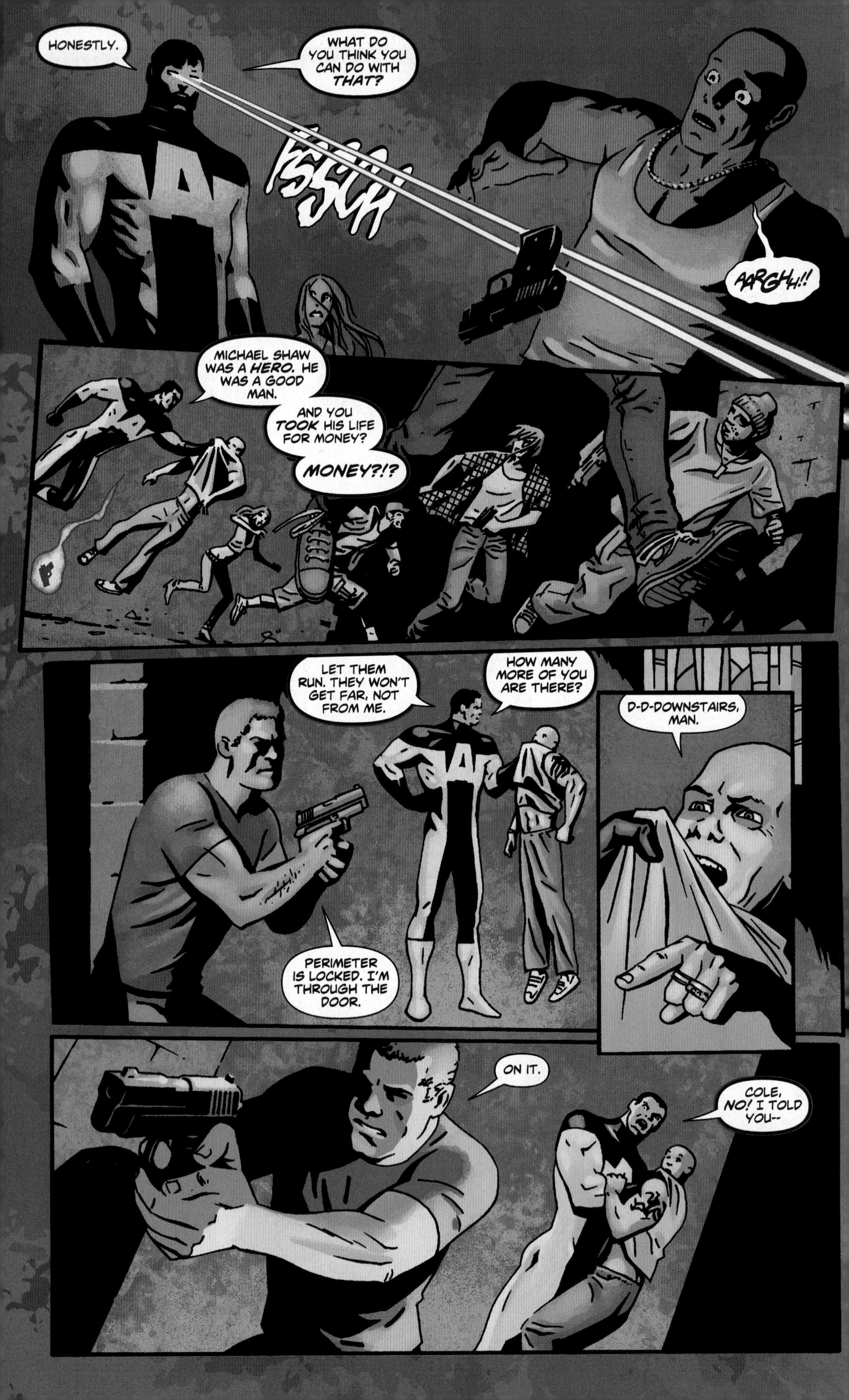
HONESTLY.
WHAT DO YOU THINK YOU CAN DO WITH *THAT?*
AARGHHH!!
MICHAEL SHAW WAS A *HERO.* HE WAS A GOOD MAN.
AND YOU *TOOK* HIS LIFE FOR MONEY?
MONEY?!?
LET THEM RUN. THEY WON'T GET FAR, NOT FROM ME.
HOW MANY MORE OF YOU ARE THERE?
D-D-DOWNSTAIRS, MAN.
PERIMETER IS LOCKED. I'M THROUGH THE DOOR.
ON IT.
COLE, *NO!* I TOLD YOU--

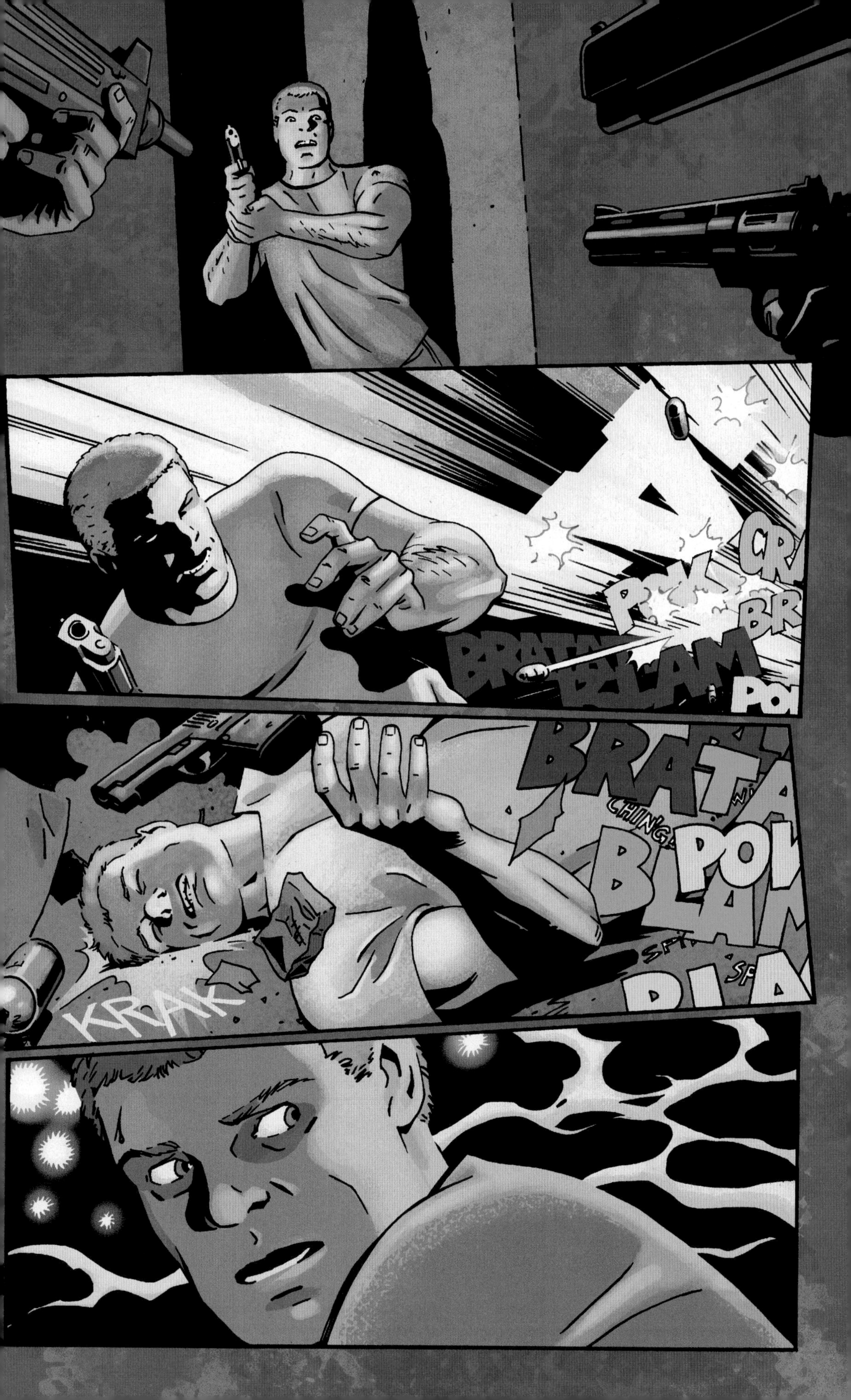
BLAM
CHING
KRAK

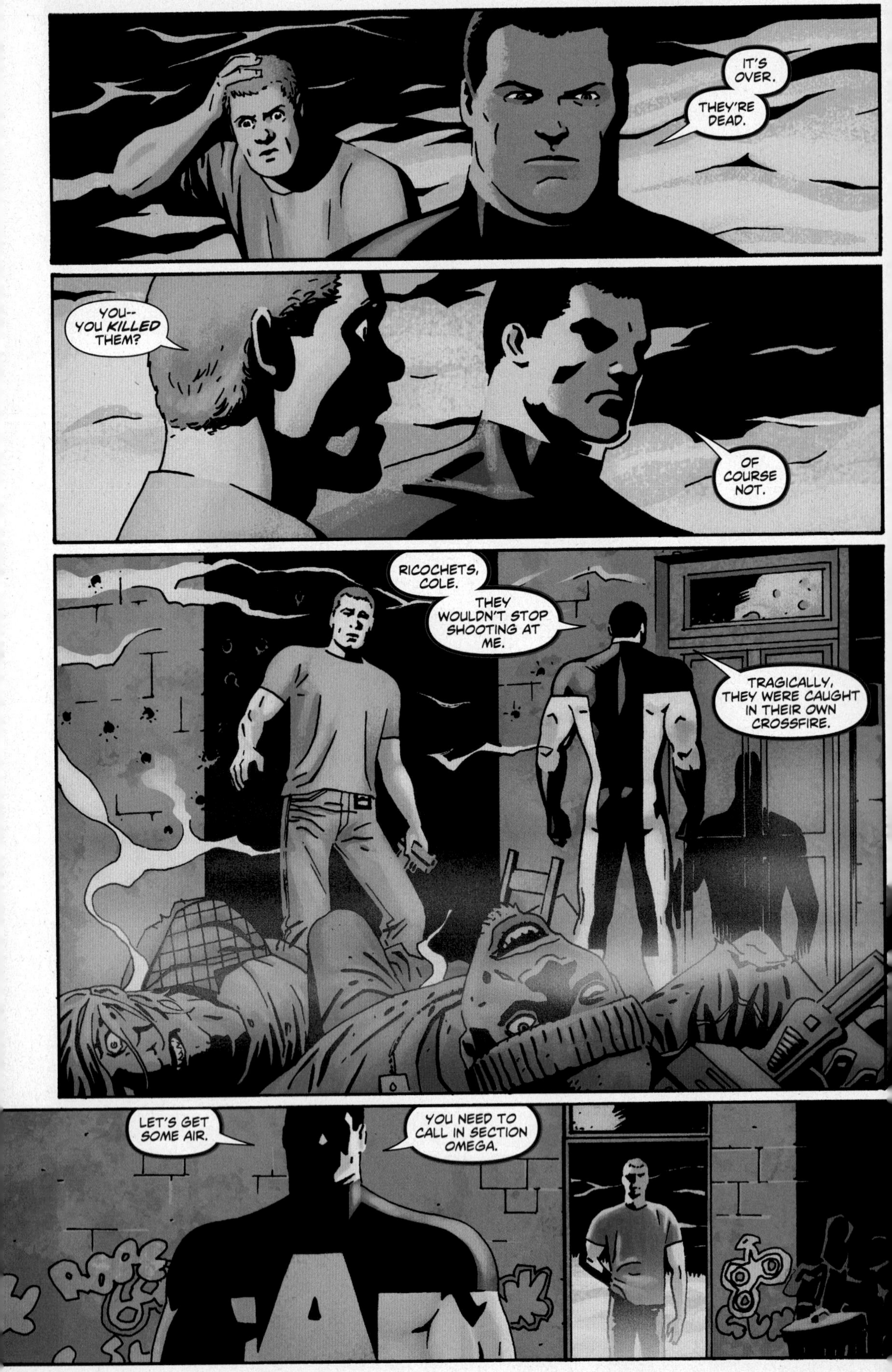
IT'S OVER.
THEY'RE DEAD.
YOU-- YOU KILLED THEM?
OF COURSE NOT.
RICOCHETS, COLE.
THEY WOULDN'T STOP SHOOTING AT ME.
TRAGICALLY, THEY WERE CAUGHT IN THEIR OWN CROSSFIRE.
LET'S GET SOME AIR.
YOU NEED TO CALL IN SECTION OMEGA.

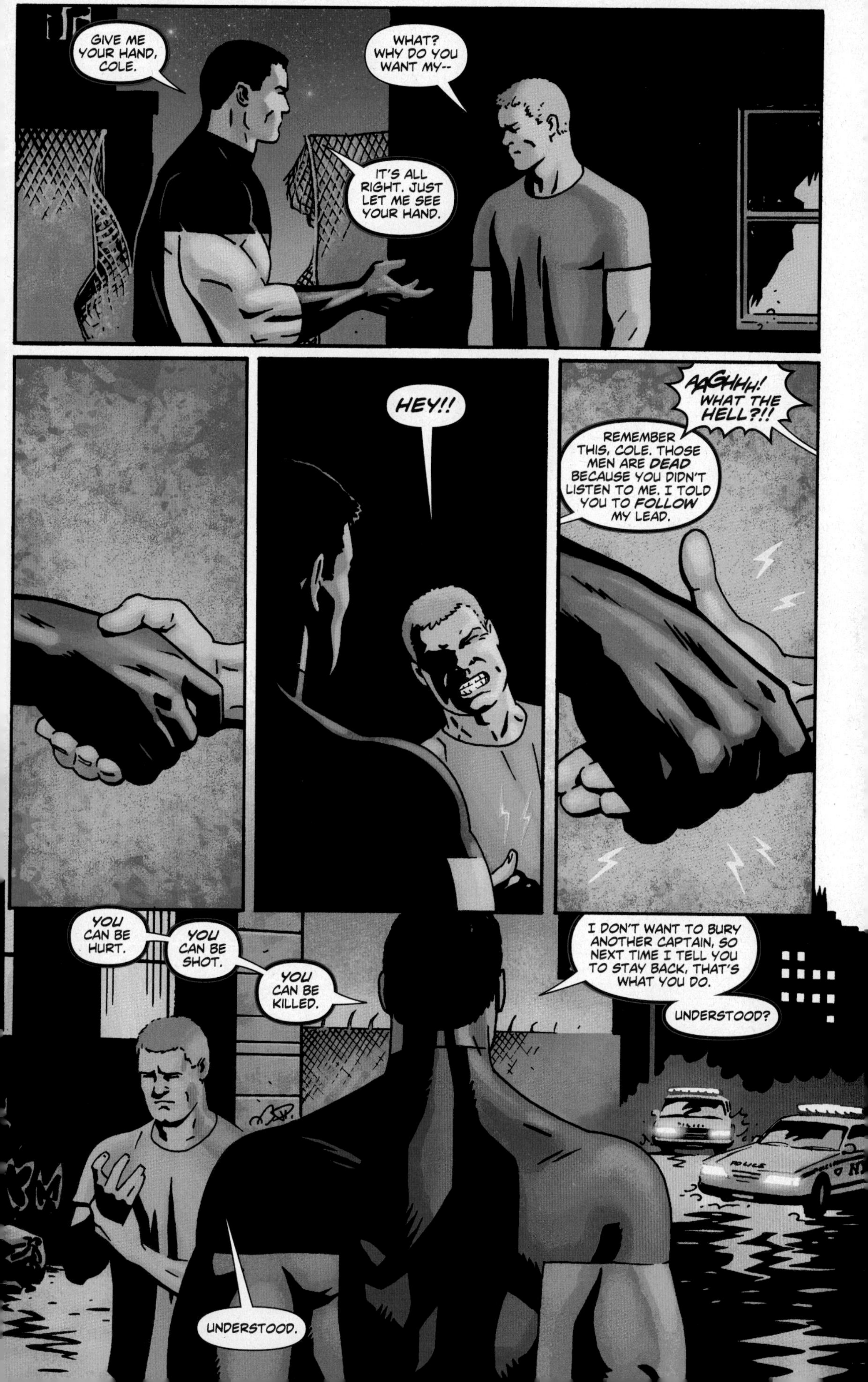
GIVE ME YOUR HAND, COLE.
WHAT? WHY DO YOU WANT MY--
IT'S ALL RIGHT. JUST LET ME SEE YOUR HAND.
HEY!!
AAGHHH! WHAT THE HELL?!!
REMEMBER THIS, COLE. THOSE MEN ARE DEAD BECAUSE YOU DIDN'T LISTEN TO ME. I TOLD YOU TO FOLLOW MY LEAD.
YOU CAN BE HURT.
YOU CAN BE SHOT.
YOU CAN BE KILLED.
I DON'T WANT TO BURY ANOTHER CAPTAIN, SO NEXT TIME I TELL YOU TO STAY BACK, THAT'S WHAT YOU DO.
UNDERSTOOD?
UNDERSTOOD.

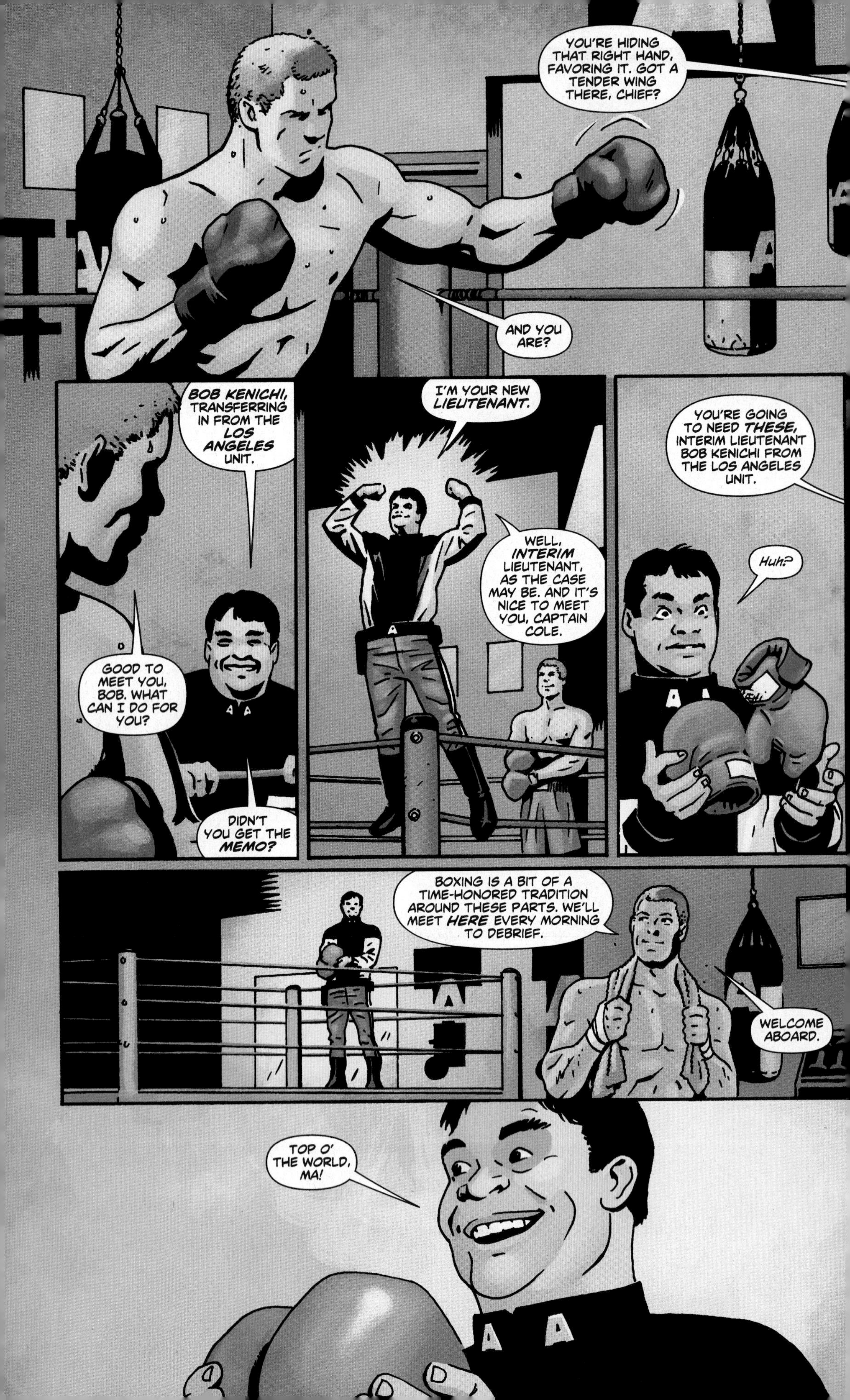
YOU'RE HIDING THAT RIGHT HAND, FAVORING IT. GOT A TENDER WING THERE, CHIEF?
AND YOU ARE?
BOB KENICHI, TRANSFERRING IN FROM THE LOS ANGELES UNIT.
GOOD TO MEET YOU, BOB. WHAT CAN I DO FOR YOU?
DIDN'T YOU GET THE MEMO?
I'M YOUR NEW LIEUTENANT.
WELL, INTERIM LIEUTENANT, AS THE CASE MAY BE. AND IT'S NICE TO MEET YOU, CAPTAIN COLE.
YOU'RE GOING TO NEED THESE, INTERIM LIEUTENANT BOB KENICHI FROM THE LOS ANGELES UNIT.
Huh?
BOXING IS A BIT OF A TIME-HONORED TRADITION AROUND THESE PARTS. WE'LL MEET HERE EVERY MORNING TO DEBRIEF.
WELCOME ABOARD.
TOP O' THE WORLD, MA!

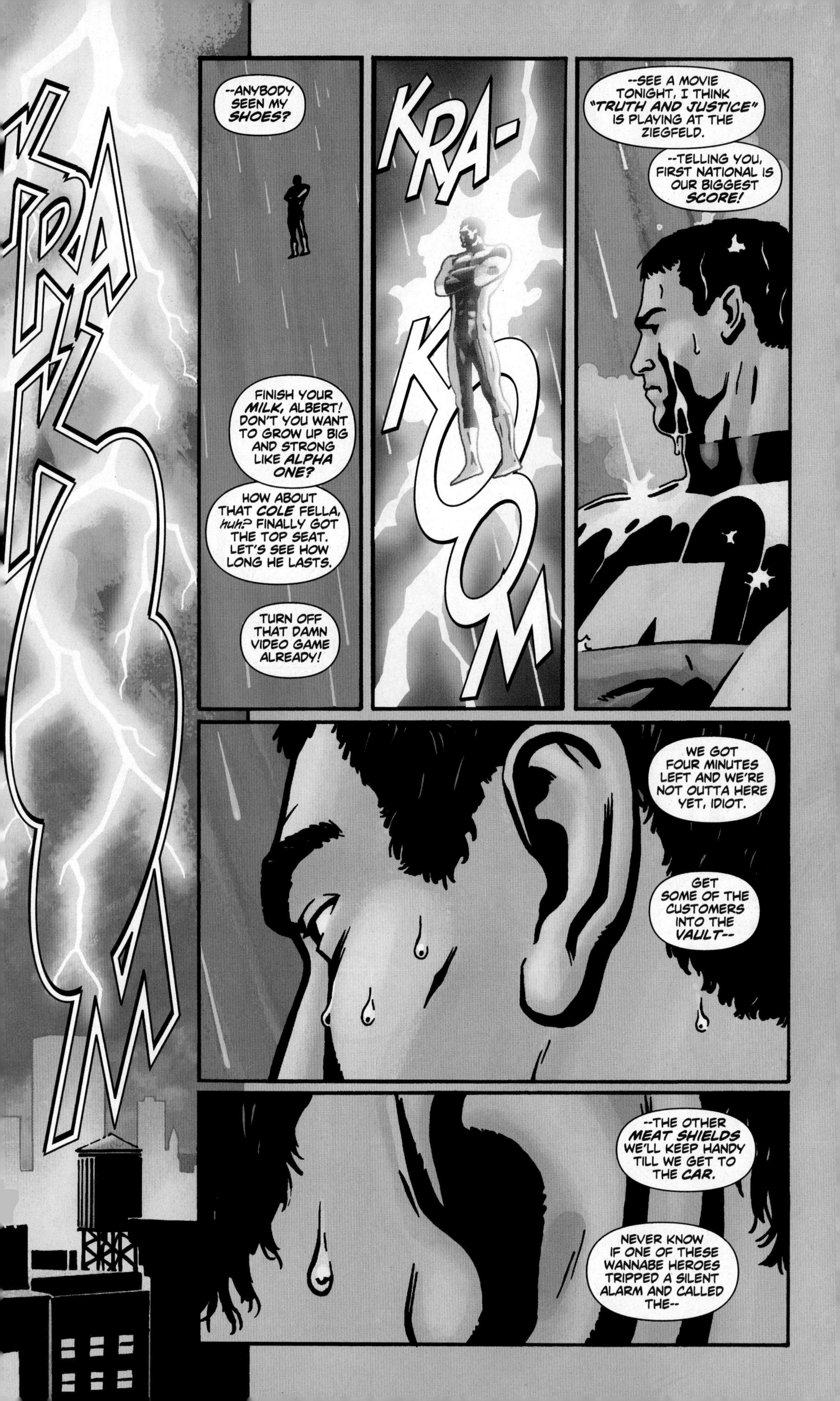

KRA-BLAM
--ANYBODY SEEN MY SHOES?
FINISH YOUR MILK, ALBERT! DON'T YOU WANT TO GROW UP BIG AND STRONG LIKE ALPHA ONE?
HOW ABOUT THAT COLE FELLA, huh? FINALLY GOT THE TOP SEAT. LET'S SEE HOW LONG HE LASTS.
TURN OFF THAT DAMN VIDEO GAME ALREADY!
KRA-KOOM
--SEE A MOVIE TONIGHT, I THINK "TRUTH AND JUSTICE" IS PLAYING AT THE ZIEGFELD.
--TELLING YOU, FIRST NATIONAL IS OUR BIGGEST SCORE!
WE GOT FOUR MINUTES LEFT AND WE'RE NOT OUTTA HERE YET, IDIOT.
GET SOME OF THE CUSTOMERS INTO THE VAULT--
--THE OTHER MEAT SHIELDS WE'LL KEEP HANDY TILL WE GET TO THE CAR.
NEVER KNOW IF ONE OF THESE WANNABE HEROES TRIPPED A SILENT ALARM AND CALLED THE--

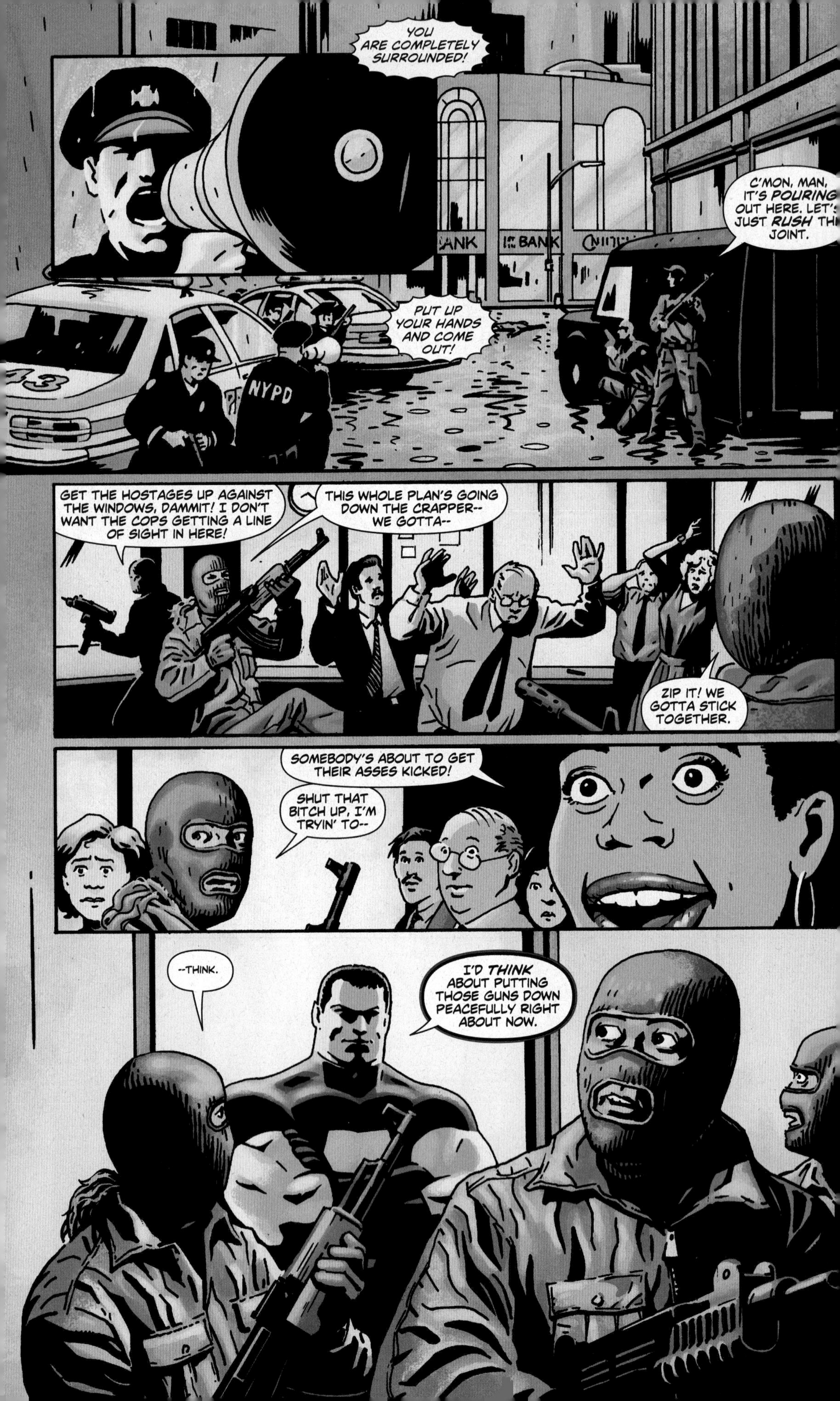
YOU ARE COMPLETELY SURROUNDED!
C'MON, MAN, IT'S POURING OUT HERE. LET'S JUST RUSH THE JOINT.
PUT UP YOUR HANDS AND COME OUT!
BANK
BANK
GET THE HOSTAGES UP AGAINST THE WINDOWS, DAMMIT! I DON'T WANT THE COPS GETTING A LINE OF SIGHT IN HERE!
THIS WHOLE PLAN'S GOING DOWN THE CRAPPER-- WE GOTTA--
ZIP IT! WE GOTTA STICK TOGETHER.
SOMEBODY'S ABOUT TO GET THEIR ASSES KICKED!
SHUT THAT BITCH UP, I'M TRYIN' TO--
--THINK.
I'D THINK ABOUT PUTTING THOSE GUNS DOWN PEACEFULLY RIGHT ABOUT NOW.

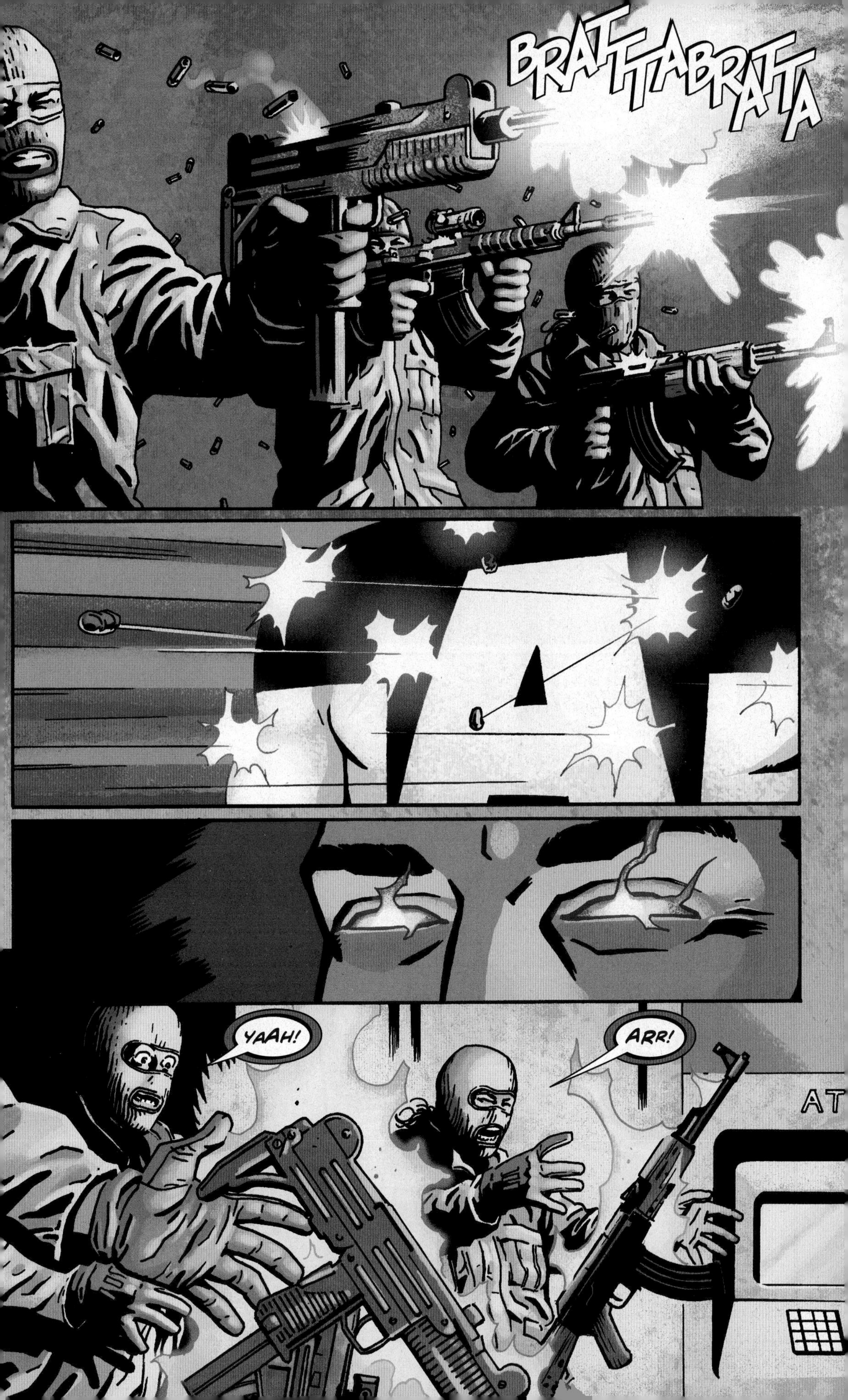
BRATTTABRATTA
YAAH!
ARR!
AT

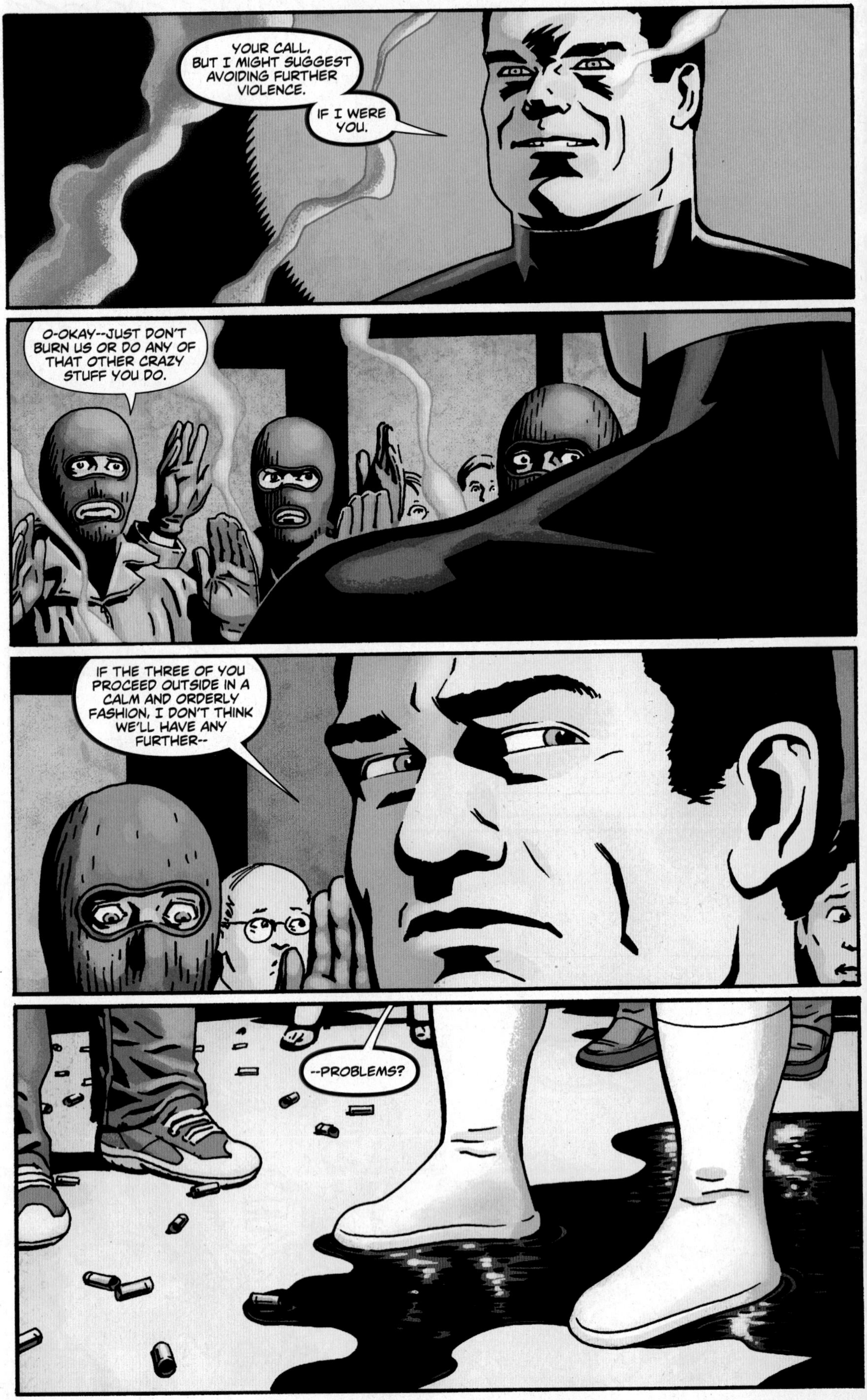
YOUR CALL, BUT I MIGHT SUGGEST AVOIDING FURTHER VIOLENCE.
IF I WERE YOU.
O-OKAY--JUST DON'T BURN US OR DO ANY OF THAT OTHER CRAZY STUFF YOU DO.
IF THE THREE OF YOU PROCEED OUTSIDE IN A CALM AND ORDERLY FASHION, I DON'T THINK WE'LL HAVE ANY FURTHER--
--PROBLEMS?

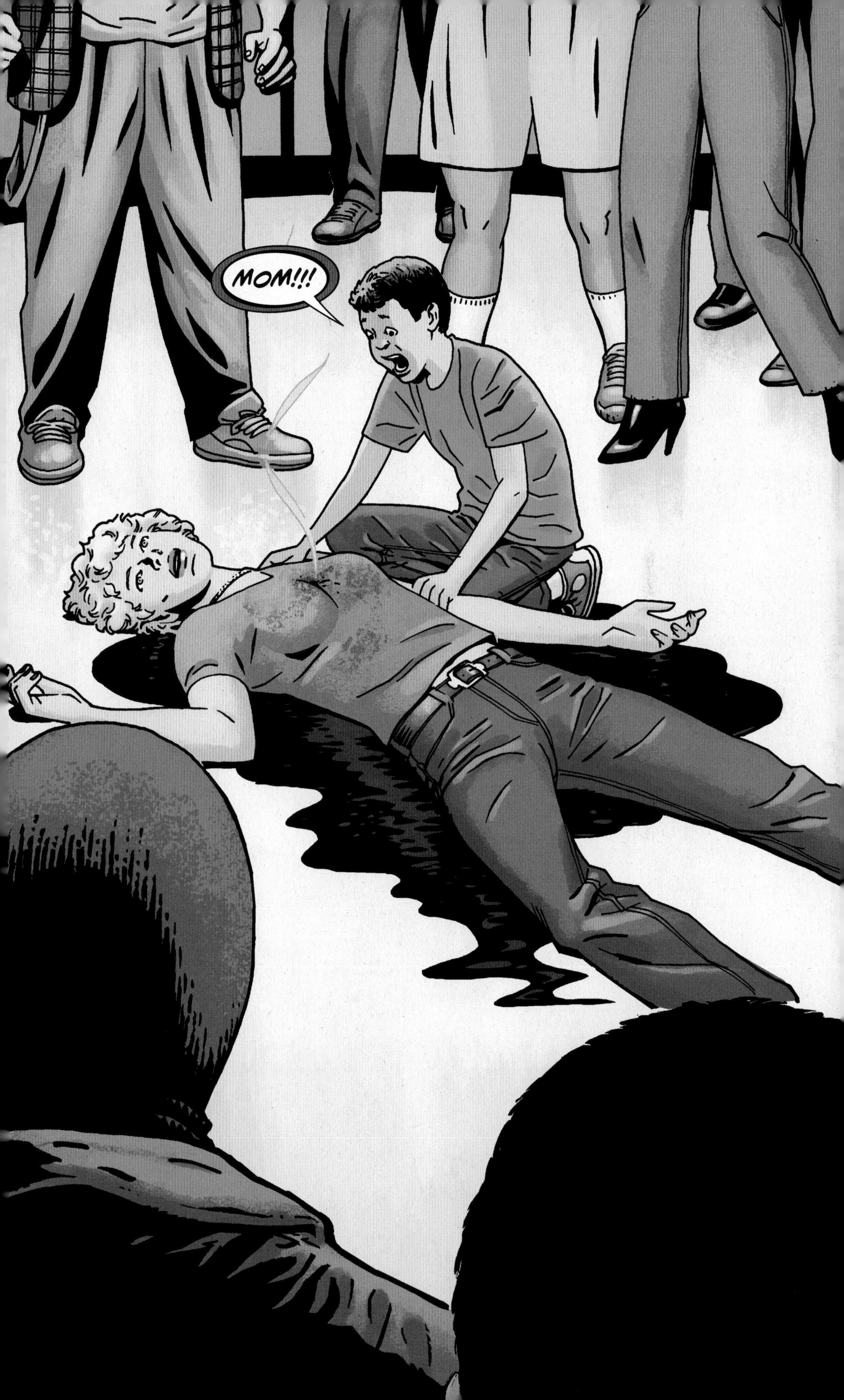
MOM!!!

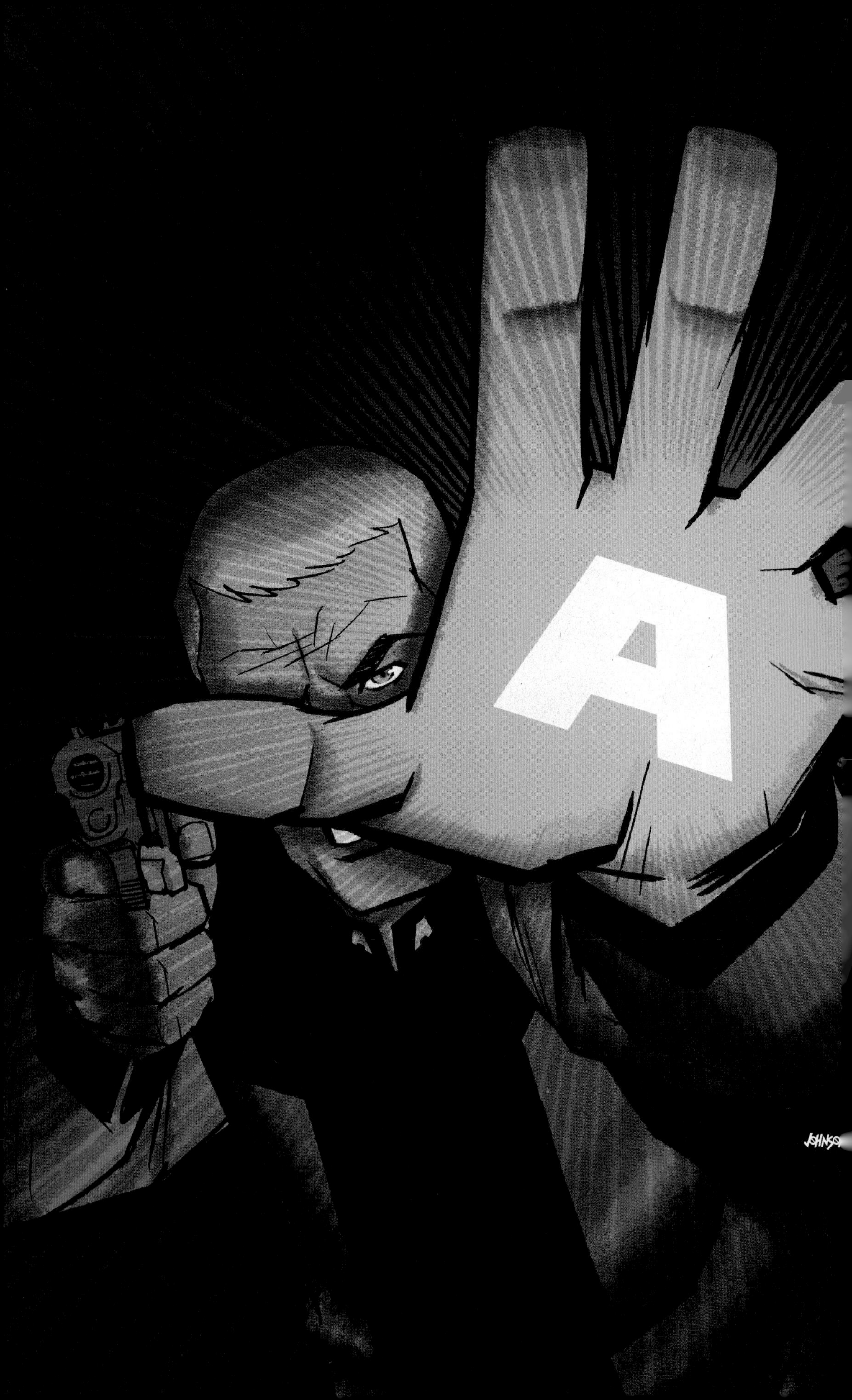

DIRGE

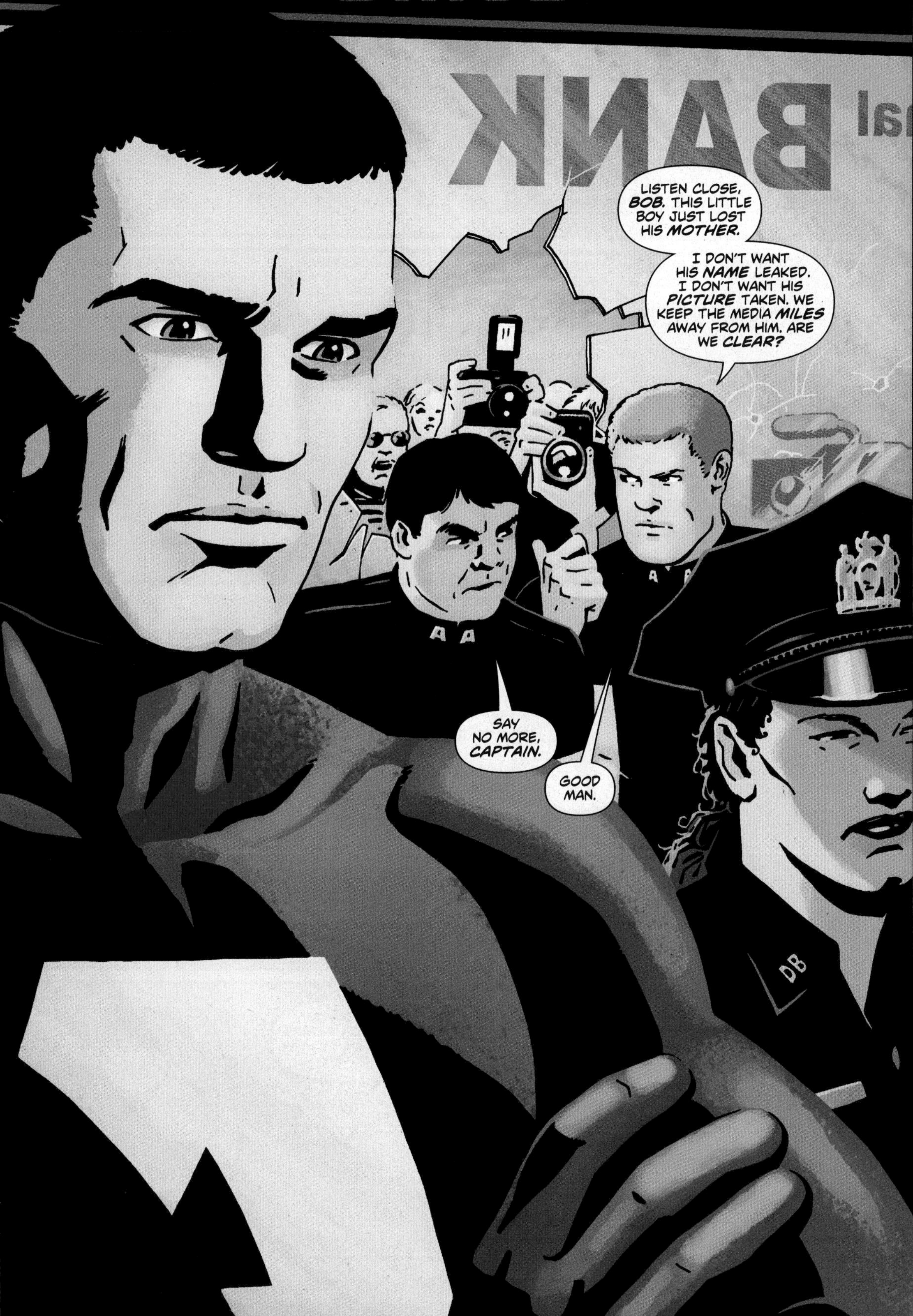
LISTEN CLOSE, BOB. THIS LITTLE BOY JUST LOST HIS MOTHER.
I DON'T WANT HIS NAME LEAKED. I DON'T WANT HIS PICTURE TAKEN. WE KEEP THE MEDIA MILES AWAY FROM HIM. ARE WE CLEAR?
SAY NO MORE, CAPTAIN.
GOOD MAN.
DB

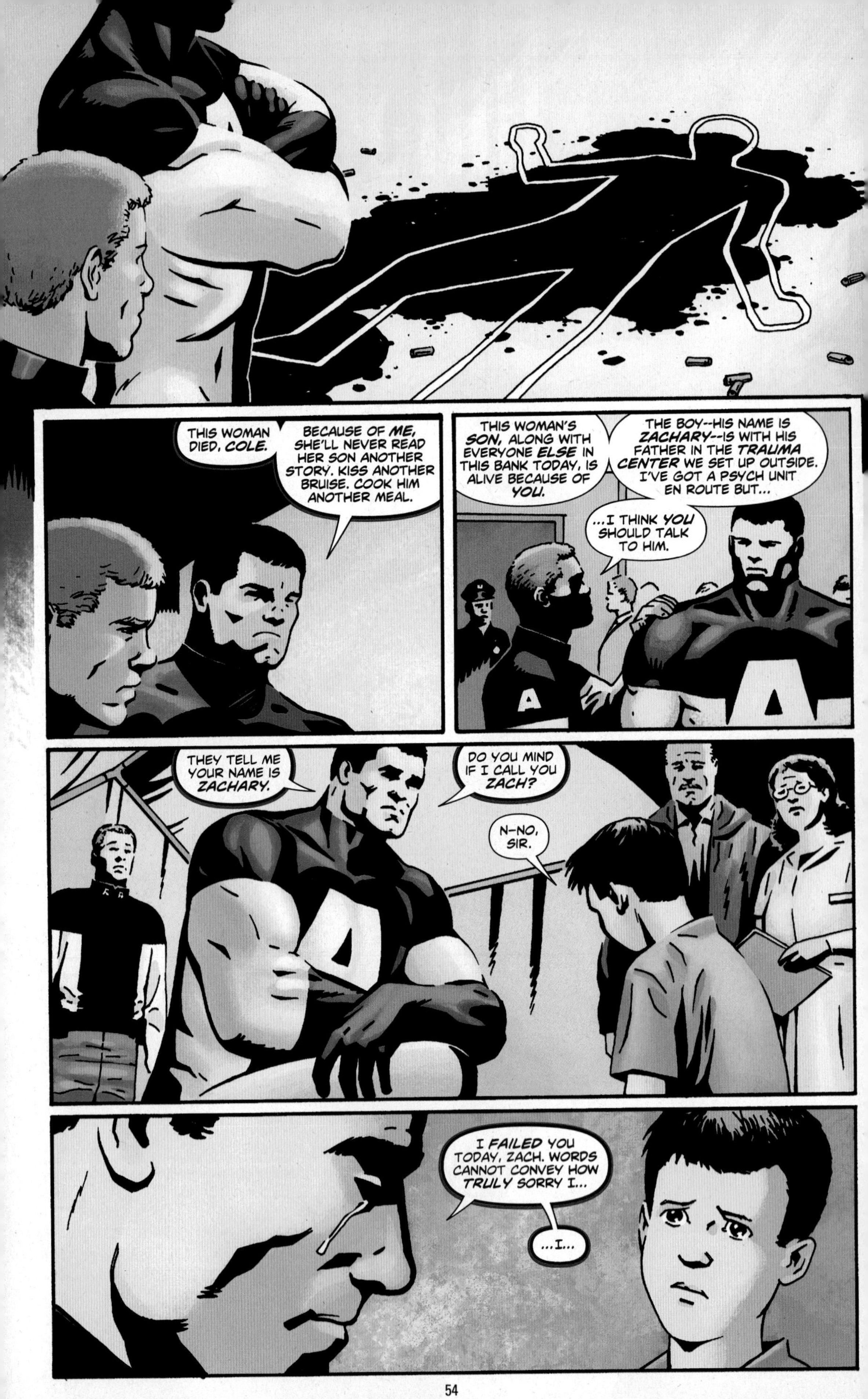
THIS WOMAN DIED, COLE.
BECAUSE OF ME, SHE'LL NEVER READ HER SON ANOTHER STORY. KISS ANOTHER BRUISE. COOK HIM ANOTHER MEAL.
THIS WOMAN'S SON, ALONG WITH EVERYONE ELSE IN THIS BANK TODAY, IS ALIVE BECAUSE OF YOU.
THE BOY--HIS NAME IS ZACHARY--IS WITH HIS FATHER IN THE TRAUMA CENTER WE SET UP OUTSIDE. I'VE GOT A PSYCH UNIT EN ROUTE BUT...
...I THINK YOU SHOULD TALK TO HIM.
THEY TELL ME YOUR NAME IS ZACHARY.
DO YOU MIND IF I CALL YOU ZACH?
N-NO, SIR.
I FAILED YOU TODAY, ZACH. WORDS CANNOT CONVEY HOW TRULY SORRY I...
...I...

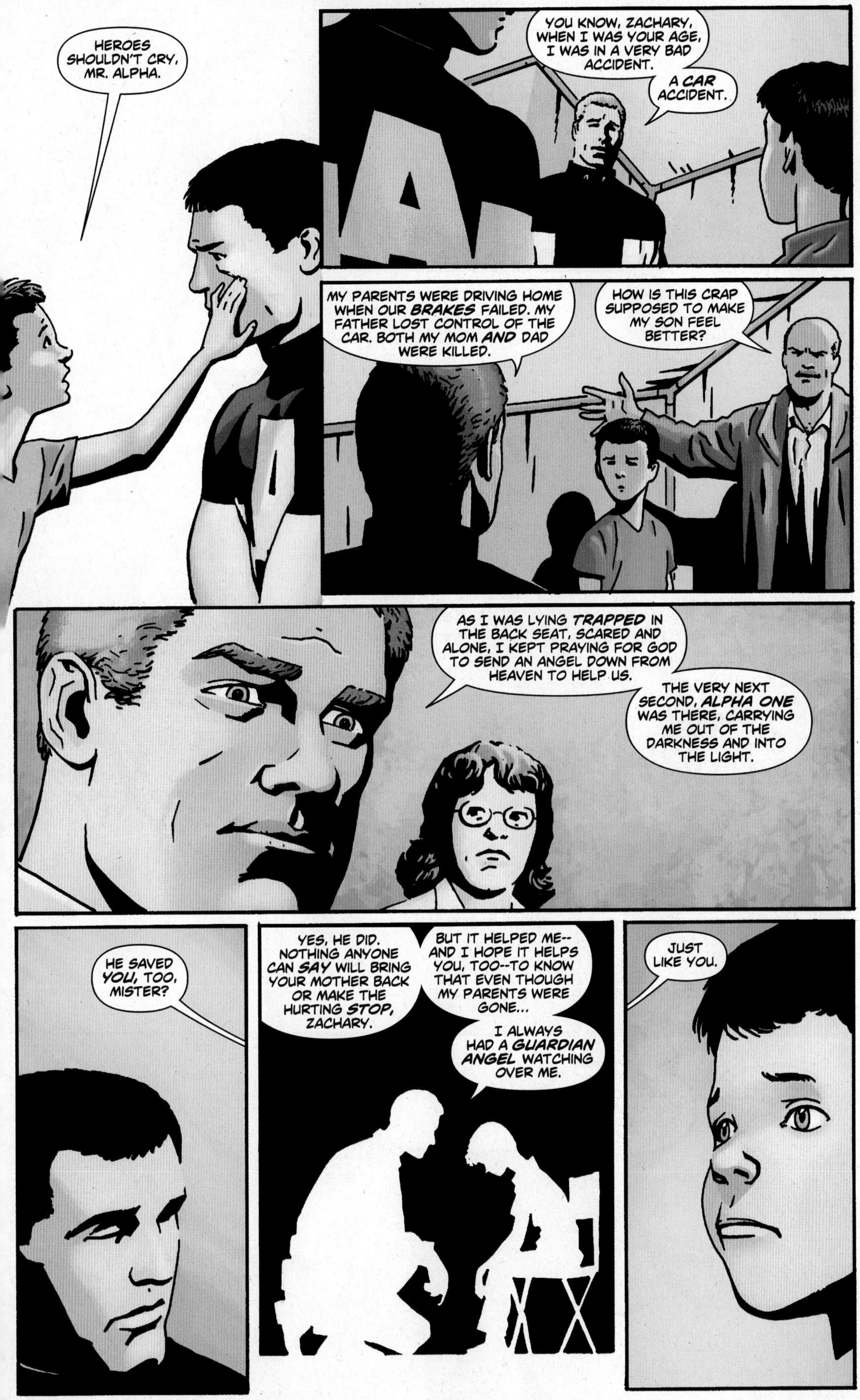

HEROES SHOULDN'T CRY, MR. ALPHA.
YOU KNOW, ZACHARY, WHEN I WAS YOUR AGE, I WAS IN A VERY BAD ACCIDENT.
A CAR ACCIDENT.
MY PARENTS WERE DRIVING HOME WHEN OUR BRAKES FAILED. MY FATHER LOST CONTROL OF THE CAR. BOTH MY MOM AND DAD WERE KILLED.
HOW IS THIS CRAP SUPPOSED TO MAKE MY SON FEEL BETTER?
AS I WAS LYING TRAPPED IN THE BACK SEAT, SCARED AND ALONE, I KEPT PRAYING FOR GOD TO SEND AN ANGEL DOWN FROM HEAVEN TO HELP US.
THE VERY NEXT SECOND, ALPHA ONE WAS THERE, CARRYING ME OUT OF THE DARKNESS AND INTO THE LIGHT.
HE SAVED YOU, TOO, MISTER?
YES, HE DID. NOTHING ANYONE CAN SAY WILL BRING YOUR MOTHER BACK OR MAKE THE HURTING STOP, ZACHARY.
BUT IT HELPED ME-- AND I HOPE IT HELPS YOU, TOO--TO KNOW THAT EVEN THOUGH MY PARENTS WERE GONE...
I ALWAYS HAD A GUARDIAN ANGEL WATCHING OVER ME.
JUST LIKE YOU.

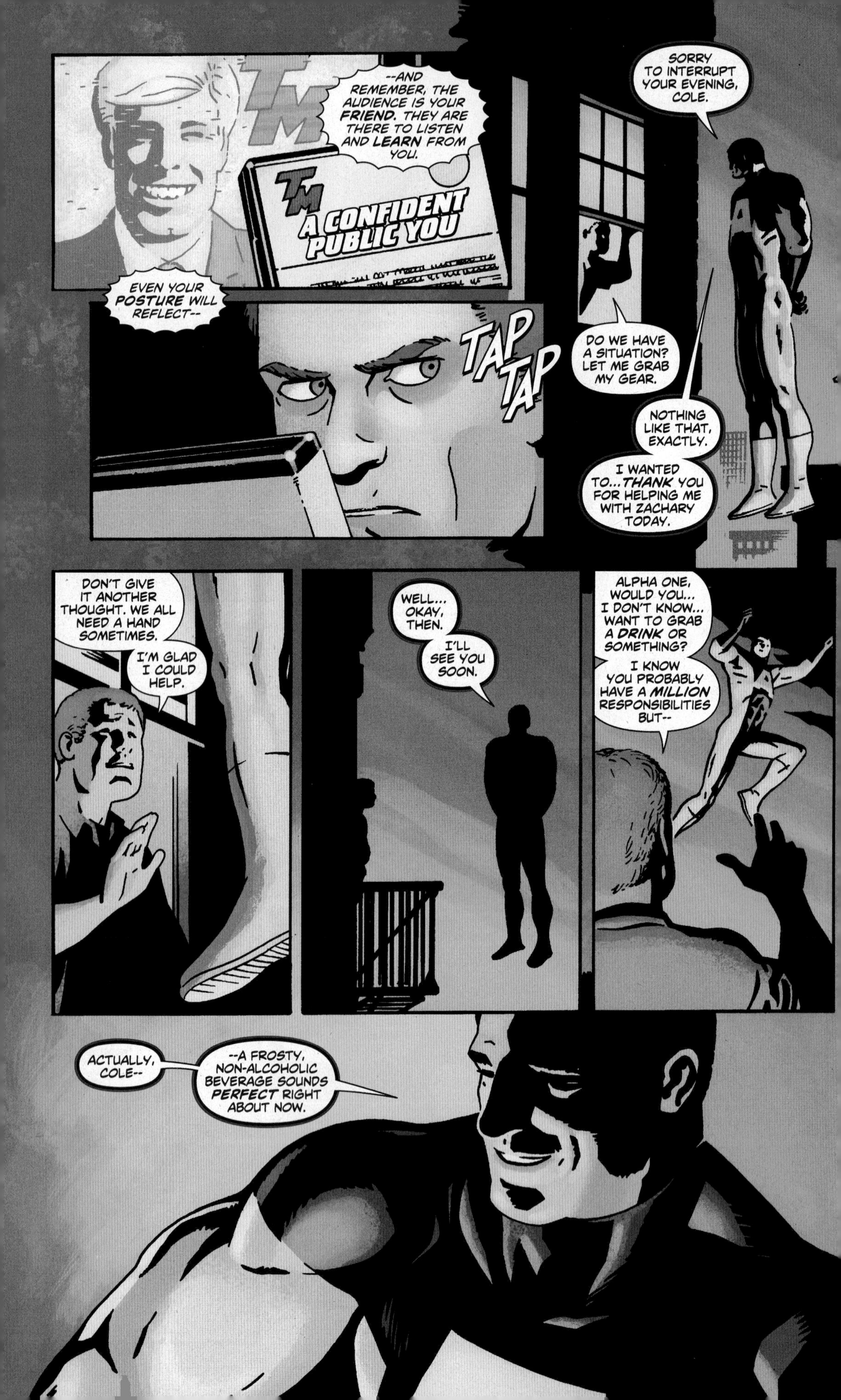
--AND REMEMBER, THE AUDIENCE IS YOUR FRIEND. THEY ARE THERE TO LISTEN AND LEARN FROM YOU.
TM A CONFIDENT PUBLIC YOU
SORRY TO INTERRUPT YOUR EVENING, COLE.
EVEN YOUR POSTURE WILL REFLECT--
TAP TAP
DO WE HAVE A SITUATION? LET ME GRAB MY GEAR.
NOTHING LIKE THAT, EXACTLY.
I WANTED TO...THANK YOU FOR HELPING ME WITH ZACHARY TODAY.
DON'T GIVE IT ANOTHER THOUGHT. WE ALL NEED A HAND SOMETIMES.
I'M GLAD I COULD HELP.
WELL... OKAY, THEN.
I'LL SEE YOU SOON.
ALPHA ONE, WOULD YOU... I DON'T KNOW... WANT TO GRAB A DRINK OR SOMETHING?
I KNOW YOU PROBABLY HAVE A MILLION RESPONSIBILITIES BUT--
ACTUALLY, COLE--
--A FROSTY, NON-ALCOHOLIC BEVERAGE SOUNDS PERFECT RIGHT ABOUT NOW.

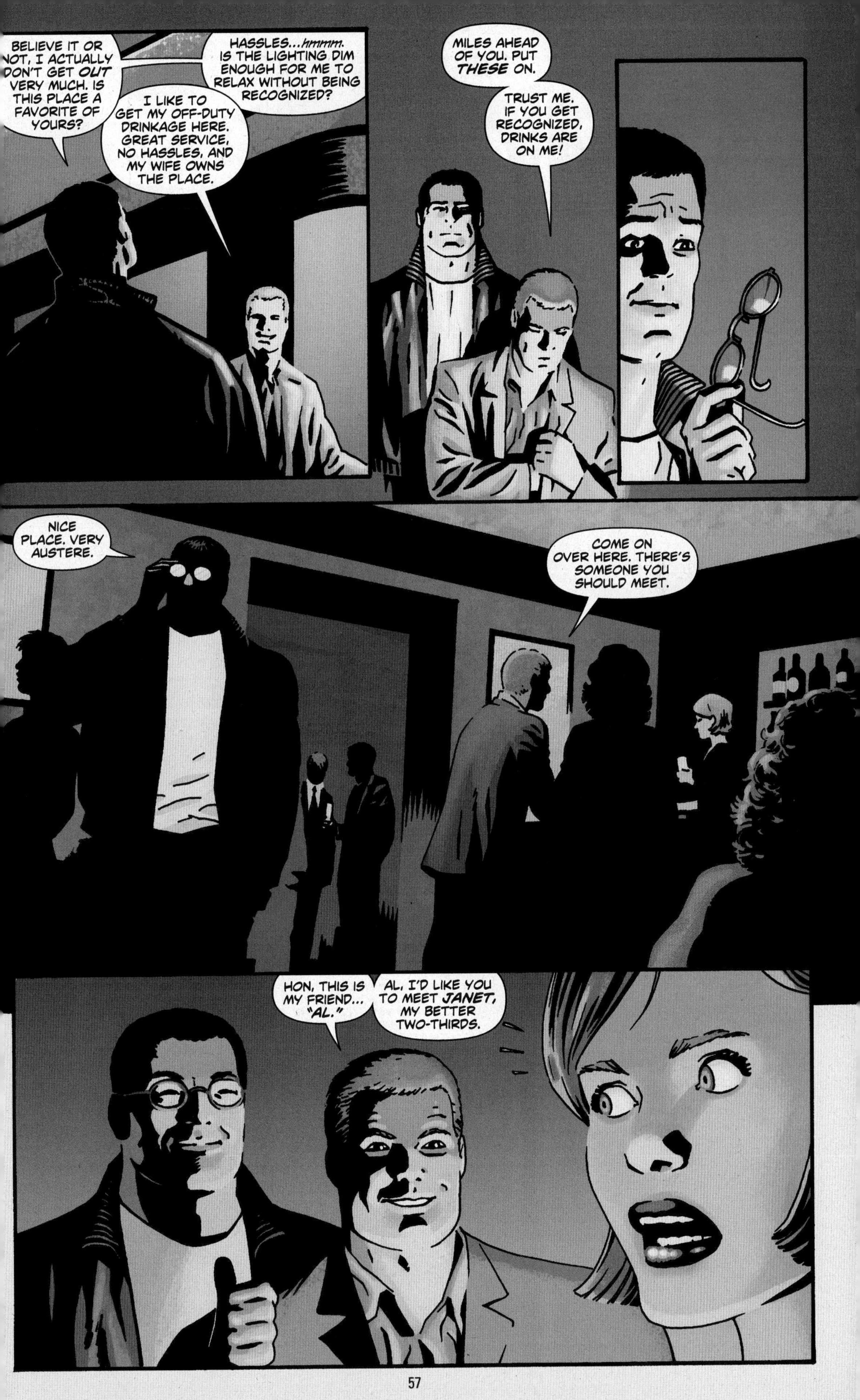

BELIEVE IT OR NOT, I ACTUALLY DON'T GET *OUT* VERY MUCH. IS THIS PLACE A FAVORITE OF YOURS?
I LIKE TO GET MY OFF-DUTY DRINKAGE HERE. GREAT SERVICE, NO HASSLES, AND MY WIFE OWNS THE PLACE.
HASSLES... *hmmm.* IS THE LIGHTING DIM ENOUGH FOR ME TO RELAX WITHOUT BEING RECOGNIZED?
MILES AHEAD OF YOU. PUT *THESE* ON.
TRUST ME. IF YOU GET RECOGNIZED, DRINKS ARE ON ME!
NICE PLACE. VERY AUSTERE.
COME ON OVER HERE. THERE'S SOMEONE YOU SHOULD MEET.
HON, THIS IS MY FRIEND... *"AL."*
AL, I'D LIKE YOU TO MEET *JANET*, MY BETTER TWO-THIRDS.

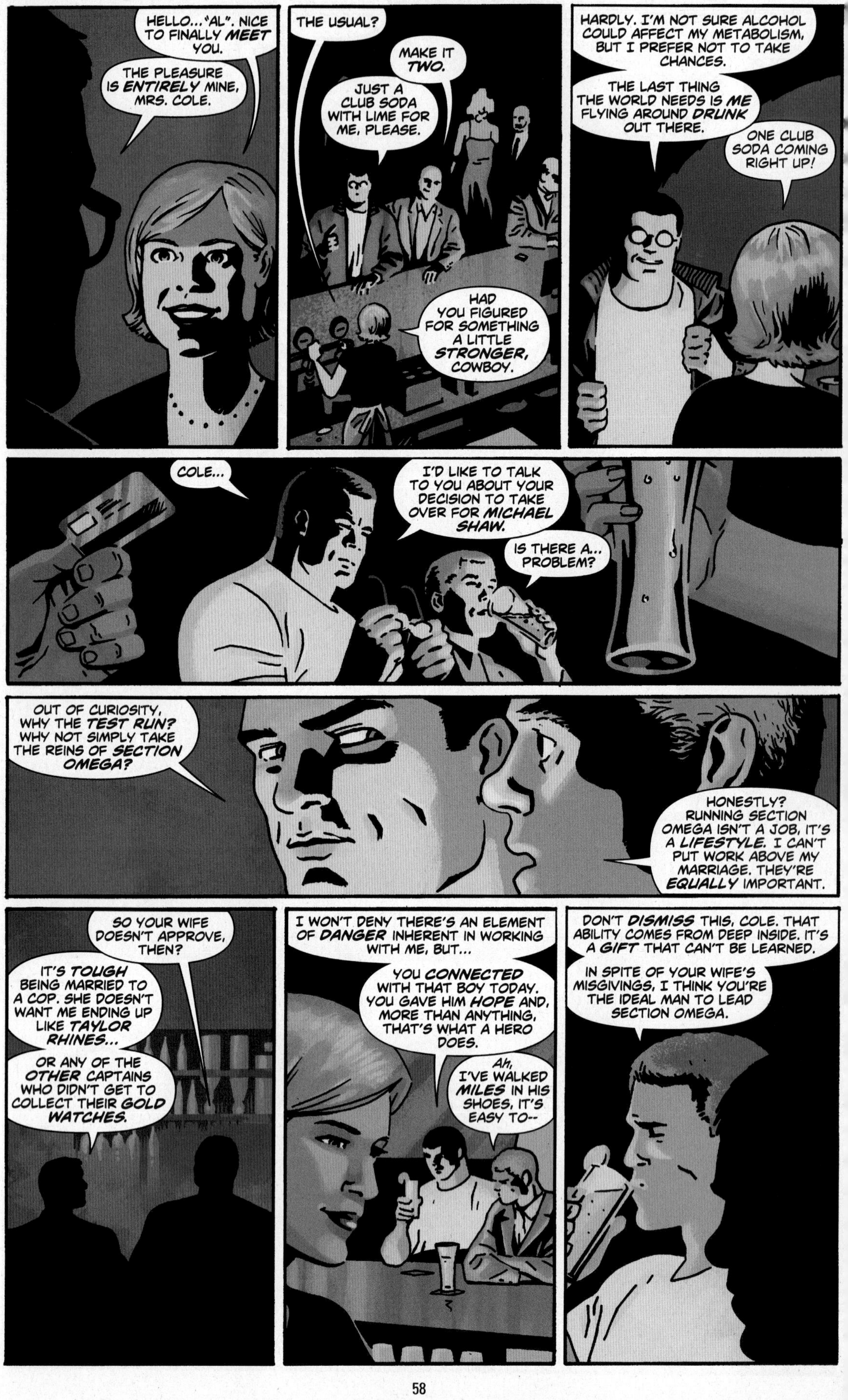
HELLO... "AL". NICE TO FINALLY MEET YOU.
THE PLEASURE IS ENTIRELY MINE, MRS. COLE.
THE USUAL?
MAKE IT TWO.
JUST A CLUB SODA WITH LIME FOR ME, PLEASE.
HAD YOU FIGURED FOR SOMETHING A LITTLE STRONGER, COWBOY.
HARDLY. I'M NOT SURE ALCOHOL COULD AFFECT MY METABOLISM, BUT I PREFER NOT TO TAKE CHANCES.
THE LAST THING THE WORLD NEEDS IS ME FLYING AROUND DRUNK OUT THERE.
ONE CLUB SODA COMING RIGHT UP!
COLE...
I'D LIKE TO TALK TO YOU ABOUT YOUR DECISION TO TAKE OVER FOR MICHAEL SHAW.
IS THERE A... PROBLEM?
OUT OF CURIOSITY, WHY THE TEST RUN? WHY NOT SIMPLY TAKE THE REINS OF SECTION OMEGA?
HONESTLY? RUNNING SECTION OMEGA ISN'T A JOB, IT'S A LIFESTYLE. I CAN'T PUT WORK ABOVE MY MARRIAGE. THEY'RE EQUALLY IMPORTANT.
SO YOUR WIFE DOESN'T APPROVE, THEN?
IT'S TOUGH BEING MARRIED TO A COP. SHE DOESN'T WANT ME ENDING UP LIKE TAYLOR RHINES...
OR ANY OF THE OTHER CAPTAINS WHO DIDN'T GET TO COLLECT THEIR GOLD WATCHES.
I WON'T DENY THERE'S AN ELEMENT OF DANGER INHERENT IN WORKING WITH ME, BUT...
YOU CONNECTED WITH THAT BOY TODAY. YOU GAVE HIM HOPE AND, MORE THAN ANYTHING, THAT'S WHAT A HERO DOES.
Ah, I'VE WALKED MILES IN HIS SHOES, IT'S EASY TO--
DON'T DISMISS THIS, COLE. THAT ABILITY COMES FROM DEEP INSIDE. IT'S A GIFT THAT CAN'T BE LEARNED.
IN SPITE OF YOUR WIFE'S MISGIVINGS, I THINK YOU'RE THE IDEAL MAN TO LEAD SECTION OMEGA.

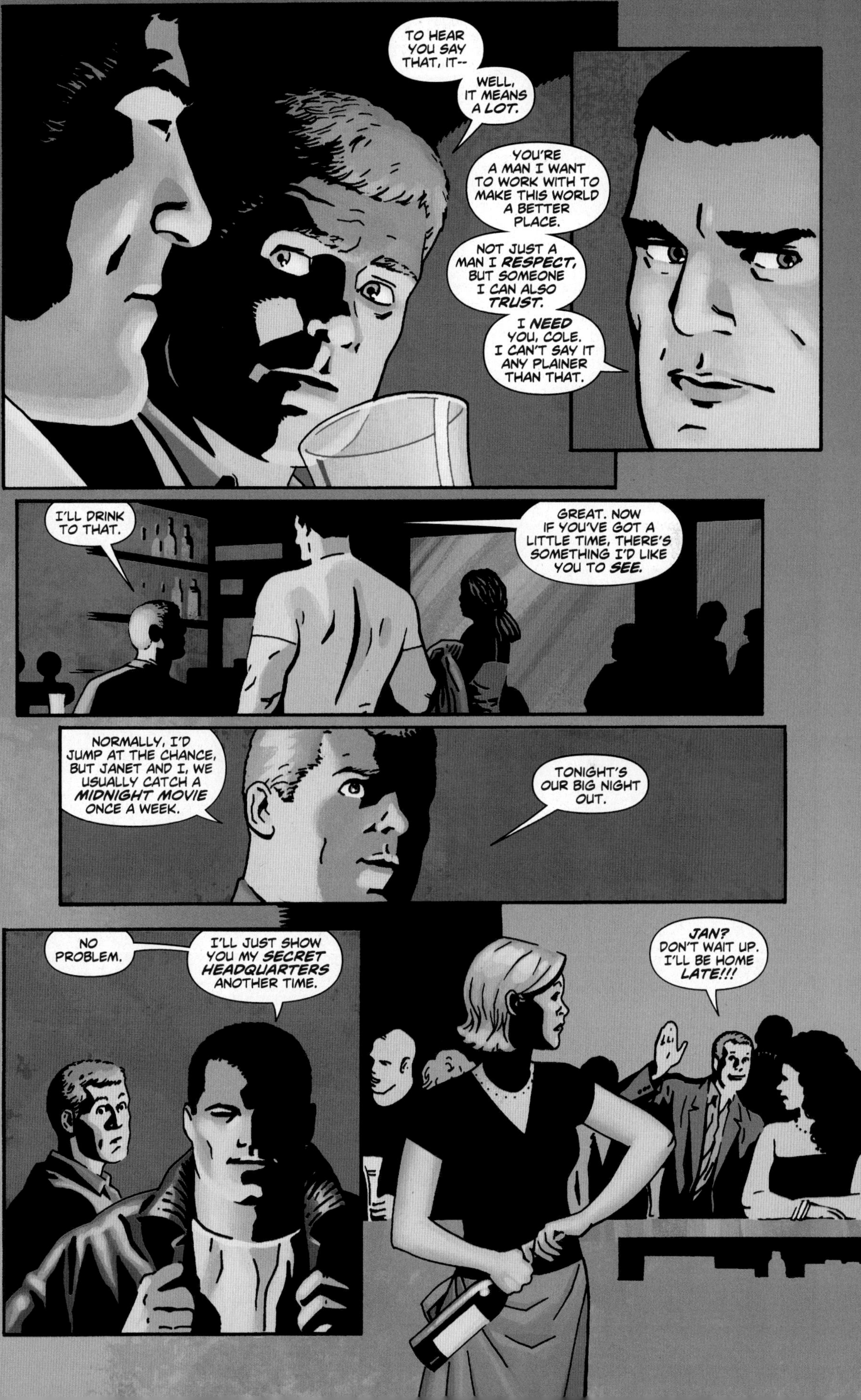
TO HEAR YOU SAY THAT, IT--
WELL, IT MEANS A LOT.
YOU'RE A MAN I WANT TO WORK WITH TO MAKE THIS WORLD A BETTER PLACE.
NOT JUST A MAN I RESPECT, BUT SOMEONE I CAN ALSO TRUST.
I NEED YOU, COLE. I CAN'T SAY IT ANY PLAINER THAN THAT.
I'LL DRINK TO THAT.
GREAT. NOW IF YOU'VE GOT A LITTLE TIME, THERE'S SOMETHING I'D LIKE YOU TO SEE.
NORMALLY, I'D JUMP AT THE CHANCE, BUT JANET AND I, WE USUALLY CATCH A MIDNIGHT MOVIE ONCE A WEEK.
TONIGHT'S OUR BIG NIGHT OUT.
NO PROBLEM.
I'LL JUST SHOW YOU MY SECRET HEADQUARTERS ANOTHER TIME.
JAN? DON'T WAIT UP. I'LL BE HOME LATE!!!

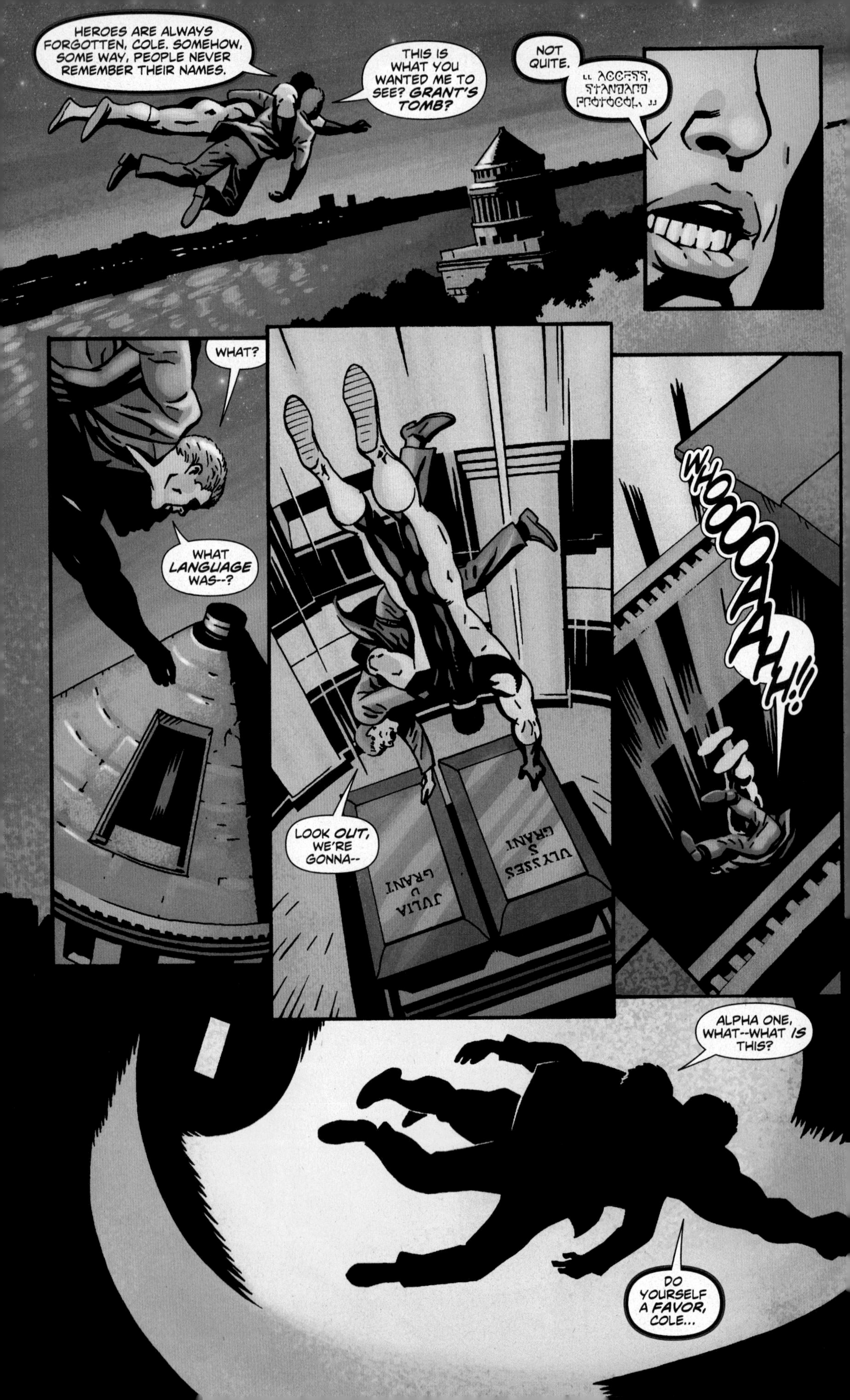
HEROES ARE ALWAYS FORGOTTEN, COLE. SOMEHOW, SOME WAY, PEOPLE NEVER REMEMBER THEIR NAMES.
THIS IS WHAT YOU WANTED ME TO SEE? GRANT'S TOMB?
NOT QUITE.
«ACCESS, STANDARD PROTOCOL.»
WHAT?
WHAT LANGUAGE WAS--?
LOOK OUT, WE'RE GONNA--
ULYSSES S GRANT
JULIA D GRANT
WHOOOAAHH!!
ALPHA ONE, WHAT--WHAT IS THIS?
DO YOURSELF A FAVOR, COLE...

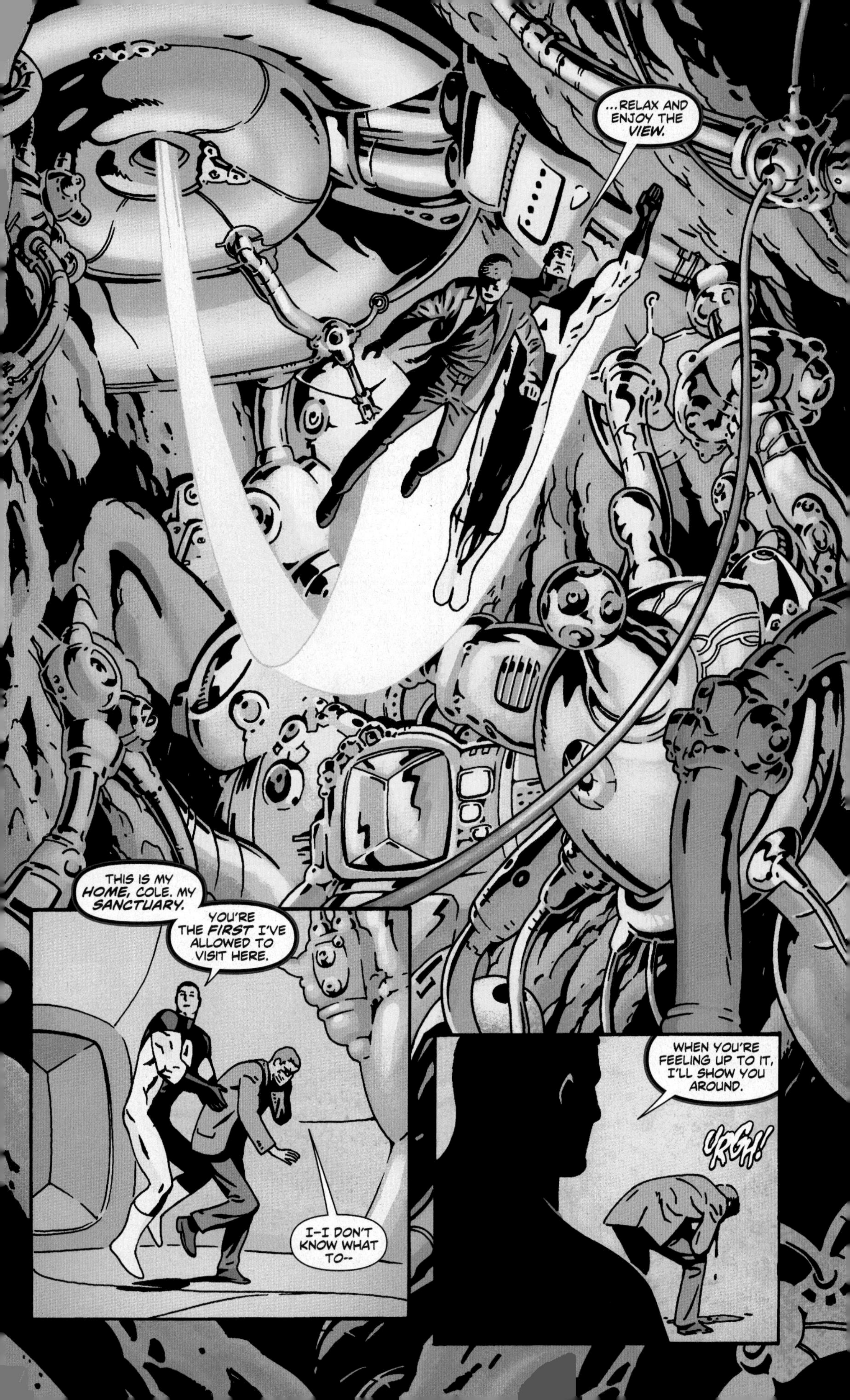
...RELAX AND ENJOY THE VIEW.
THIS IS MY HOME, COLE. MY SANCTUARY.
YOU'RE THE FIRST I'VE ALLOWED TO VISIT HERE.
I--I DON'T KNOW WHAT TO--
WHEN YOU'RE FEELING UP TO IT, I'LL SHOW YOU AROUND.
URGH!

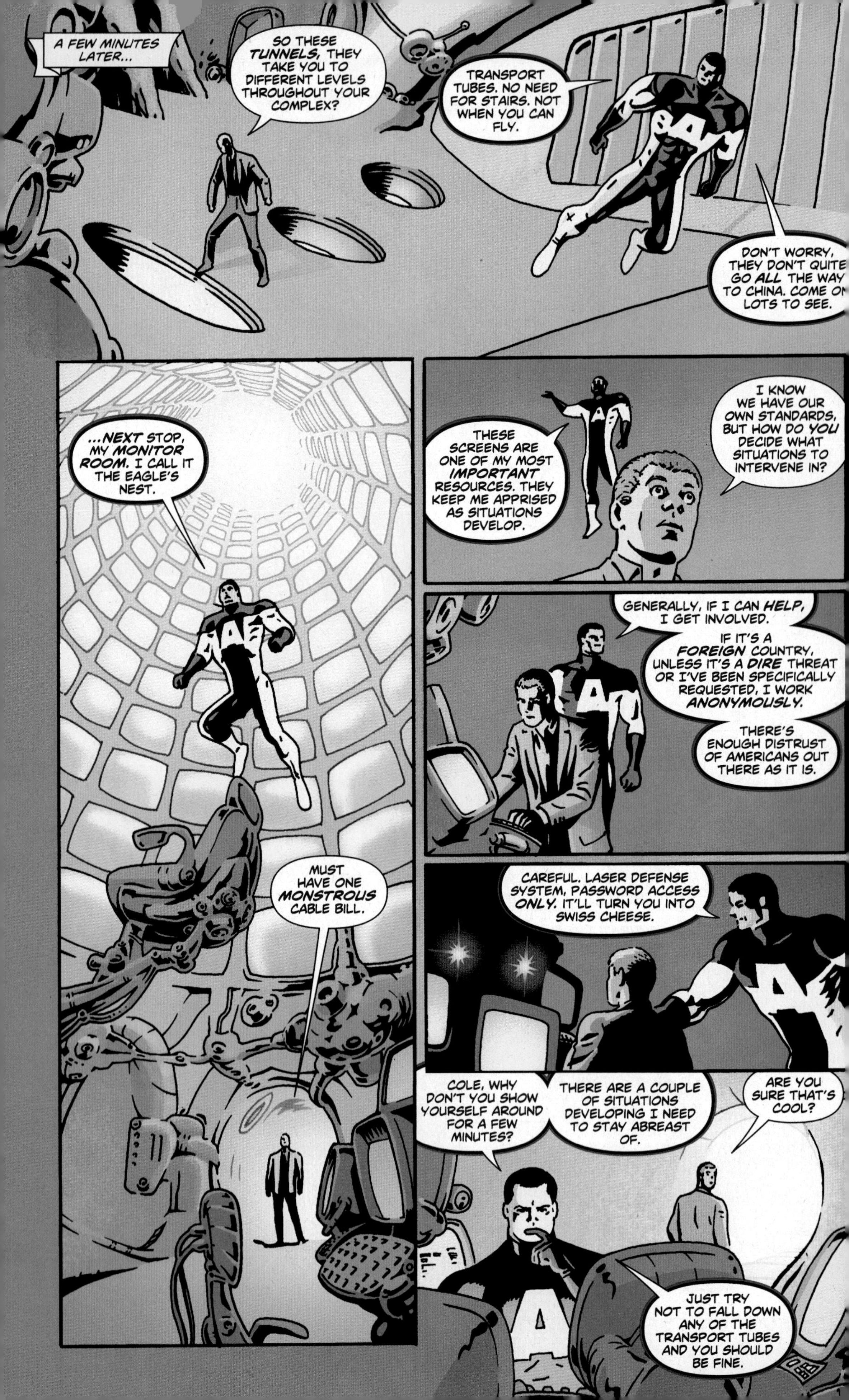
A FEW MINUTES LATER...
SO THESE TUNNELS, THEY TAKE YOU TO DIFFERENT LEVELS THROUGHOUT YOUR COMPLEX?
TRANSPORT TUBES. NO NEED FOR STAIRS. NOT WHEN YOU CAN FLY.
DON'T WORRY, THEY DON'T QUITE GO ALL THE WAY TO CHINA. COME ON LOTS TO SEE.
...NEXT STOP, MY MONITOR ROOM. I CALL IT THE EAGLE'S NEST.
MUST HAVE ONE MONSTROUS CABLE BILL.
THESE SCREENS ARE ONE OF MY MOST IMPORTANT RESOURCES. THEY KEEP ME APPRISED AS SITUATIONS DEVELOP.
I KNOW WE HAVE OUR OWN STANDARDS, BUT HOW DO YOU DECIDE WHAT SITUATIONS TO INTERVENE IN?
GENERALLY, IF I CAN HELP, I GET INVOLVED.
IF IT'S A FOREIGN COUNTRY, UNLESS IT'S A DIRE THREAT OR I'VE BEEN SPECIFICALLY REQUESTED, I WORK ANONYMOUSLY.
THERE'S ENOUGH DISTRUST OF AMERICANS OUT THERE AS IT IS.
CAREFUL. LASER DEFENSE SYSTEM, PASSWORD ACCESS ONLY. IT'LL TURN YOU INTO SWISS CHEESE.
COLE, WHY DON'T YOU SHOW YOURSELF AROUND FOR A FEW MINUTES?
THERE ARE A COUPLE OF SITUATIONS DEVELOPING I NEED TO STAY ABREAST OF.
ARE YOU SURE THAT'S COOL?
JUST TRY NOT TO FALL DOWN ANY OF THE TRANSPORT TUBES AND YOU SHOULD BE FINE.

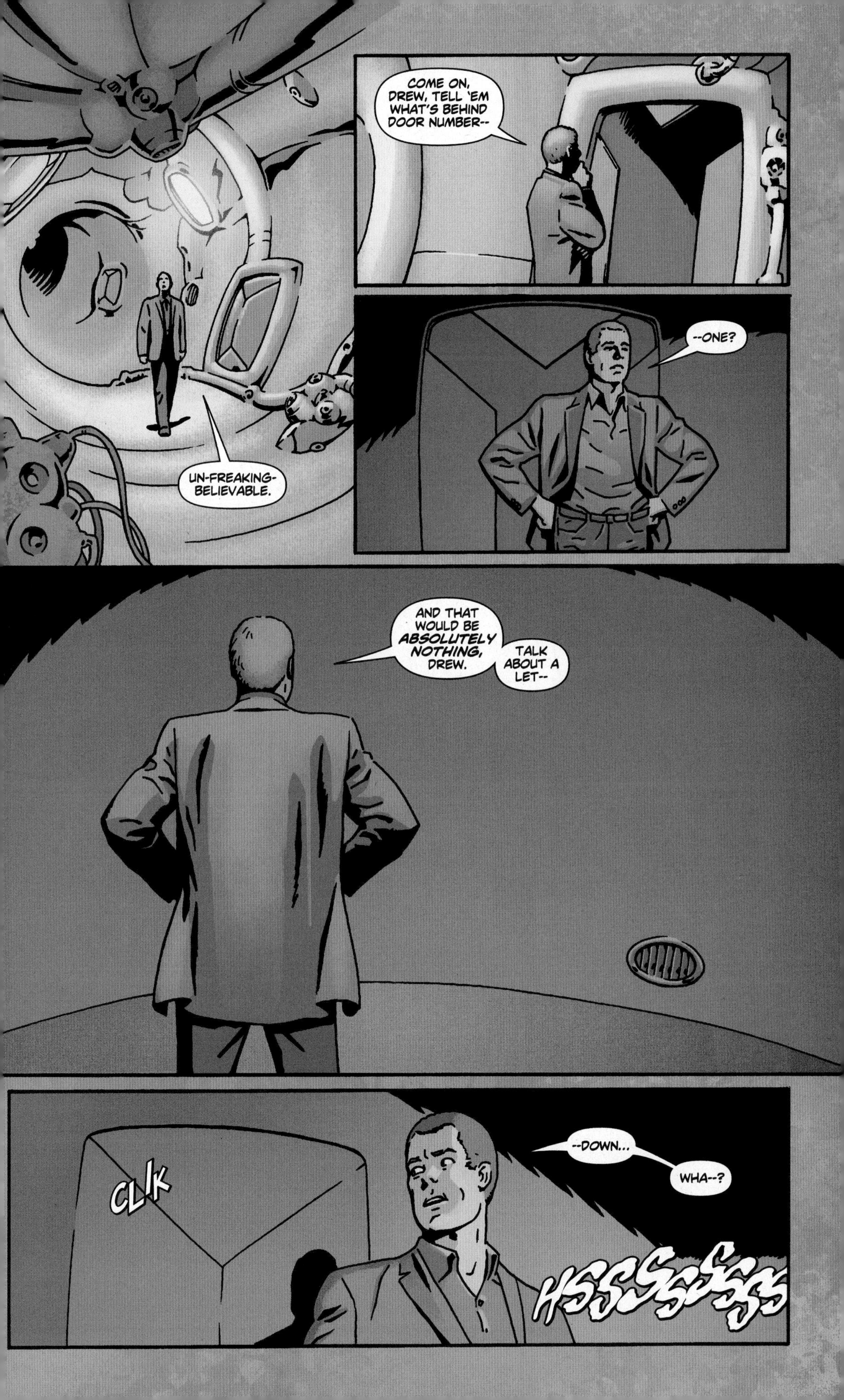
COME ON, DREW, TELL 'EM WHAT'S BEHIND DOOR NUMBER--
UN-FREAKING-BELIEVABLE.
--ONE?
AND THAT WOULD BE *ABSOLUTELY NOTHING,* DREW.
TALK ABOUT A LET--
--DOWN...
WHA--?
CLIK
HSSSSSSSS

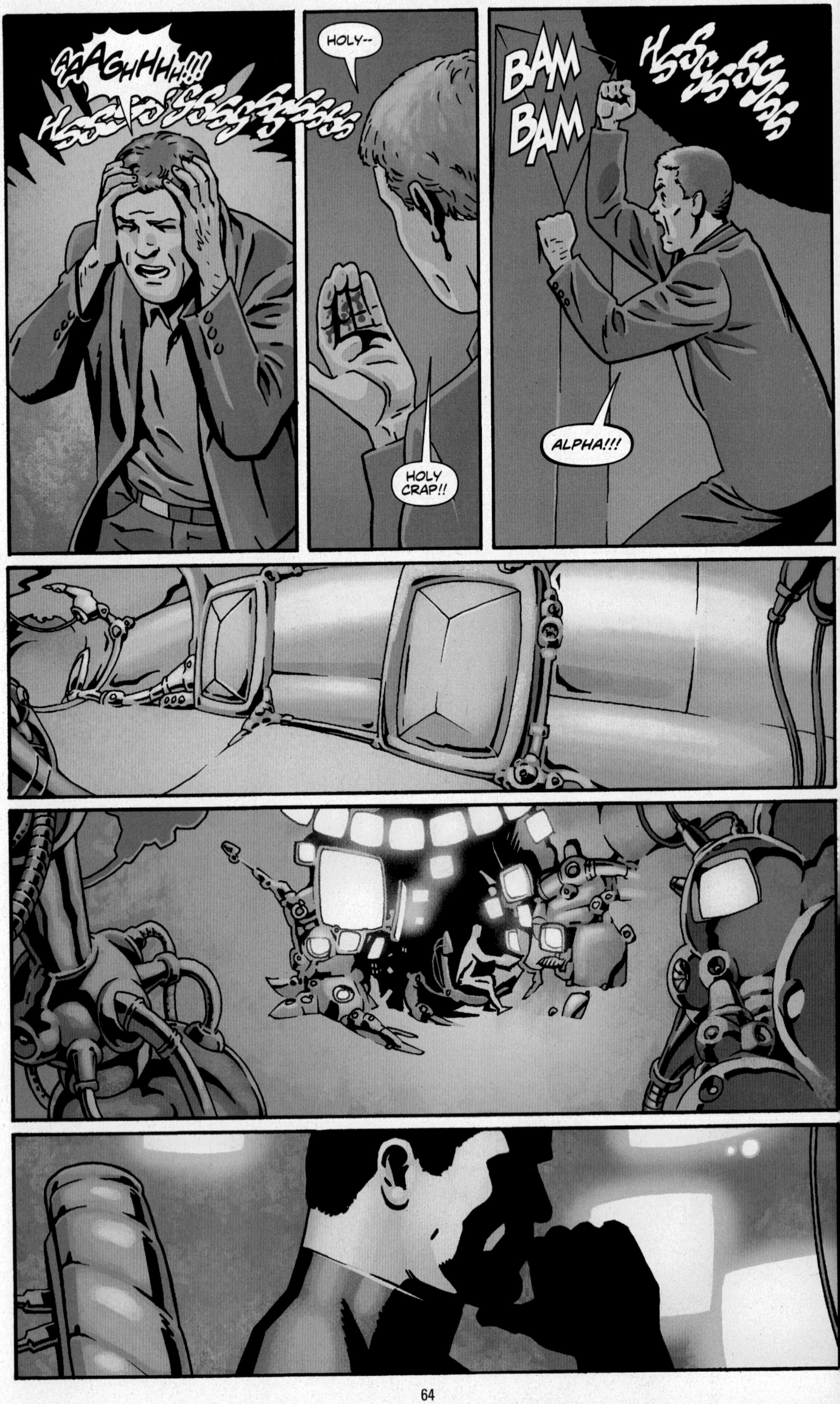
AAAGHHHH!!!
HSSSSSSSSSSSSSSSSSS
HOLY--
HOLY
CRAP!!
BAM
BAM
HSSSSSSSSS
ALPHA!!!

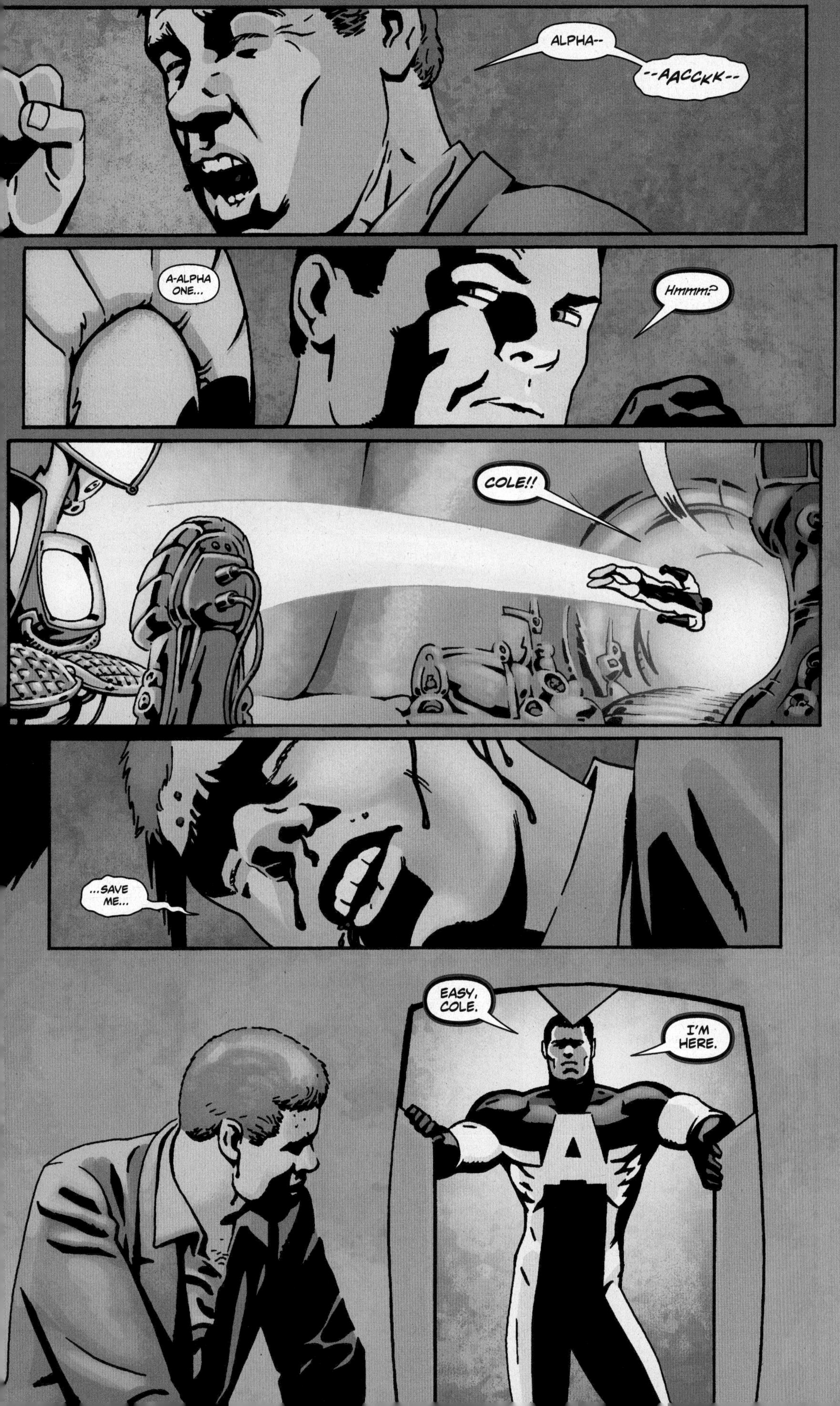
ALPHA--
--AACCKK--
A-ALPHA ONE...
Hmmm?
COLE!!
...SAVE ME...
EASY, COLE.
I'M HERE.

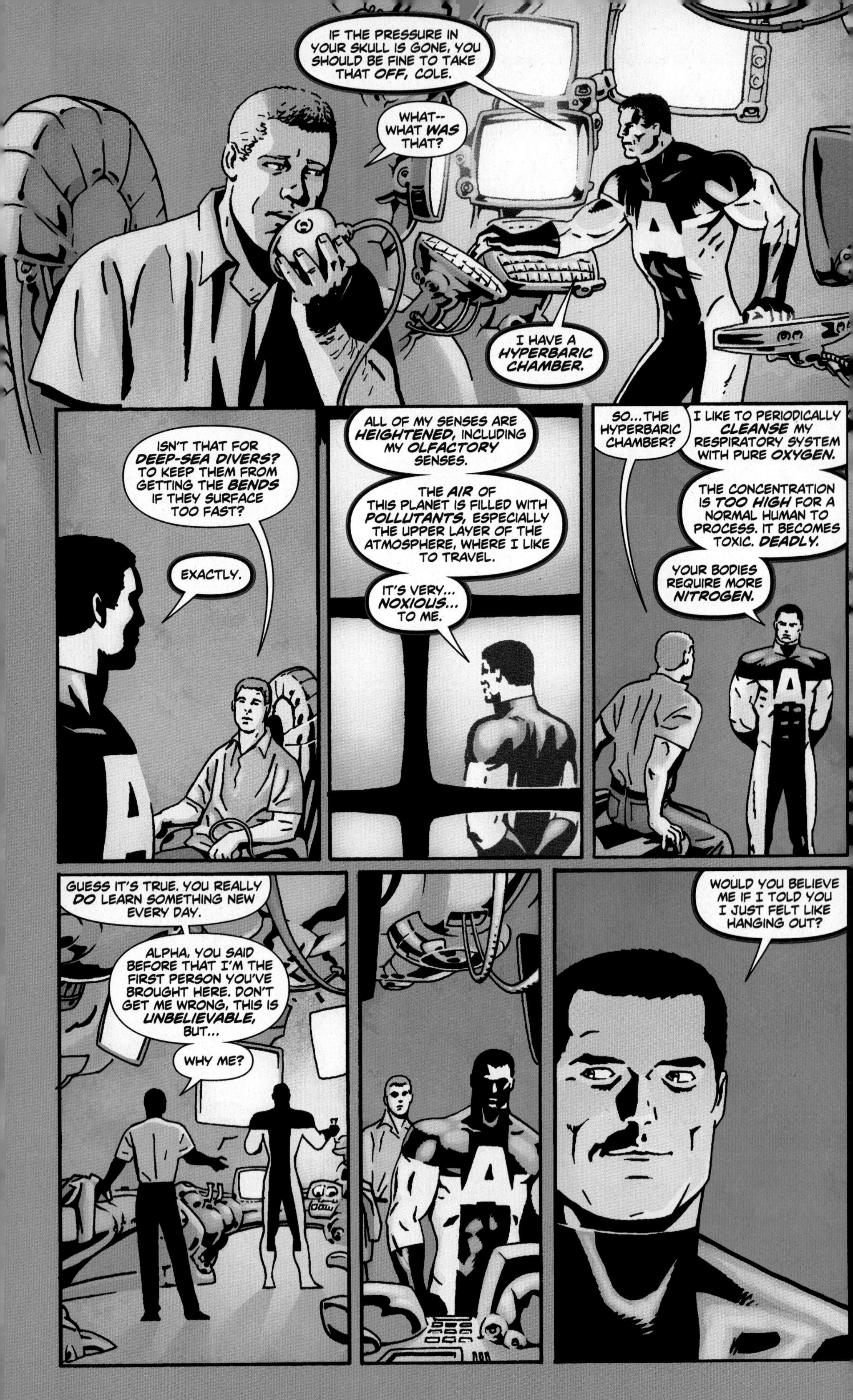

IF THE PRESSURE IN YOUR SKULL IS GONE, YOU SHOULD BE FINE TO TAKE THAT OFF, COLE.
WHAT-- WHAT WAS THAT?
I HAVE A HYPERBARIC CHAMBER.
ISN'T THAT FOR DEEP-SEA DIVERS? TO KEEP THEM FROM GETTING THE BENDS IF THEY SURFACE TOO FAST?
EXACTLY.
ALL OF MY SENSES ARE HEIGHTENED, INCLUDING MY OLFACTORY SENSES.
THE AIR OF THIS PLANET IS FILLED WITH POLLUTANTS, ESPECIALLY THE UPPER LAYER OF THE ATMOSPHERE, WHERE I LIKE TO TRAVEL.
IT'S VERY... NOXIOUS... TO ME.
SO...THE HYPERBARIC CHAMBER?
I LIKE TO PERIODICALLY CLEANSE MY RESPIRATORY SYSTEM WITH PURE OXYGEN.
THE CONCENTRATION IS TOO HIGH FOR A NORMAL HUMAN TO PROCESS. IT BECOMES TOXIC. DEADLY.
YOUR BODIES REQUIRE MORE NITROGEN.
GUESS IT'S TRUE. YOU REALLY DO LEARN SOMETHING NEW EVERY DAY.
ALPHA, YOU SAID BEFORE THAT I'M THE FIRST PERSON YOU'VE BROUGHT HERE. DON'T GET ME WRONG, THIS IS UNBELIEVABLE, BUT...
WHY ME?
WOULD YOU BELIEVE ME IF I TOLD YOU I JUST FELT LIKE HANGING OUT?

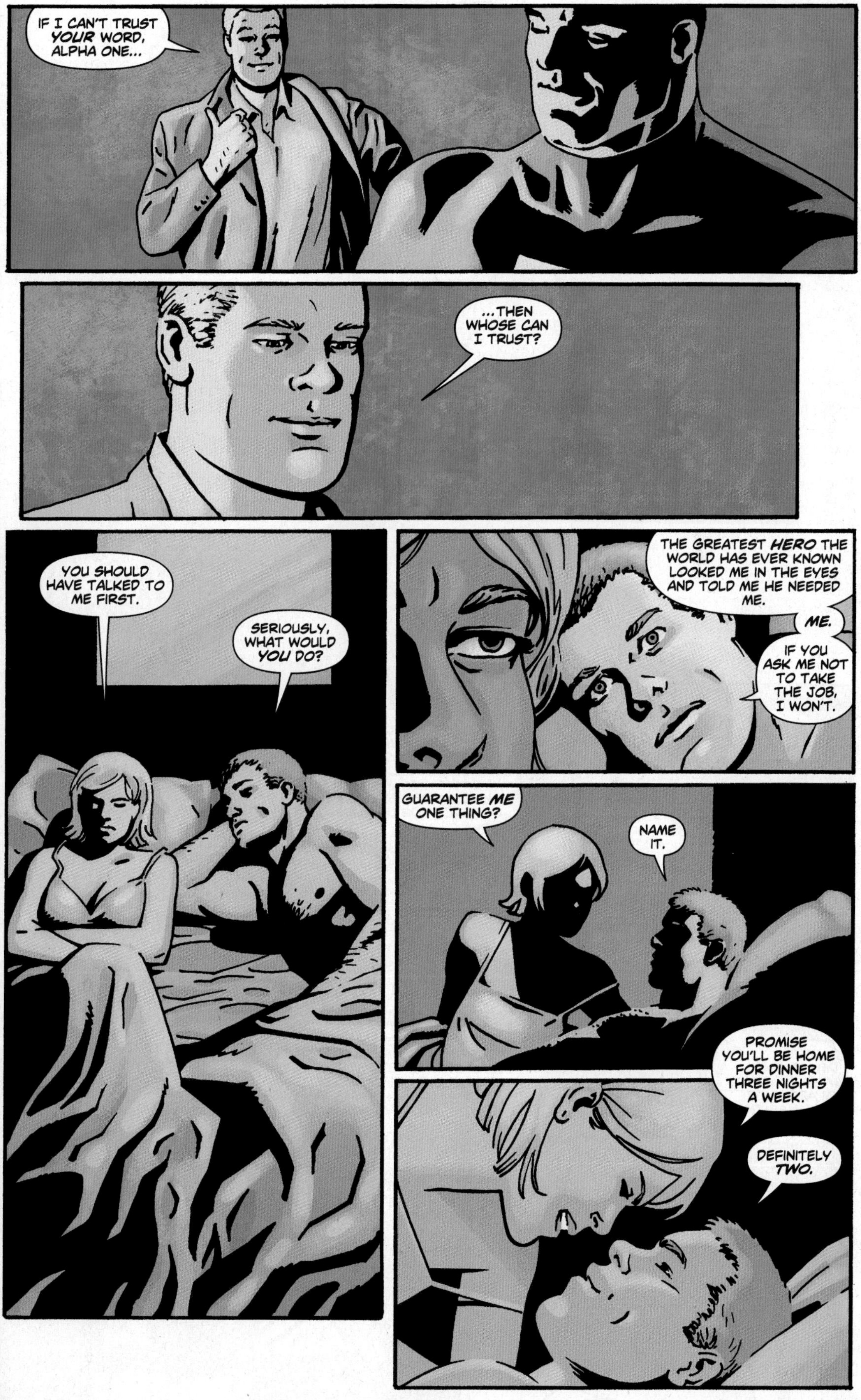
IF I CAN'T TRUST YOUR WORD, ALPHA ONE...
...THEN WHOSE CAN I TRUST?
YOU SHOULD HAVE TALKED TO ME FIRST.
SERIOUSLY, WHAT WOULD YOU DO?
THE GREATEST HERO THE WORLD HAS EVER KNOWN LOOKED ME IN THE EYES AND TOLD ME HE NEEDED ME.
ME.
IF YOU ASK ME NOT TO TAKE THE JOB, I WON'T.
GUARANTEE ME ONE THING?
NAME IT.
PROMISE YOU'LL BE HOME FOR DINNER THREE NIGHTS A WEEK.
DEFINITELY TWO.

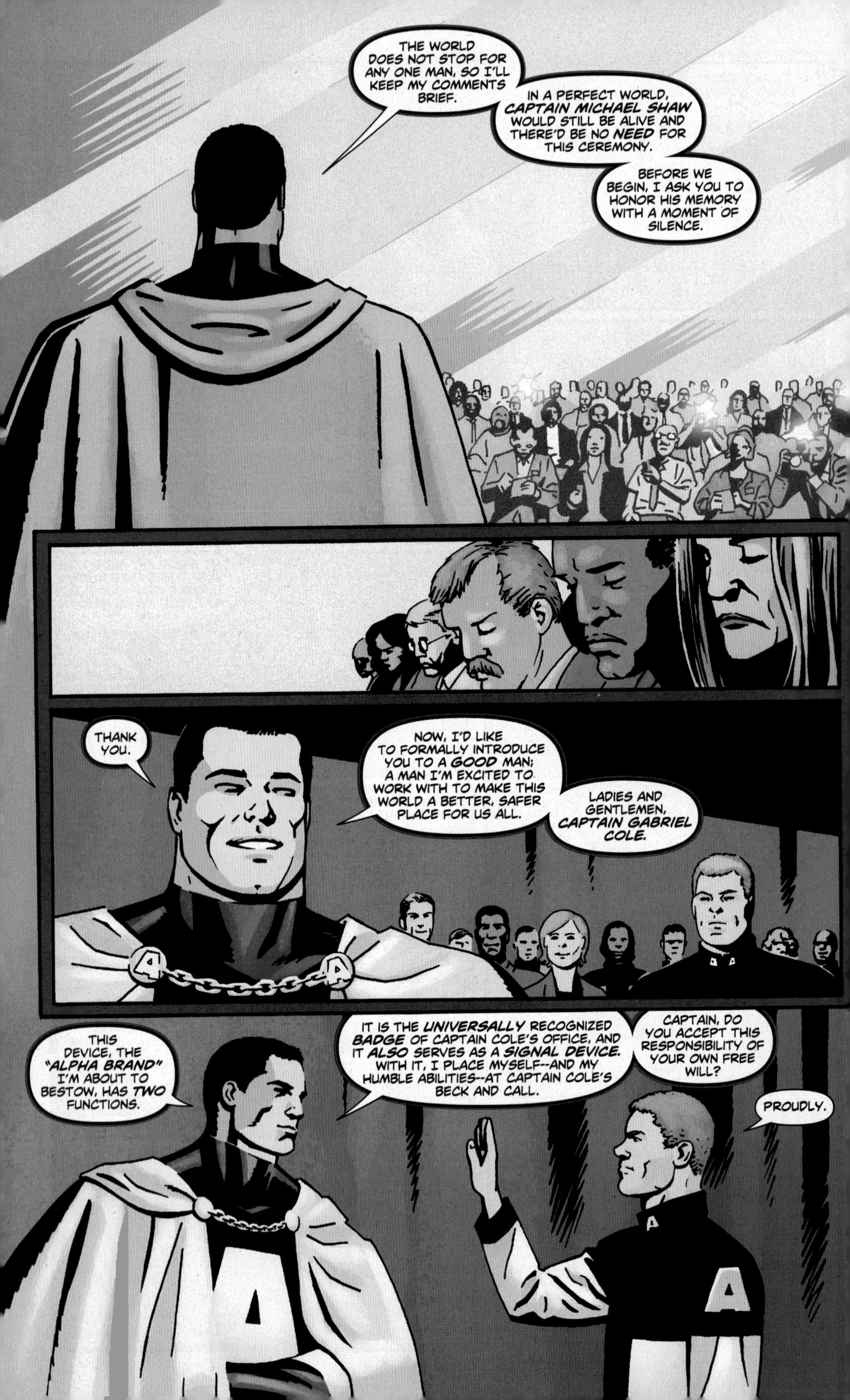
THE WORLD DOES NOT STOP FOR ANY ONE MAN, SO I'LL KEEP MY COMMENTS BRIEF.
IN A PERFECT WORLD, CAPTAIN MICHAEL SHAW WOULD STILL BE ALIVE AND THERE'D BE NO NEED FOR THIS CEREMONY.
BEFORE WE BEGIN, I ASK YOU TO HONOR HIS MEMORY WITH A MOMENT OF SILENCE.
THANK YOU.
NOW, I'D LIKE TO FORMALLY INTRODUCE YOU TO A GOOD MAN; A MAN I'M EXCITED TO WORK WITH TO MAKE THIS WORLD A BETTER, SAFER PLACE FOR US ALL.
LADIES AND GENTLEMEN, CAPTAIN GABRIEL COLE.
THIS DEVICE, THE "ALPHA BRAND" I'M ABOUT TO BESTOW, HAS TWO FUNCTIONS.
IT IS THE UNIVERSALLY RECOGNIZED BADGE OF CAPTAIN COLE'S OFFICE, AND IT ALSO SERVES AS A SIGNAL DEVICE. WITH IT, I PLACE MYSELF--AND MY HUMBLE ABILITIES--AT CAPTAIN COLE'S BECK AND CALL.
CAPTAIN, DO YOU ACCEPT THIS RESPONSIBILITY OF YOUR OWN FREE WILL?
PROUDLY.

THEN LET US *BEGIN.*

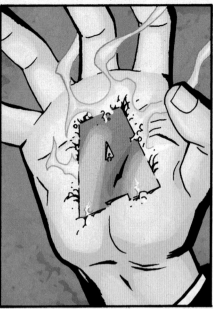

CALL ME IF YOU NEED ME.

THIS SHOULD HOLD YOU OVER UNTIL YOUR *OFFICIAL* CELEBRATION DINNER IS READY.

I SWEAR, THE THINGS YOU DO TO GET ME TO COOK.

YOU KNOW ME, ALL WILE AND GUILE.

NNNN.

AAHHH.

YOU'VE GOT TO KEEP THE ICE ON IT, GABE. I SWEAR YOU'RE LIKE A *TWO-YEAR-OLD.*

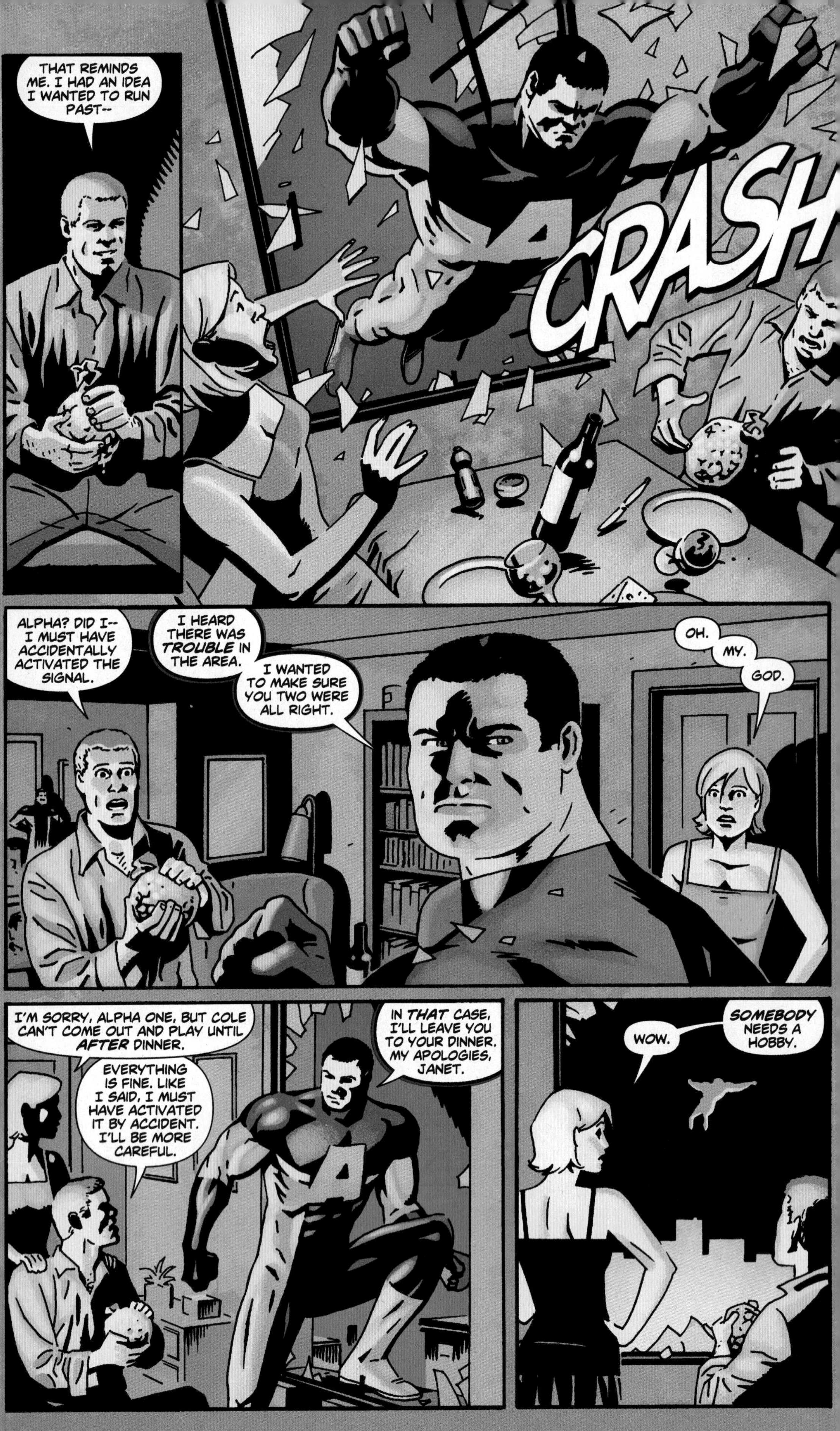

THAT REMINDS ME. I HAD AN IDEA I WANTED TO RUN PAST--
CRASH
ALPHA? DID I-- I MUST HAVE ACCIDENTALLY ACTIVATED THE SIGNAL.
I HEARD THERE WAS TROUBLE IN THE AREA.
I WANTED TO MAKE SURE YOU TWO WERE ALL RIGHT.
OH.
MY.
GOD.
I'M SORRY, ALPHA ONE, BUT COLE CAN'T COME OUT AND PLAY UNTIL AFTER DINNER.
EVERYTHING IS FINE. LIKE I SAID, I MUST HAVE ACTIVATED IT BY ACCIDENT. I'LL BE MORE CAREFUL.
IN THAT CASE, I'LL LEAVE YOU TO YOUR DINNER. MY APOLOGIES, JANET.
WOW.
SOMEBODY NEEDS A HOBBY.

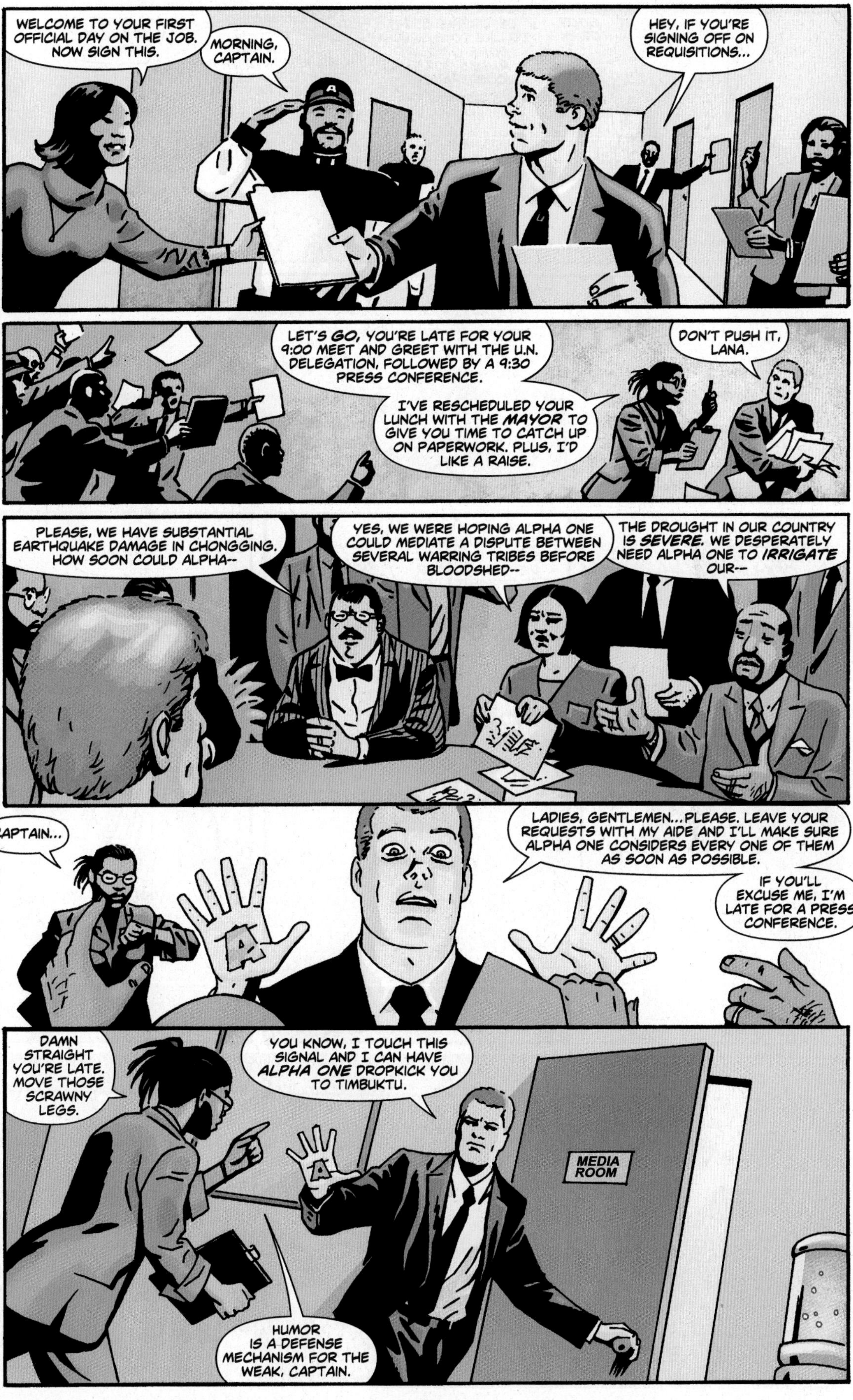
WELCOME TO YOUR FIRST OFFICIAL DAY ON THE JOB. NOW SIGN THIS.
MORNING, CAPTAIN.
HEY, IF YOU'RE SIGNING OFF ON REQUISITIONS...
LET'S GO, YOU'RE LATE FOR YOUR 9:00 MEET AND GREET WITH THE U.N. DELEGATION, FOLLOWED BY A 9:30 PRESS CONFERENCE.
I'VE RESCHEDULED YOUR LUNCH WITH THE MAYOR TO GIVE YOU TIME TO CATCH UP ON PAPERWORK. PLUS, I'D LIKE A RAISE.
DON'T PUSH IT, LANA.
PLEASE, WE HAVE SUBSTANTIAL EARTHQUAKE DAMAGE IN CHONGGING. HOW SOON COULD ALPHA--
YES, WE WERE HOPING ALPHA ONE COULD MEDIATE A DISPUTE BETWEEN SEVERAL WARRING TRIBES BEFORE BLOODSHED--
THE DROUGHT IN OUR COUNTRY IS SEVERE. WE DESPERATELY NEED ALPHA ONE TO IRRIGATE OUR--
CAPTAIN...
LADIES, GENTLEMEN...PLEASE. LEAVE YOUR REQUESTS WITH MY AIDE AND I'LL MAKE SURE ALPHA ONE CONSIDERS EVERY ONE OF THEM AS SOON AS POSSIBLE.
IF YOU'LL EXCUSE ME, I'M LATE FOR A PRESS CONFERENCE.
DAMN STRAIGHT YOU'RE LATE. MOVE THOSE SCRAWNY LEGS.
YOU KNOW, I TOUCH THIS SIGNAL AND I CAN HAVE ALPHA ONE DROPKICK YOU TO TIMBUKTU.
MEDIA ROOM
HUMOR IS A DEFENSE MECHANISM FOR THE WEAK, CAPTAIN.

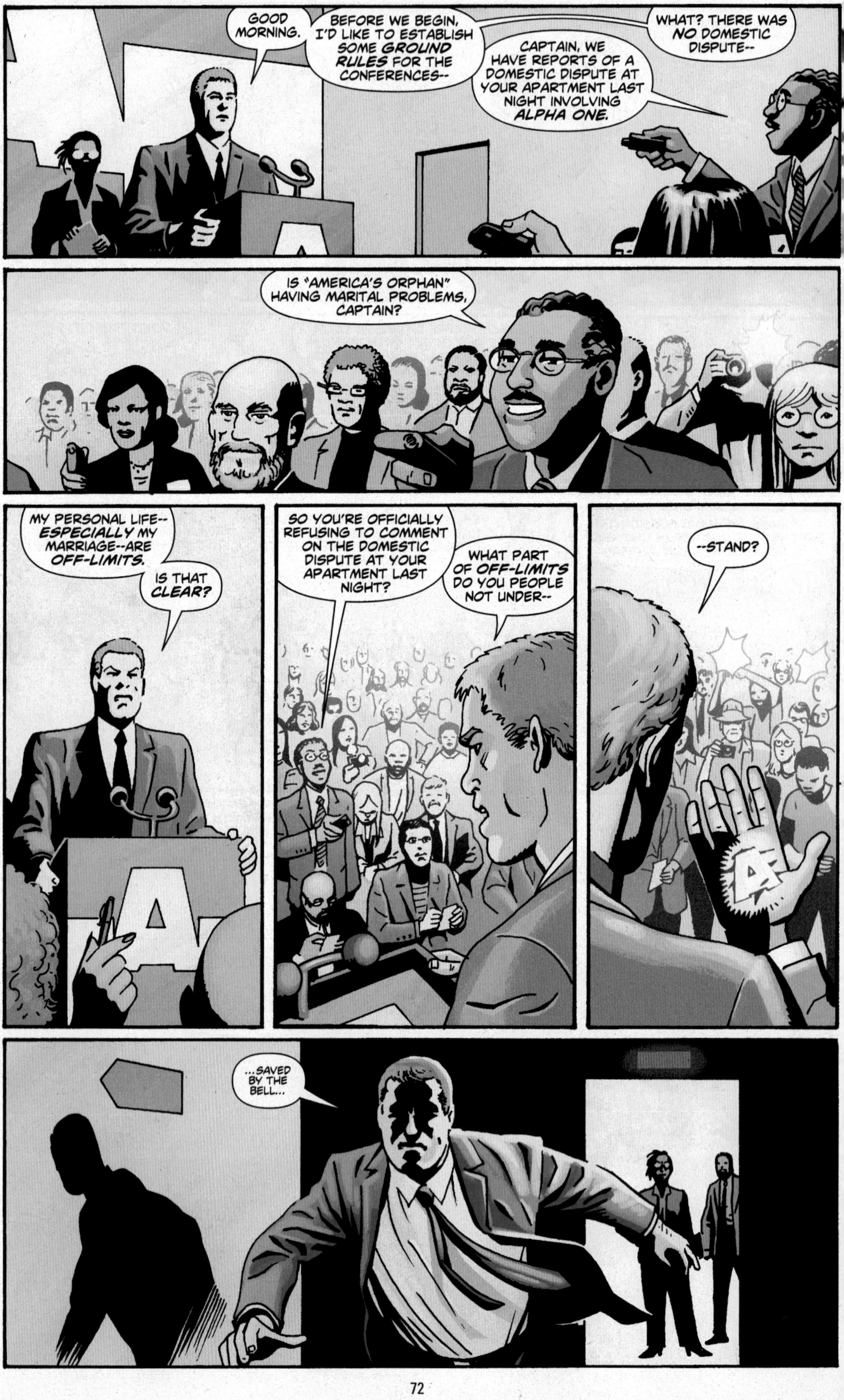
GOOD MORNING.
BEFORE WE BEGIN, I'D LIKE TO ESTABLISH SOME GROUND RULES FOR THE CONFERENCES--
CAPTAIN, WE HAVE REPORTS OF A DOMESTIC DISPUTE AT YOUR APARTMENT LAST NIGHT INVOLVING ALPHA ONE.
WHAT? THERE WAS NO DOMESTIC DISPUTE--
IS "AMERICA'S ORPHAN" HAVING MARITAL PROBLEMS, CAPTAIN?
MY PERSONAL LIFE--ESPECIALLY MY MARRIAGE--ARE OFF-LIMITS.
IS THAT CLEAR?
SO YOU'RE OFFICIALLY REFUSING TO COMMENT ON THE DOMESTIC DISPUTE AT YOUR APARTMENT LAST NIGHT?
WHAT PART OF OFF-LIMITS DO YOU PEOPLE NOT UNDER--
--STAND?
...SAVED BY THE BELL...

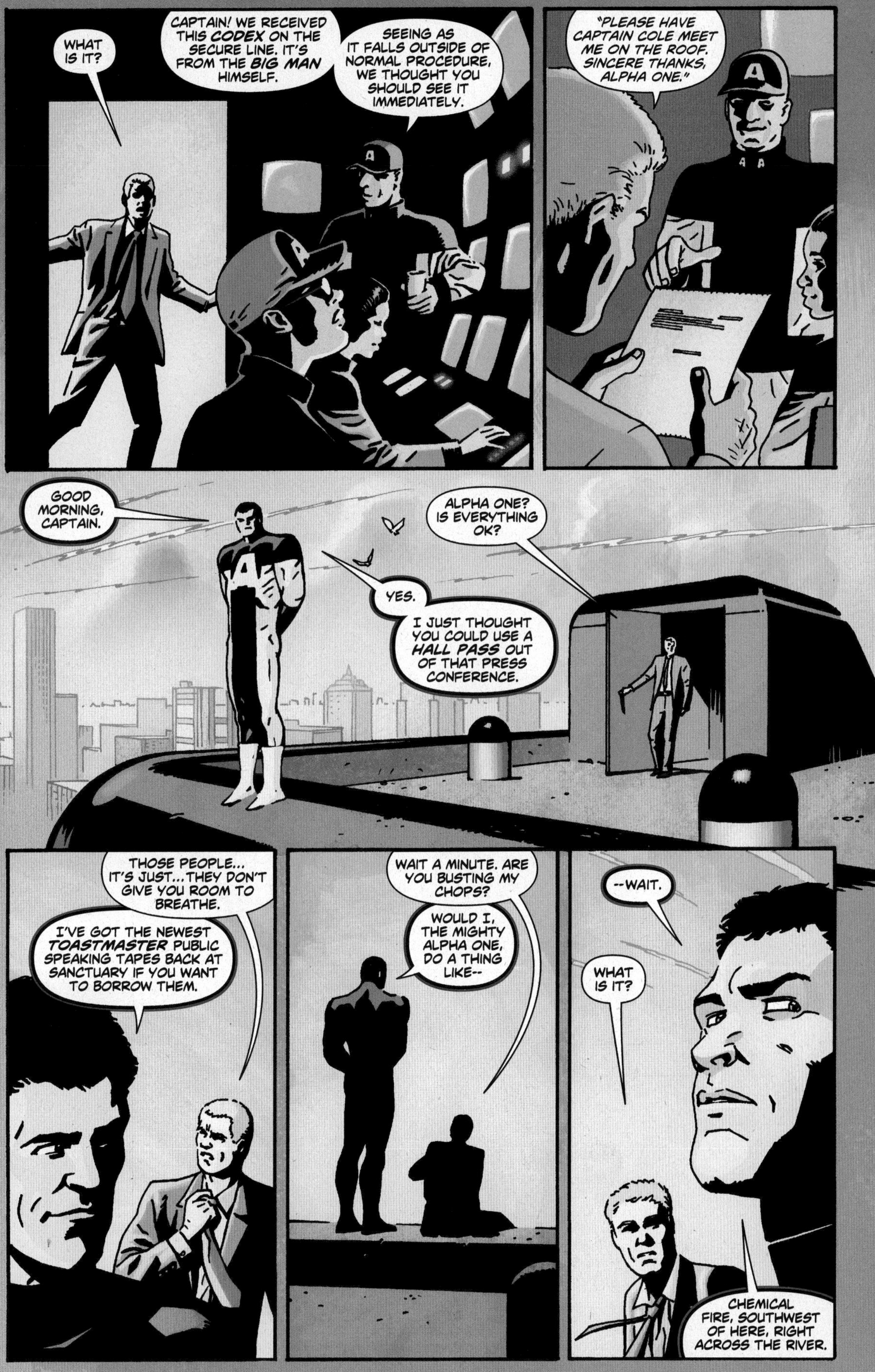
WHAT IS IT?
CAPTAIN! WE RECEIVED THIS CODEX ON THE SECURE LINE. IT'S FROM THE BIG MAN HIMSELF.
SEEING AS IT FALLS OUTSIDE OF NORMAL PROCEDURE, WE THOUGHT YOU SHOULD SEE IT IMMEDIATELY.
"PLEASE HAVE CAPTAIN COLE MEET ME ON THE ROOF. SINCERE THANKS, ALPHA ONE."
GOOD MORNING, CAPTAIN.
ALPHA ONE? IS EVERYTHING OK?
YES.
I JUST THOUGHT YOU COULD USE A HALL PASS OUT OF THAT PRESS CONFERENCE.
THOSE PEOPLE... IT'S JUST... THEY DON'T GIVE YOU ROOM TO BREATHE.
I'VE GOT THE NEWEST TOASTMASTER PUBLIC SPEAKING TAPES BACK AT SANCTUARY IF YOU WANT TO BORROW THEM.
WAIT A MINUTE. ARE YOU BUSTING MY CHOPS?
WOULD I, THE MIGHTY ALPHA ONE, DO A THING LIKE--
--WAIT.
WHAT IS IT?
CHEMICAL FIRE, SOUTHWEST OF HERE, RIGHT ACROSS THE RIVER.

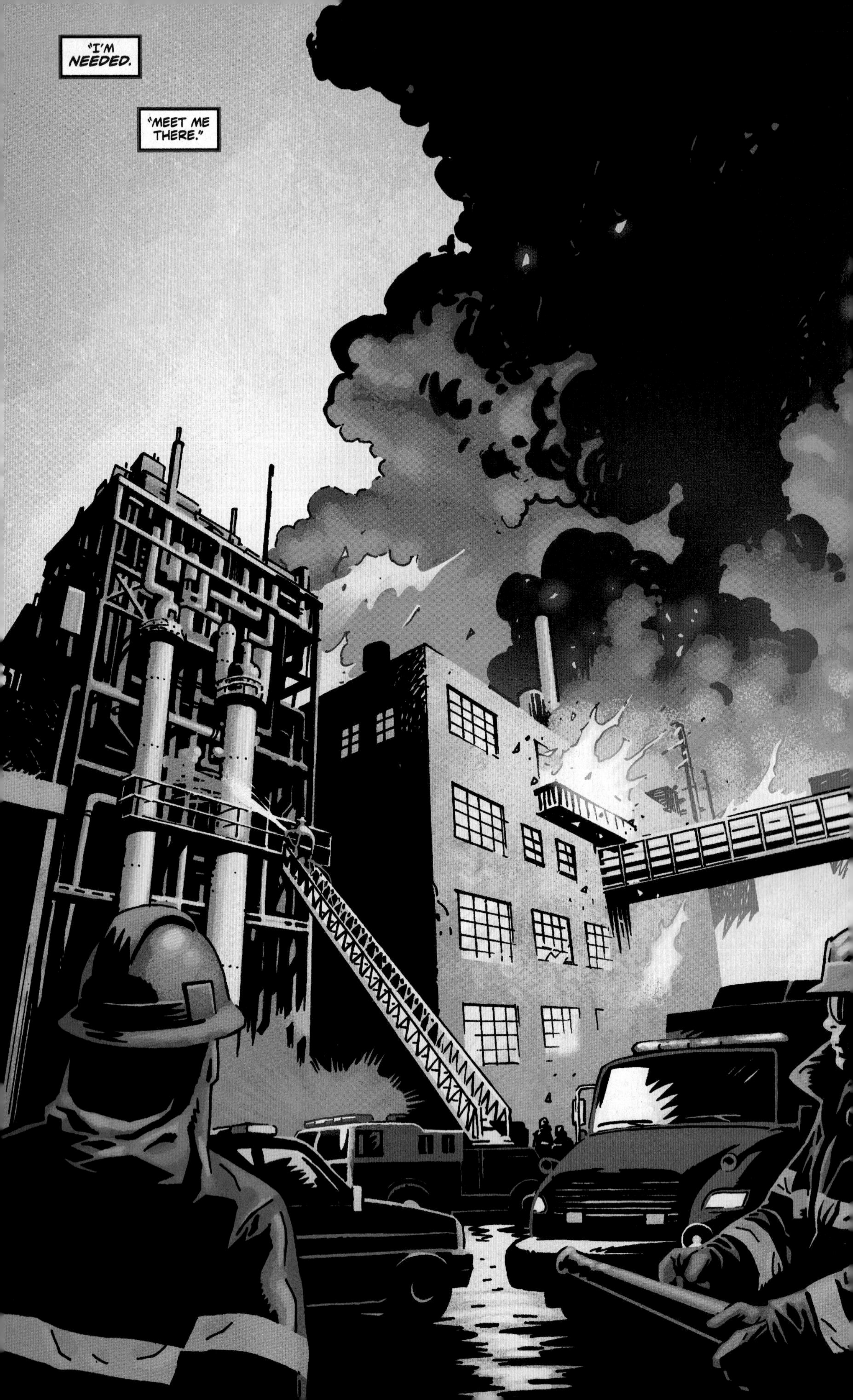
"I'M NEEDED.
"MEET ME THERE."

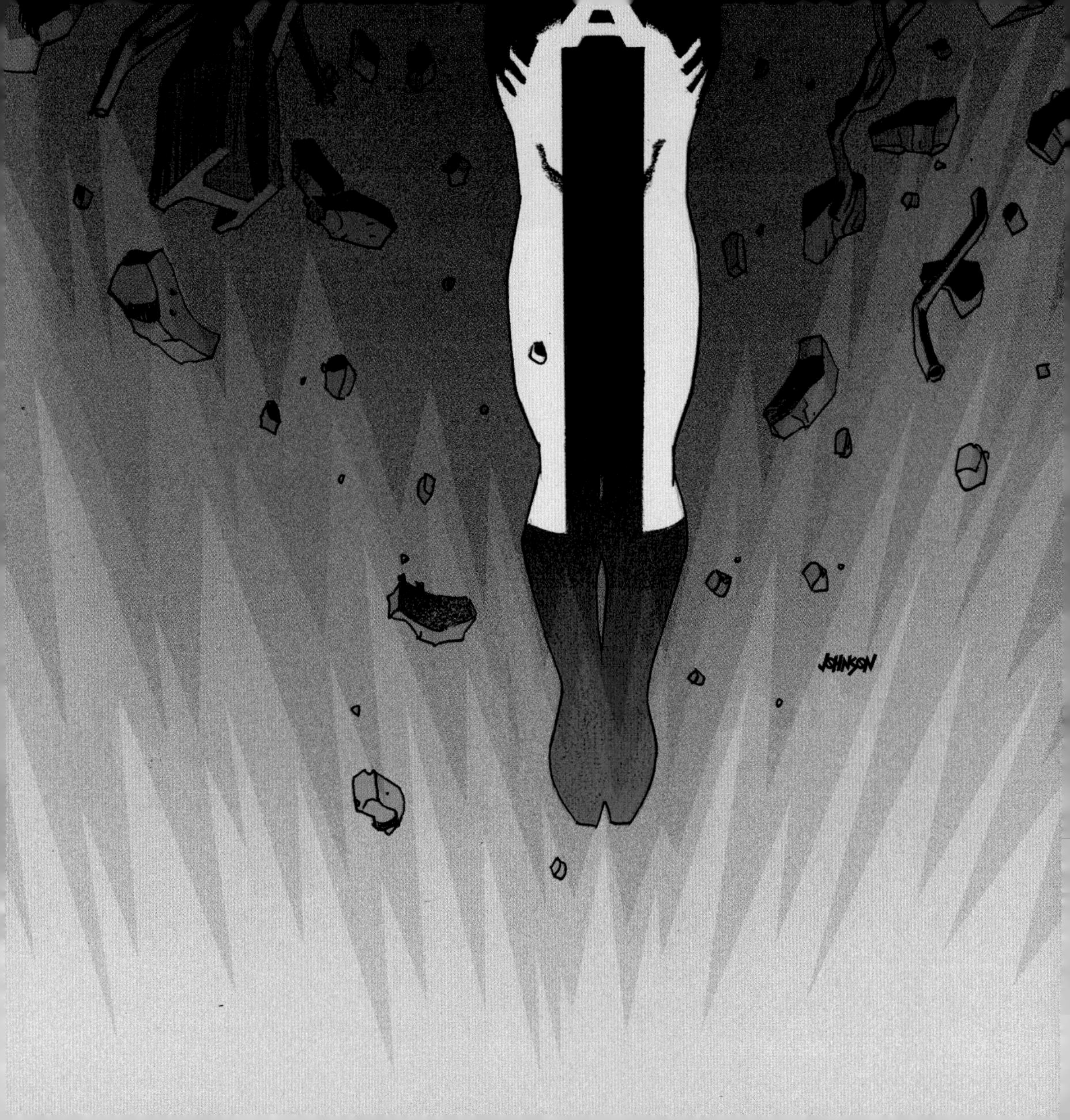
JOHNSON

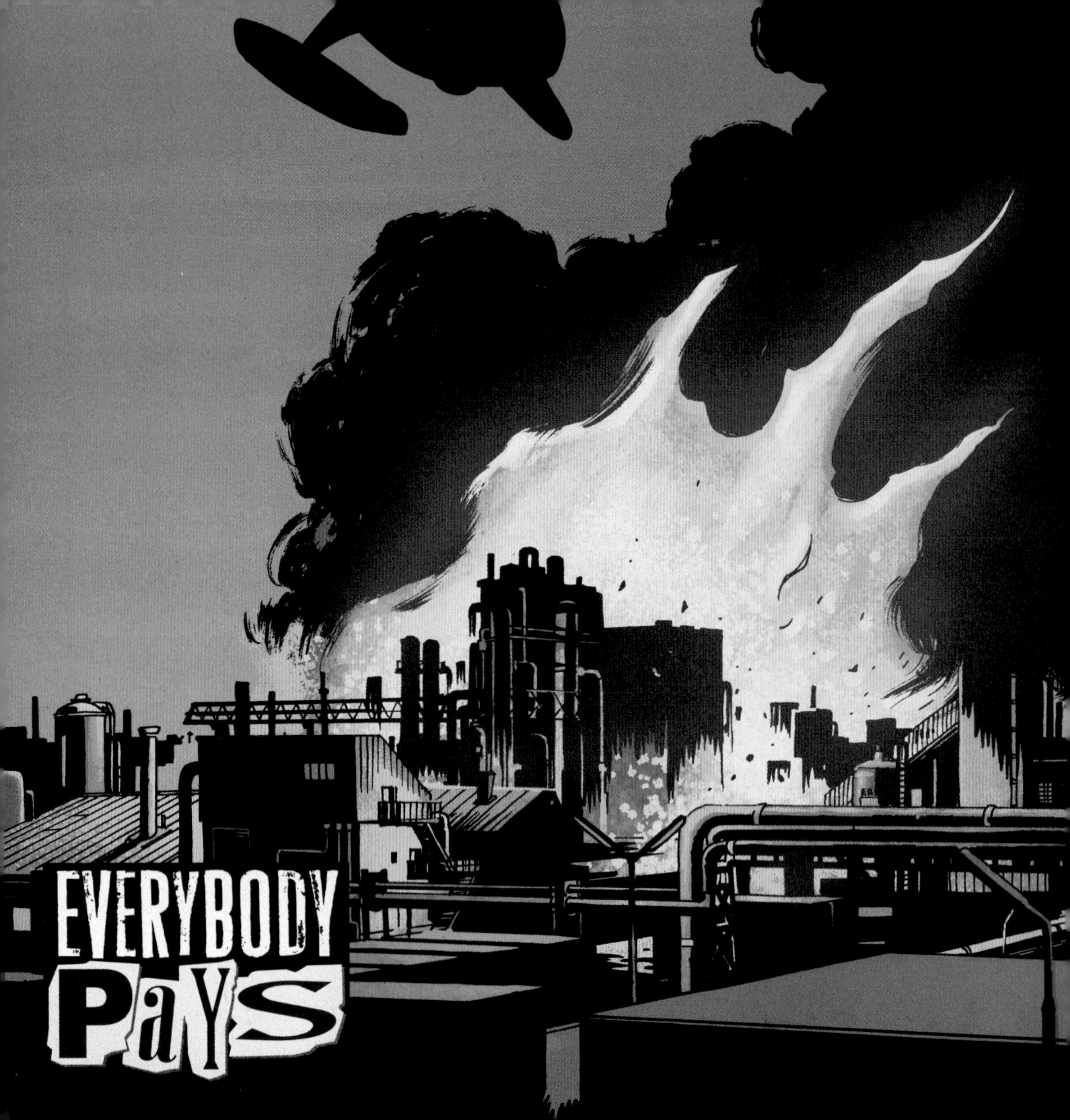
EVERYBODY
PaYS

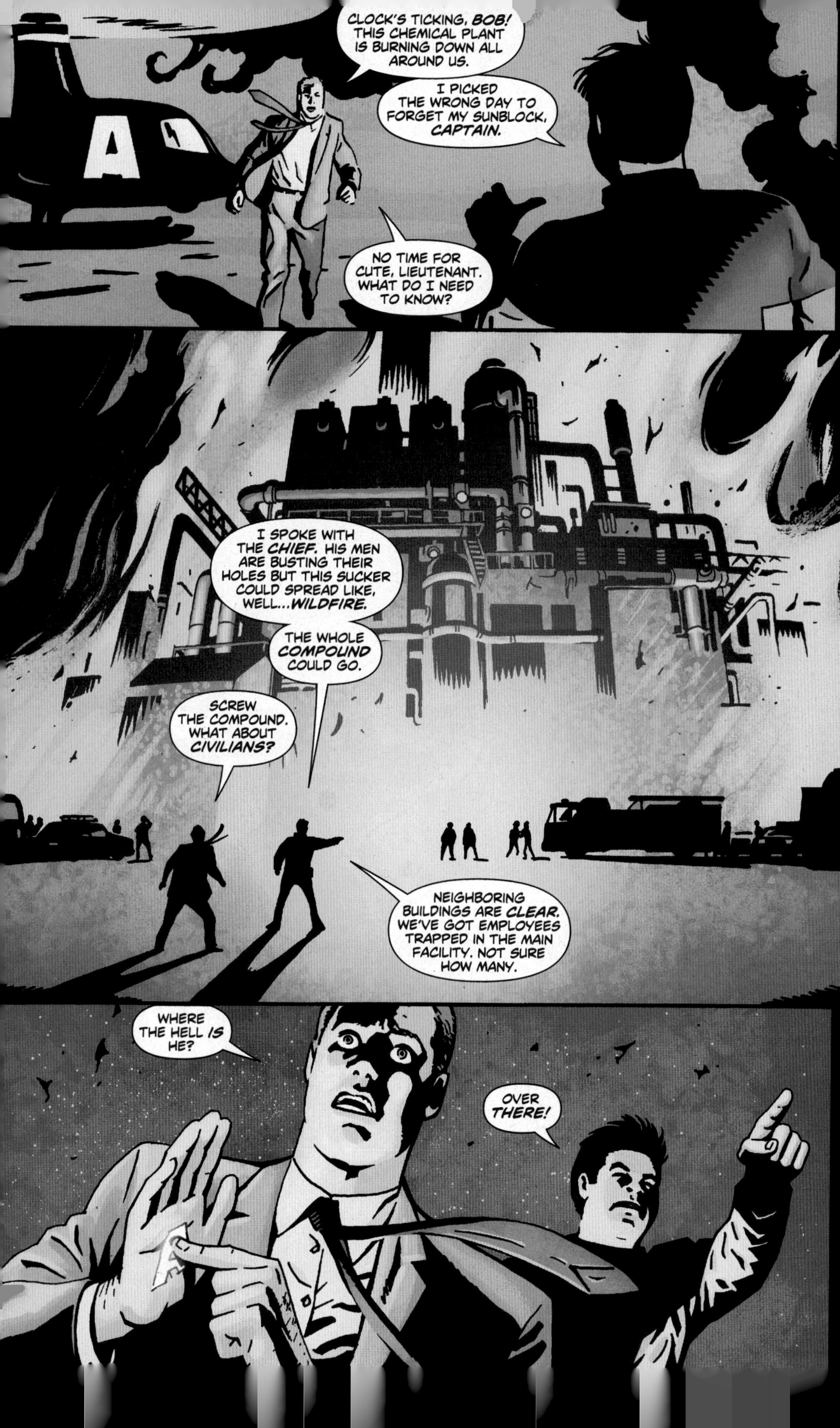
CLOCK'S TICKING, BOB! THIS CHEMICAL PLANT IS BURNING DOWN ALL AROUND US.
I PICKED THE WRONG DAY TO FORGET MY SUNBLOCK, CAPTAIN.
NO TIME FOR CUTE, LIEUTENANT. WHAT DO I NEED TO KNOW?
I SPOKE WITH THE CHIEF. HIS MEN ARE BUSTING THEIR HOLES BUT THIS SUCKER COULD SPREAD LIKE, WELL...WILDFIRE.
THE WHOLE COMPOUND COULD GO.
SCREW THE COMPOUND. WHAT ABOUT CIVILIANS?
NEIGHBORING BUILDINGS ARE CLEAR. WE'VE GOT EMPLOYEES TRAPPED IN THE MAIN FACILITY. NOT SURE HOW MANY.
WHERE THE HELL IS HE?
OVER THERE!

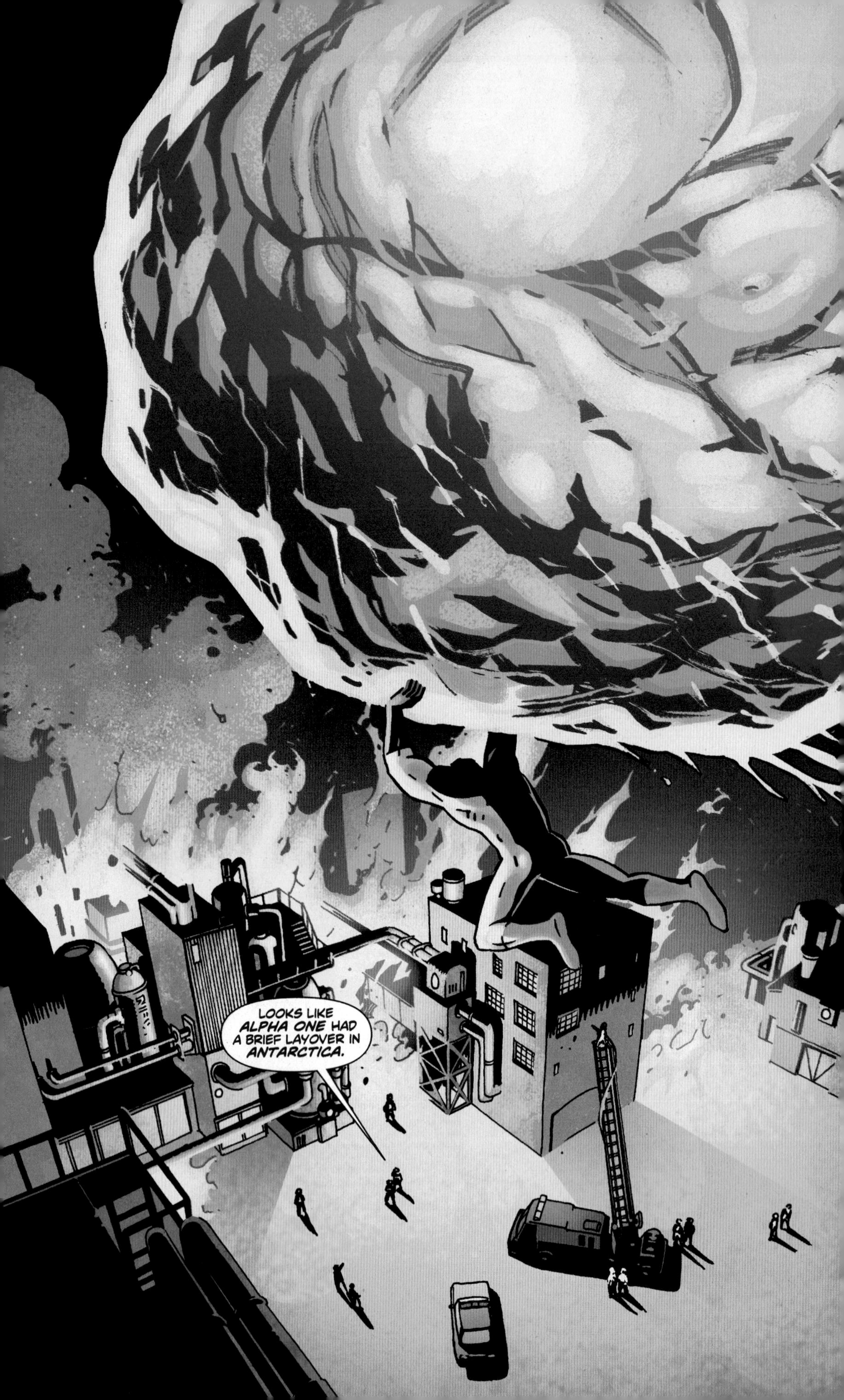
LOOKS LIKE ALPHA ONE HAD A BRIEF LAYOVER IN ANTARCTICA.

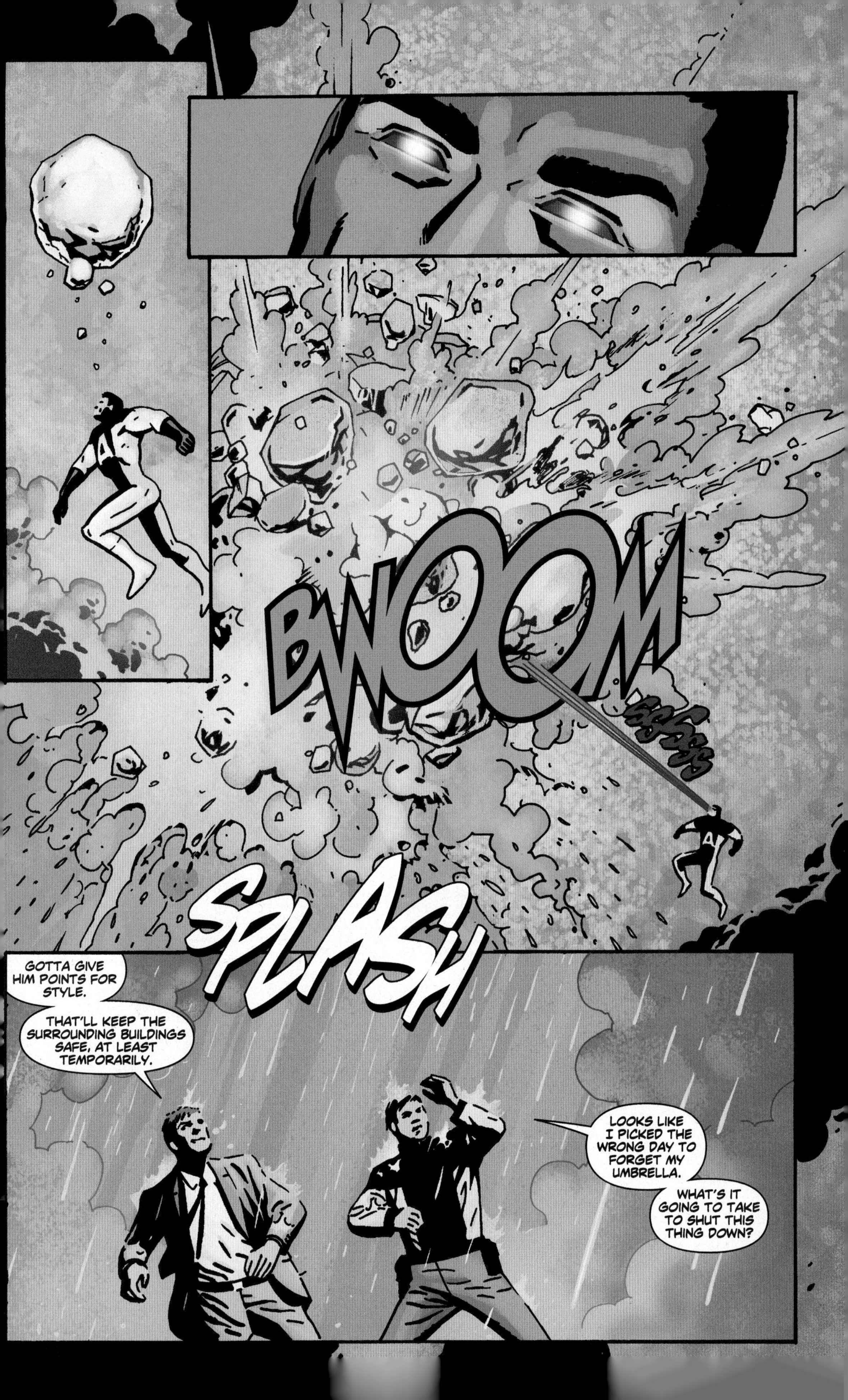
BWOOM
SSSSSS
SPLASH
GOTTA GIVE HIM POINTS FOR STYLE.
THAT'LL KEEP THE SURROUNDING BUILDINGS SAFE, AT LEAST TEMPORARILY.
LOOKS LIKE I PICKED THE WRONG DAY TO FORGET MY UMBRELLA.
WHAT'S IT GOING TO TAKE TO SHUT THIS THING DOWN?

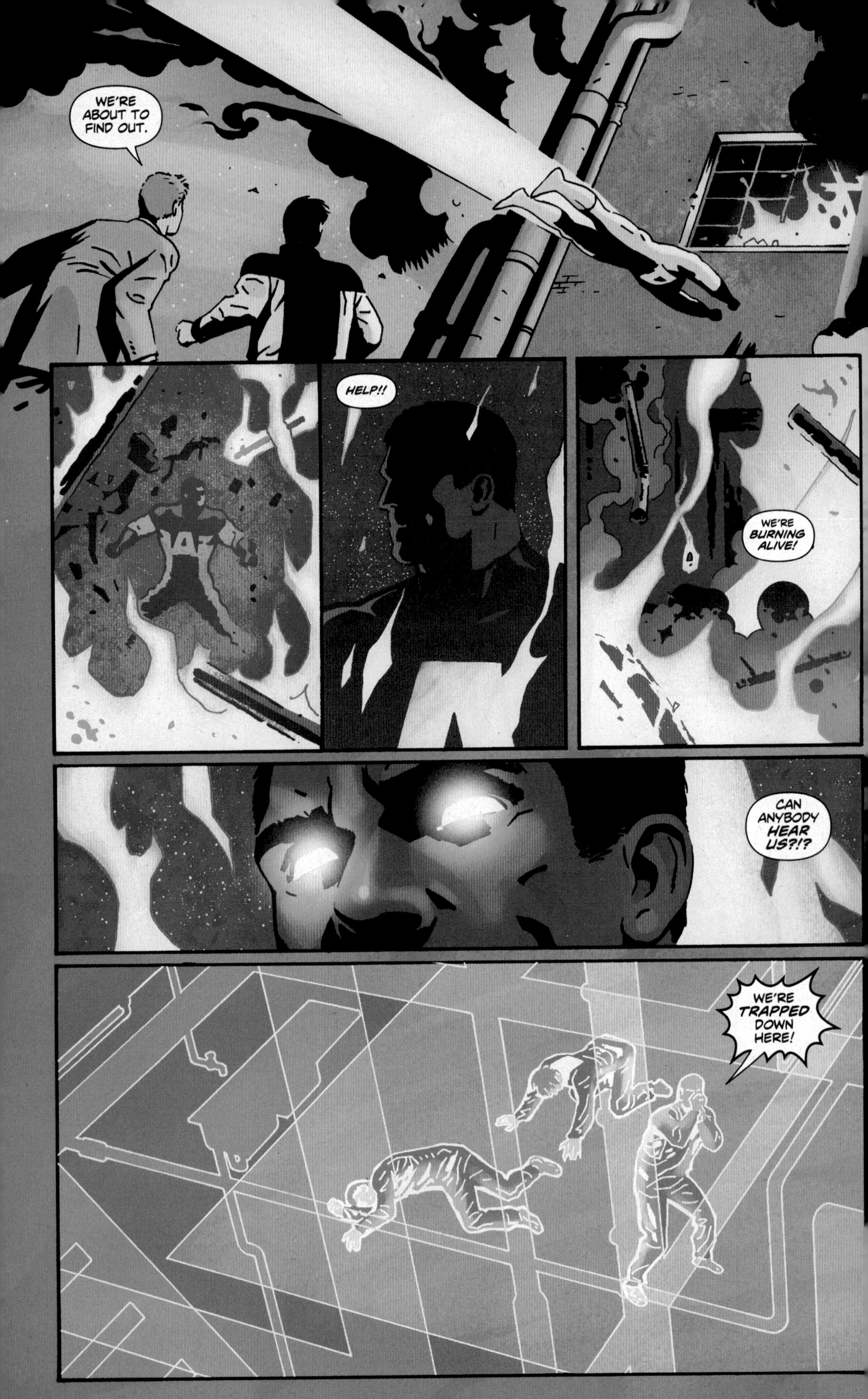
WE'RE ABOUT TO FIND OUT.
HELP!!
WE'RE BURNING ALIVE!
CAN ANYBODY HEAR US?!?
WE'RE TRAPPED DOWN HERE!

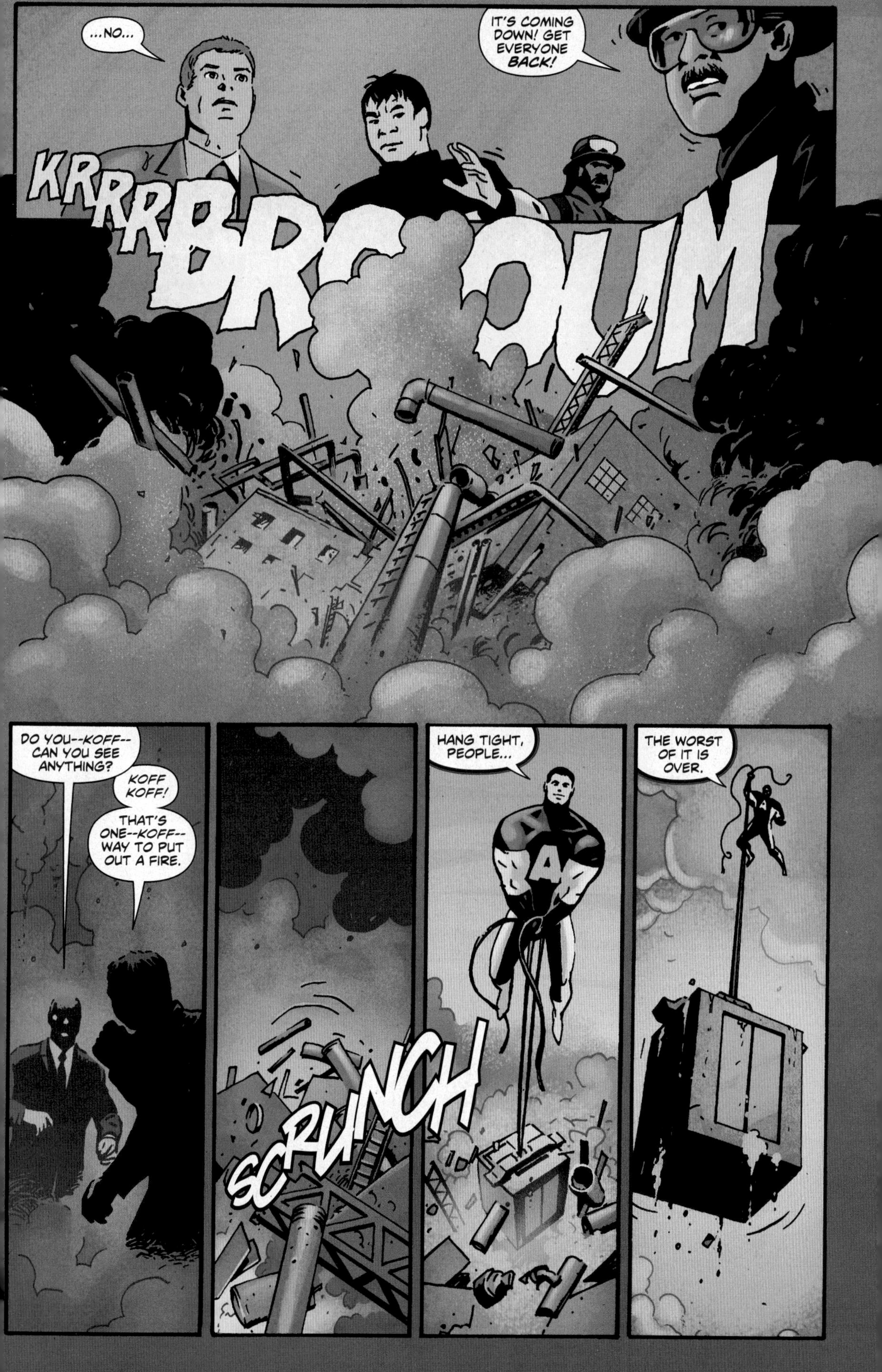
...NO...
IT'S COMING DOWN! GET EVERYONE BACK!
KRRRBROOUM
DO YOU--KOFF--CAN YOU SEE ANYTHING?
KOFF KOFF!
THAT'S ONE--KOFF--WAY TO PUT OUT A FIRE.
SCRUNCH
HANG TIGHT, PEOPLE...
THE WORST OF IT IS OVER.

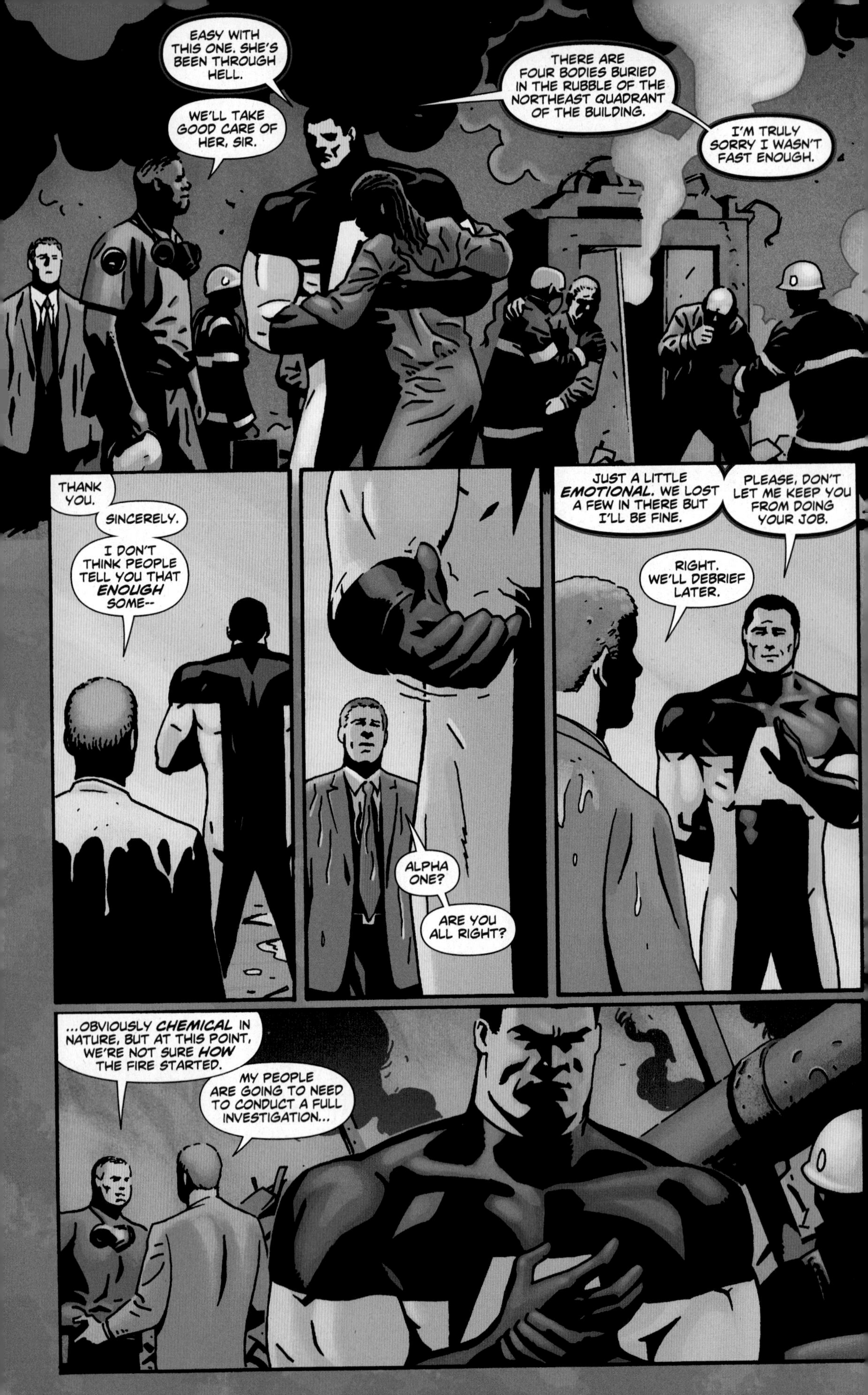
EASY WITH THIS ONE. SHE'S BEEN THROUGH HELL.
WE'LL TAKE GOOD CARE OF HER, SIR.
THERE ARE FOUR BODIES BURIED IN THE RUBBLE OF THE NORTHEAST QUADRANT OF THE BUILDING.
I'M TRULY SORRY I WASN'T FAST ENOUGH.
THANK YOU.
SINCERELY.
I DON'T THINK PEOPLE TELL YOU THAT ENOUGH SOME--
ALPHA ONE?
ARE YOU ALL RIGHT?
JUST A LITTLE EMOTIONAL. WE LOST A FEW IN THERE BUT I'LL BE FINE.
PLEASE, DON'T LET ME KEEP YOU FROM DOING YOUR JOB.
RIGHT. WE'LL DEBRIEF LATER.
...OBVIOUSLY CHEMICAL IN NATURE, BUT AT THIS POINT, WE'RE NOT SURE HOW THE FIRE STARTED.
MY PEOPLE ARE GOING TO NEED TO CONDUCT A FULL INVESTIGATION...

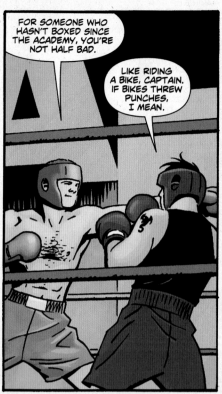

FOR SOMEONE WHO HASN'T BOXED SINCE THE ACADEMY, YOU'RE NOT HALF BAD.

LIKE RIDING A BIKE, CAPTAIN. IF BIKES THREW PUNCHES, I MEAN.

TELL ME WE GOT I.D.s ON THE FOUR CHEMICAL FIRE VICTIMS.

THEY'RE PRETTY CRISPY, SO IT'S GOING TO TAKE SOME TIME.

BASED ON THEIR LOCATION, WE KNOW THEY WORKED--

--OOF!

GET IT DONE.

WHOEVER THEY WERE, THEY HAD FAMILIES.

WE'RE ON IT.

GOOD MAN.

DO ME A FAVOR AND HANDLE THE AFTERNOON MEDIA CIRCUS, WOULD YOU?

SURE THING, BOSS. WHAT'S UP?

NOTHING MAJOR.

I JUST PROMISED THE WIFE I'D BE HOME FOR DINNER TONIGHT.

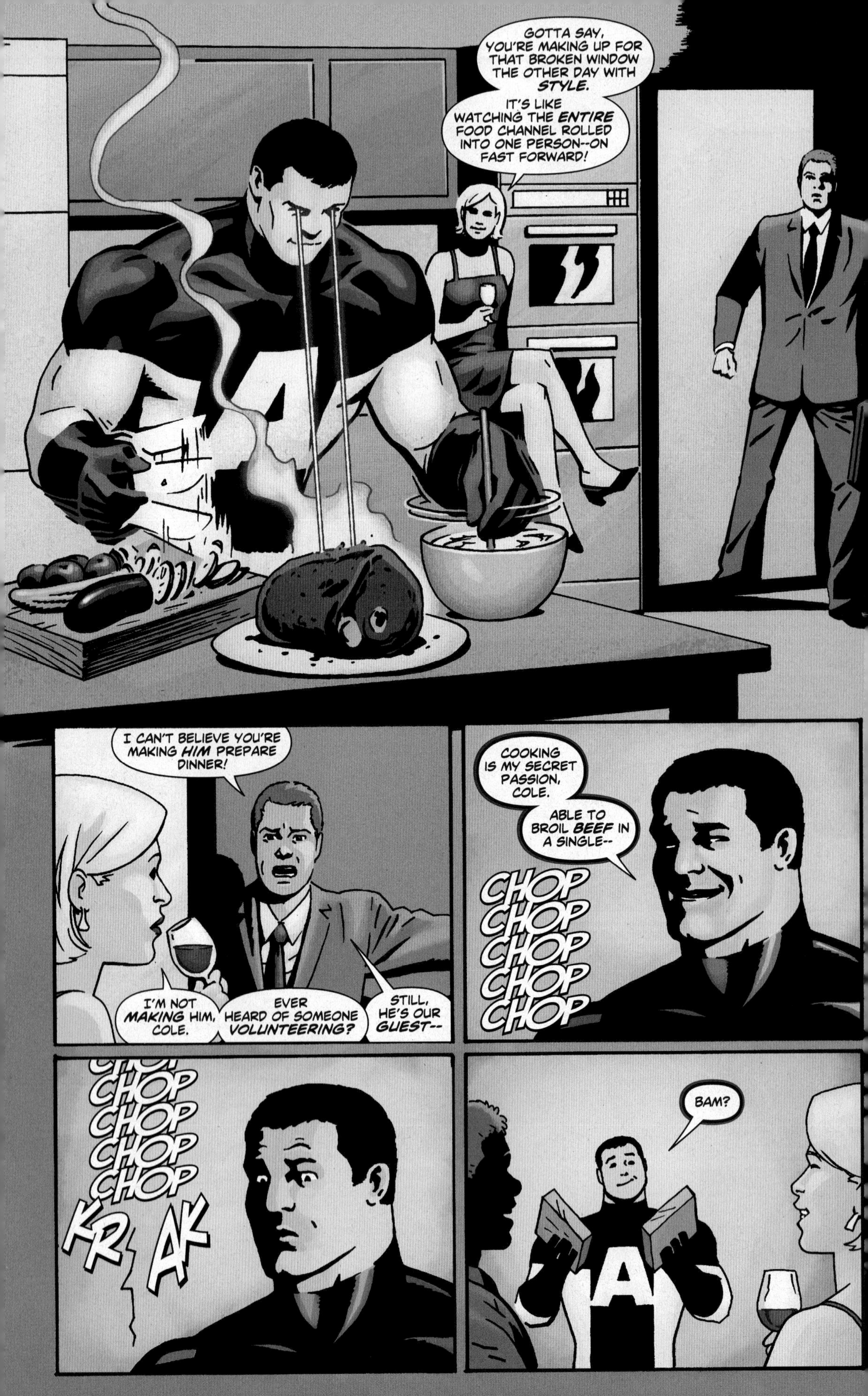
GOTTA SAY, YOU'RE MAKING UP FOR THAT BROKEN WINDOW THE OTHER DAY WITH STYLE.
IT'S LIKE WATCHING THE ENTIRE FOOD CHANNEL ROLLED INTO ONE PERSON--ON FAST FORWARD!
I CAN'T BELIEVE YOU'RE MAKING HIM PREPARE DINNER!
I'M NOT MAKING HIM, COLE.
EVER HEARD OF SOMEONE VOLUNTEERING?
STILL, HE'S OUR GUEST--
COOKING IS MY SECRET PASSION, COLE.
ABLE TO BROIL BEEF IN A SINGLE--
CHOP CHOP CHOP CHOP CHOP
CHOP CHOP CHOP CHOP
KRAK
BAM?

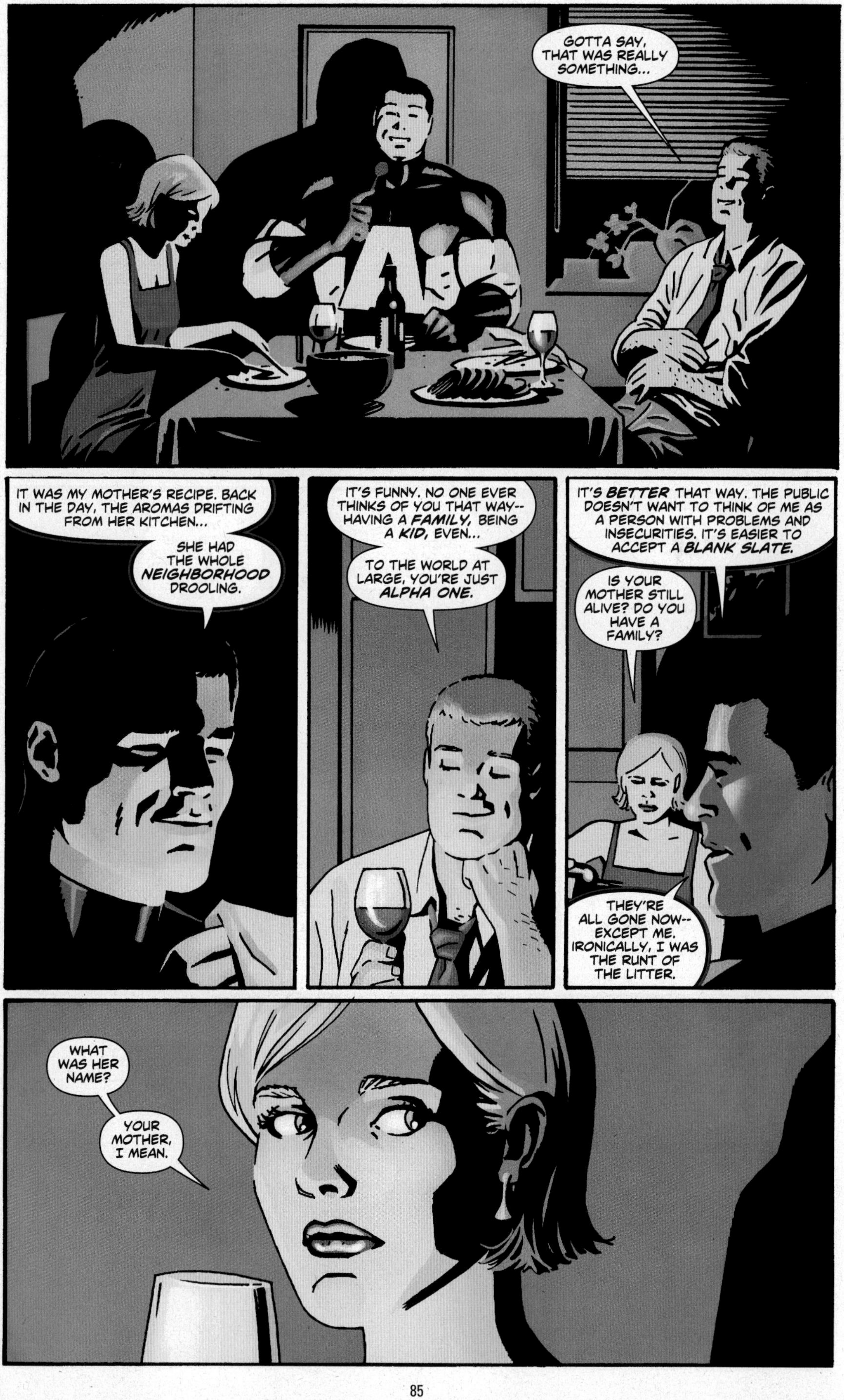
GOTTA SAY, THAT WAS REALLY SOMETHING...
IT WAS MY MOTHER'S RECIPE. BACK IN THE DAY, THE AROMAS DRIFTING FROM HER KITCHEN...
SHE HAD THE WHOLE NEIGHBORHOOD DROOLING.
IT'S FUNNY. NO ONE EVER THINKS OF YOU THAT WAY-- HAVING A FAMILY, BEING A KID, EVEN...
TO THE WORLD AT LARGE, YOU'RE JUST ALPHA ONE.
IT'S BETTER THAT WAY. THE PUBLIC DOESN'T WANT TO THINK OF ME AS A PERSON WITH PROBLEMS AND INSECURITIES. IT'S EASIER TO ACCEPT A BLANK SLATE.
IS YOUR MOTHER STILL ALIVE? DO YOU HAVE A FAMILY?
THEY'RE ALL GONE NOW-- EXCEPT ME. IRONICALLY, I WAS THE RUNT OF THE LITTER.
WHAT WAS HER NAME?
YOUR MOTHER, I MEAN.

THE DETAILS OF MY FORMER LIFE ARE *CLASSIFIED.* I REALLY CAN'T...

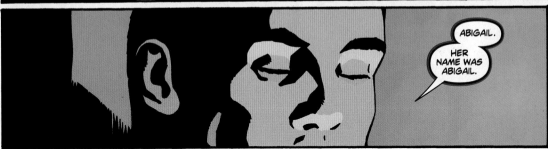

ABIGAIL.

HER NAME WAS ABIGAIL.

THAT'S A *BEAUTIFUL* NAME--

HEY, IS IT TRUE THAT WHEN YOU MET WITH *KHRUSHCHEV* BACK IN THE FIFTIES, HE TRIED TO GET YOU TO *DEFECT?*

Heh. THAT STORY HAS BEEN A *LITTLE* EXAGGERATED OVER THE YEARS.

LET ME TELL YOU WHAT REALLY HAPPENED...

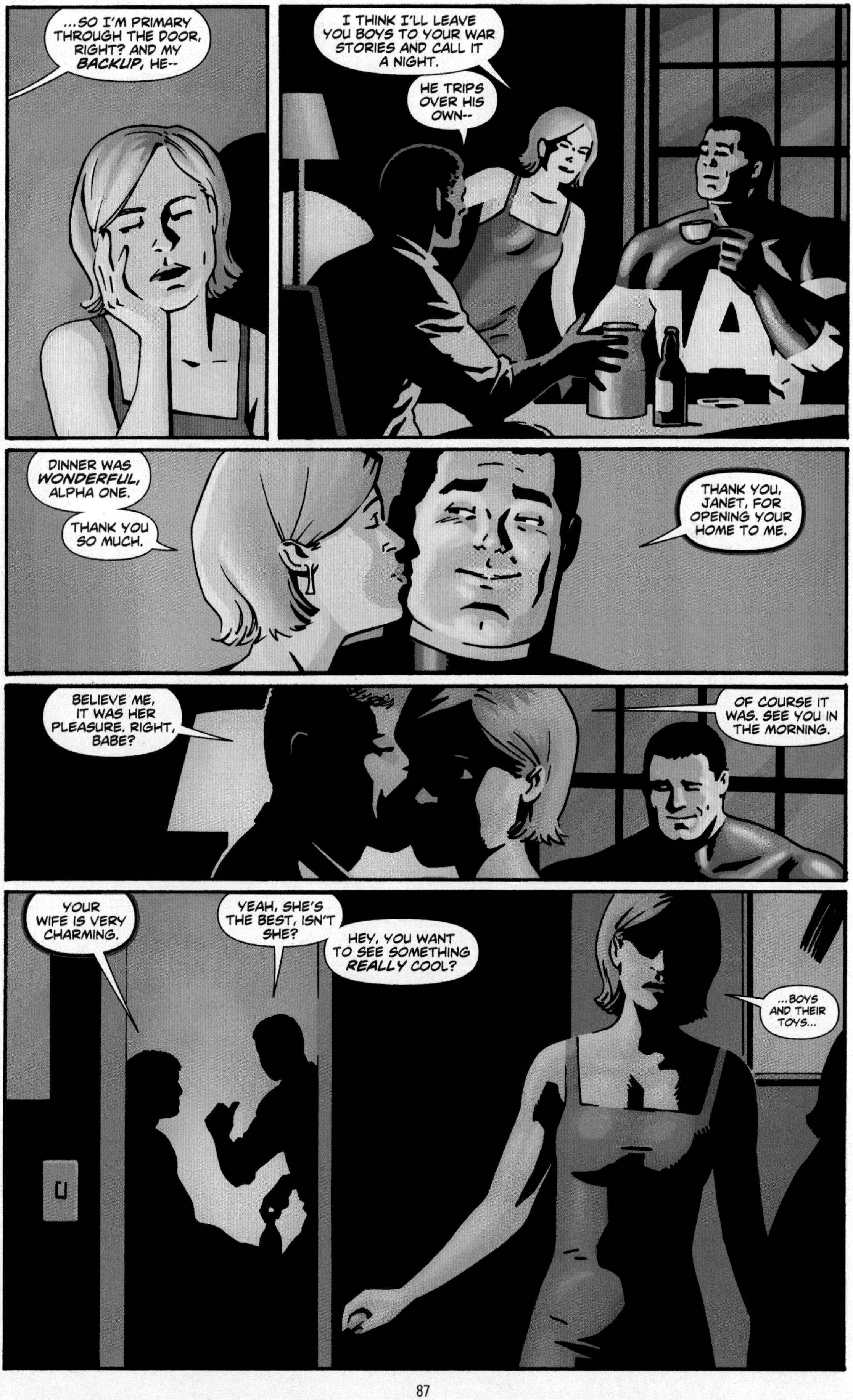
...SO I'M PRIMARY THROUGH THE DOOR, RIGHT? AND MY BACKUP, HE--
I THINK I'LL LEAVE YOU BOYS TO YOUR WAR STORIES AND CALL IT A NIGHT.
HE TRIPS OVER HIS OWN--
DINNER WAS WONDERFUL, ALPHA ONE.
THANK YOU SO MUCH.
THANK YOU, JANET, FOR OPENING YOUR HOME TO ME.
BELIEVE ME, IT WAS HER PLEASURE. RIGHT, BABE?
OF COURSE IT WAS. SEE YOU IN THE MORNING.
YOUR WIFE IS VERY CHARMING.
YEAH, SHE'S THE BEST, ISN'T SHE?
HEY, YOU WANT TO SEE SOMETHING REALLY COOL?
...BOYS AND THEIR TOYS...

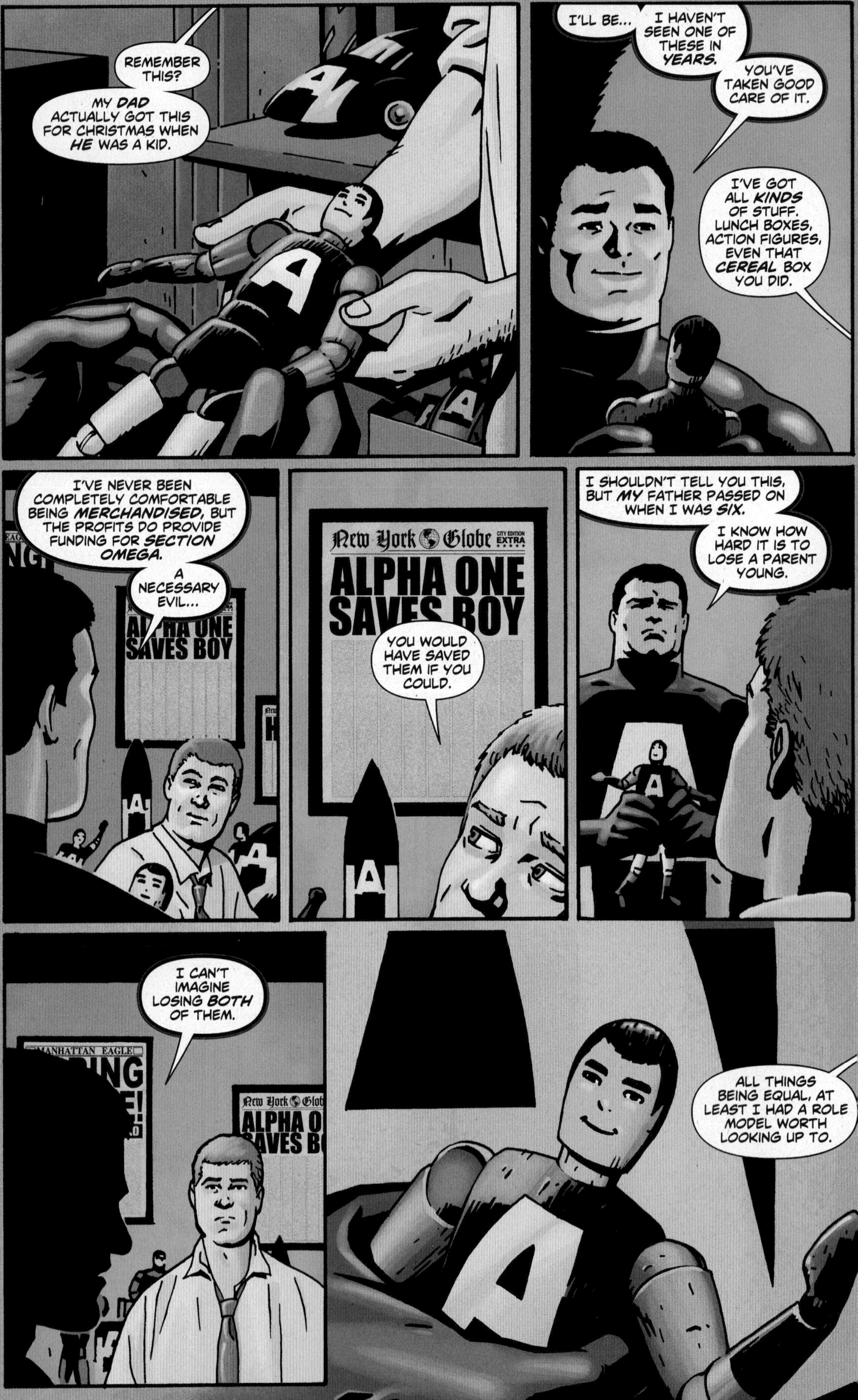
REMEMBER THIS?
MY DAD ACTUALLY GOT THIS FOR CHRISTMAS WHEN HE WAS A KID.
I'LL BE...
I HAVEN'T SEEN ONE OF THESE IN YEARS.
YOU'VE TAKEN GOOD CARE OF IT.
I'VE GOT ALL KINDS OF STUFF. LUNCH BOXES, ACTION FIGURES, EVEN THAT CEREAL BOX YOU DID.
I'VE NEVER BEEN COMPLETELY COMFORTABLE BEING MERCHANDISED, BUT THE PROFITS DO PROVIDE FUNDING FOR SECTION OMEGA.
A NECESSARY EVIL...
ALPHA ONE SAVES BOY
New York Globe
CITY EDITION EXTRA
ALPHA ONE SAVES BOY
YOU WOULD HAVE SAVED THEM IF YOU COULD.
I SHOULDN'T TELL YOU THIS, BUT MY FATHER PASSED ON WHEN I WAS SIX.
I KNOW HOW HARD IT IS TO LOSE A PARENT YOUNG.
I CAN'T IMAGINE LOSING BOTH OF THEM.
MANHATTAN EAGLE
ALL THINGS BEING EQUAL, AT LEAST I HAD A ROLE MODEL WORTH LOOKING UP TO.

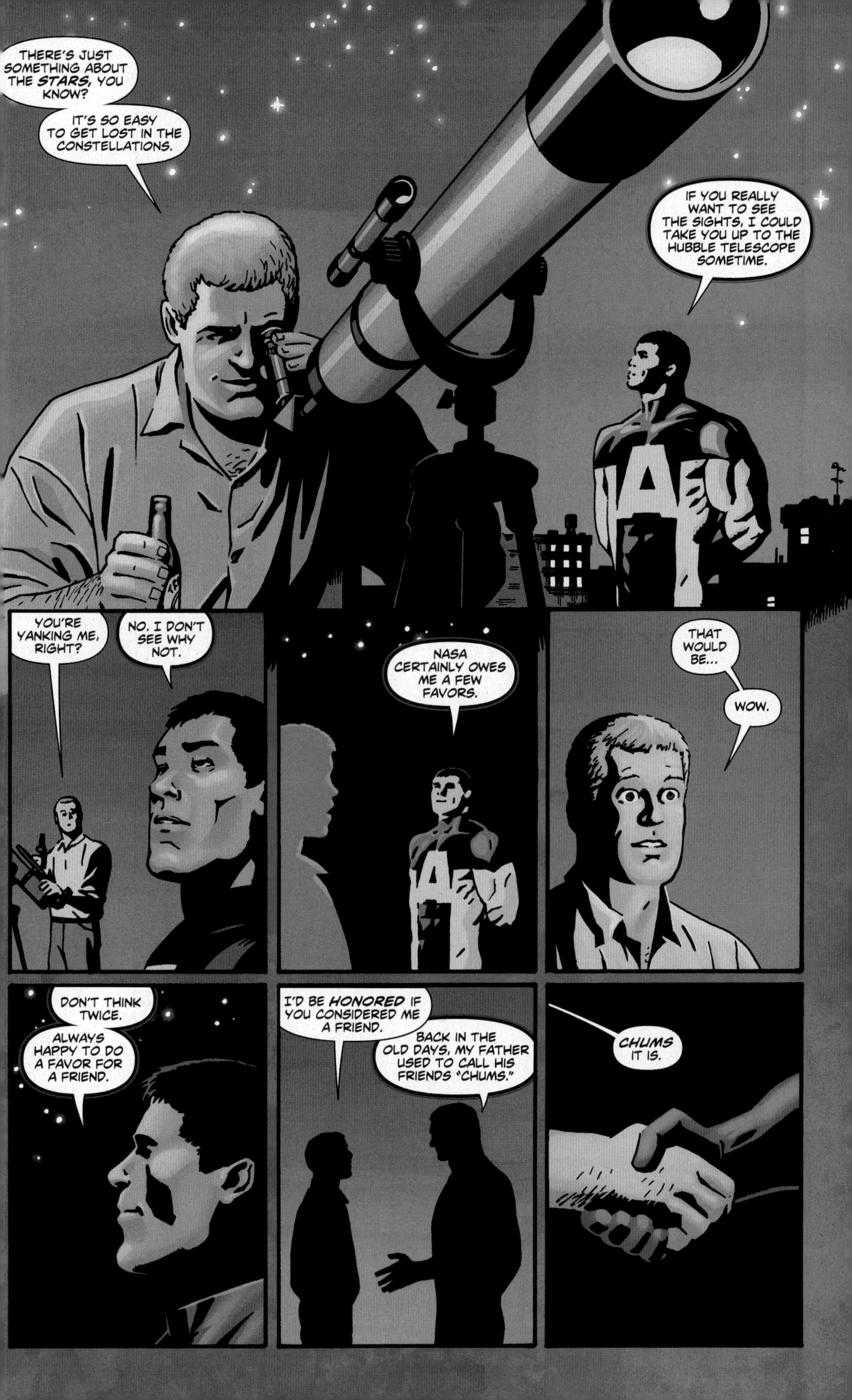
THERE'S JUST SOMETHING ABOUT THE STARS, YOU KNOW?
IT'S SO EASY TO GET LOST IN THE CONSTELLATIONS.
IF YOU REALLY WANT TO SEE THE SIGHTS, I COULD TAKE YOU UP TO THE HUBBLE TELESCOPE SOMETIME.
YOU'RE YANKING ME, RIGHT?
NO. I DON'T SEE WHY NOT.
NASA CERTAINLY OWES ME A FEW FAVORS.
THAT WOULD BE...
WOW.
DON'T THINK TWICE.
ALWAYS HAPPY TO DO A FAVOR FOR A FRIEND.
I'D BE HONORED IF YOU CONSIDERED ME A FRIEND.
BACK IN THE OLD DAYS, MY FATHER USED TO CALL HIS FRIENDS "CHUMS."
CHUMS IT IS.

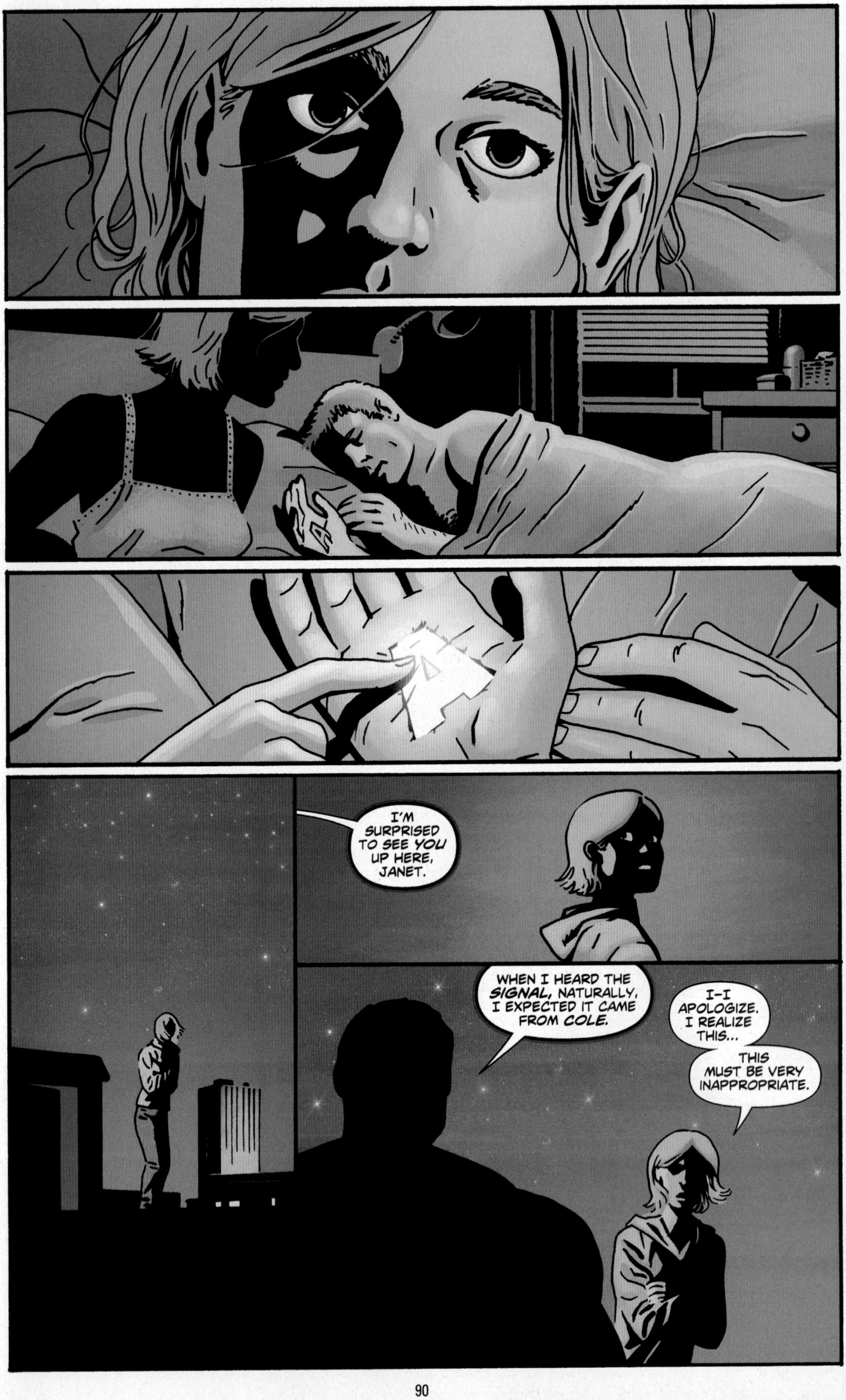
I'M SURPRISED TO SEE YOU UP HERE, JANET.
WHEN I HEARD THE SIGNAL, NATURALLY, I EXPECTED IT CAME FROM COLE.
I-I APOLOGIZE. I REALIZE THIS...
THIS MUST BE VERY INAPPROPRIATE.

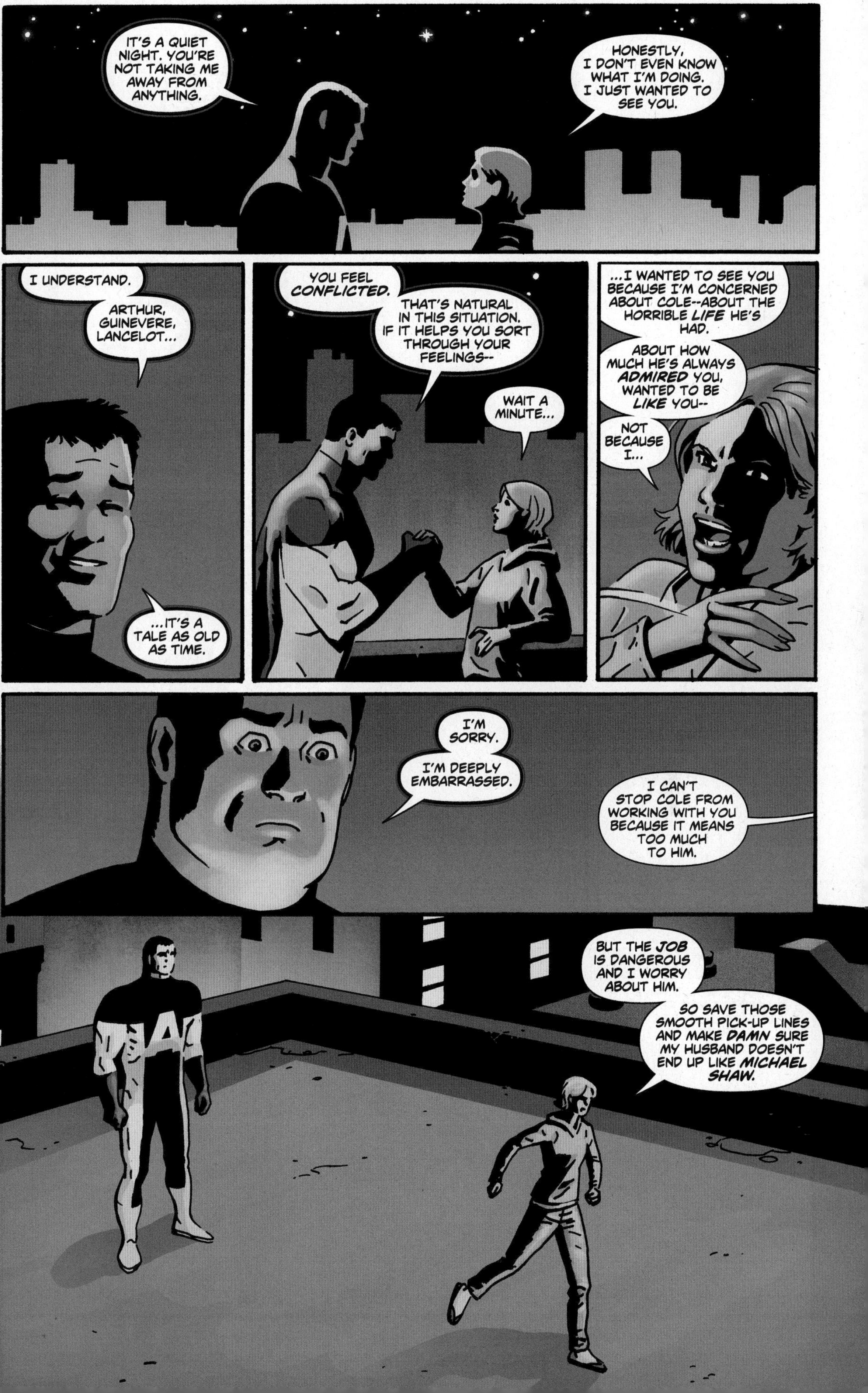
IT'S A QUIET NIGHT. YOU'RE NOT TAKING ME AWAY FROM ANYTHING.
HONESTLY, I DON'T EVEN KNOW WHAT I'M DOING. I JUST WANTED TO SEE YOU.
I UNDERSTAND.
ARTHUR, GUINEVERE, LANCELOT...
...IT'S A TALE AS OLD AS TIME.
YOU FEEL CONFLICTED.
THAT'S NATURAL IN THIS SITUATION. IF IT HELPS YOU SORT THROUGH YOUR FEELINGS--
WAIT A MINUTE...
...I WANTED TO SEE YOU BECAUSE I'M CONCERNED ABOUT COLE--ABOUT THE HORRIBLE LIFE HE'S HAD.
ABOUT HOW MUCH HE'S ALWAYS ADMIRED YOU, WANTED TO BE LIKE YOU--
NOT BECAUSE I...
I'M SORRY.
I'M DEEPLY EMBARRASSED.
I CAN'T STOP COLE FROM WORKING WITH YOU BECAUSE IT MEANS TOO MUCH TO HIM.
BUT THE JOB IS DANGEROUS AND I WORRY ABOUT HIM.
SO SAVE THOSE SMOOTH PICK-UP LINES AND MAKE DAMN SURE MY HUSBAND DOESN'T END UP LIKE MICHAEL SHAW.

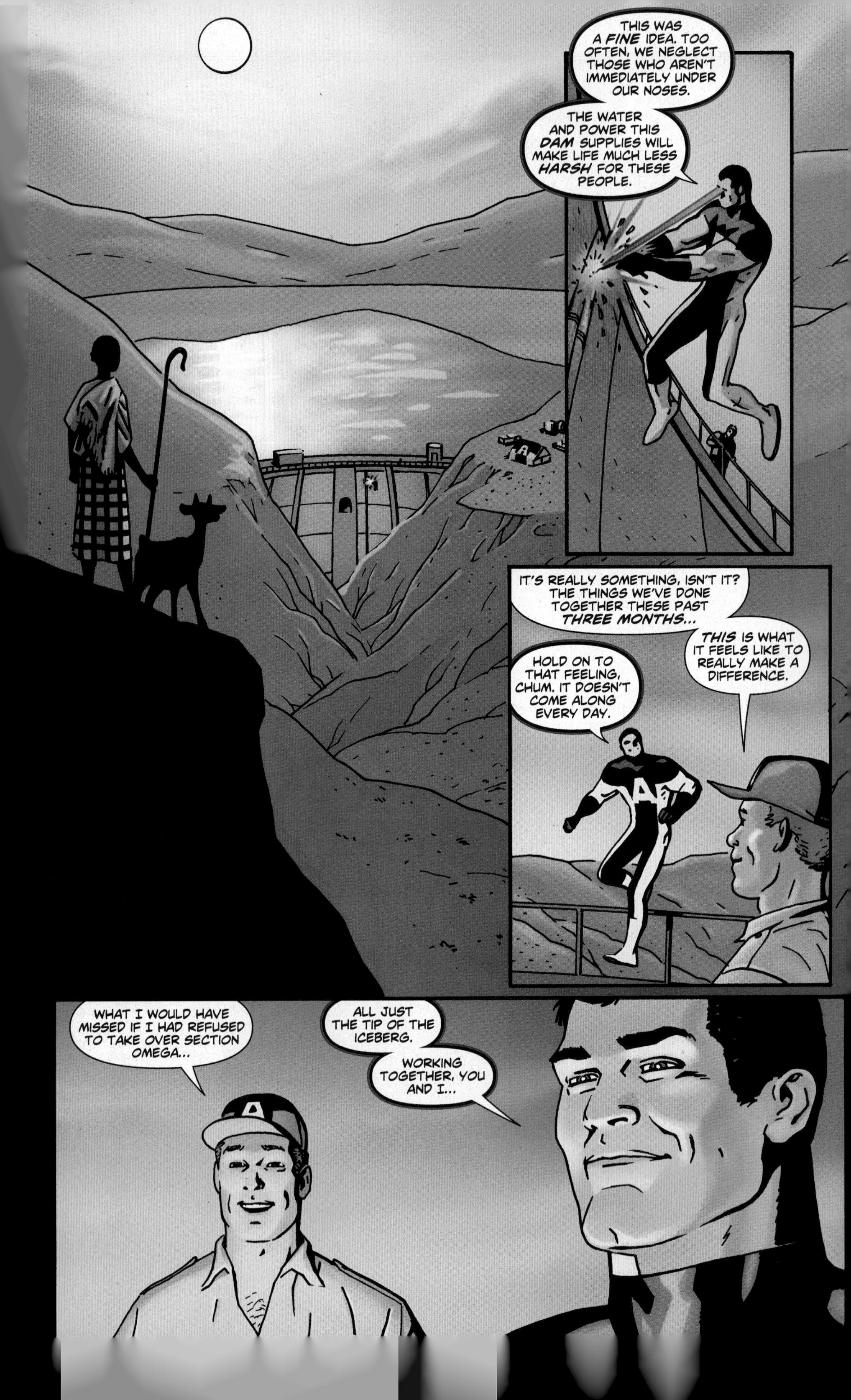
THIS WAS A FINE IDEA. TOO OFTEN, WE NEGLECT THOSE WHO AREN'T IMMEDIATELY UNDER OUR NOSES.
THE WATER AND POWER THIS DAM SUPPLIES WILL MAKE LIFE MUCH LESS HARSH FOR THESE PEOPLE.
IT'S REALLY SOMETHING, ISN'T IT? THE THINGS WE'VE DONE TOGETHER THESE PAST THREE MONTHS...
THIS IS WHAT IT FEELS LIKE TO REALLY MAKE A DIFFERENCE.
HOLD ON TO THAT FEELING, CHUM. IT DOESN'T COME ALONG EVERY DAY.
WHAT I WOULD HAVE MISSED IF I HAD REFUSED TO TAKE OVER SECTION OMEGA...
ALL JUST THE TIP OF THE ICEBERG.
WORKING TOGETHER, YOU AND I...

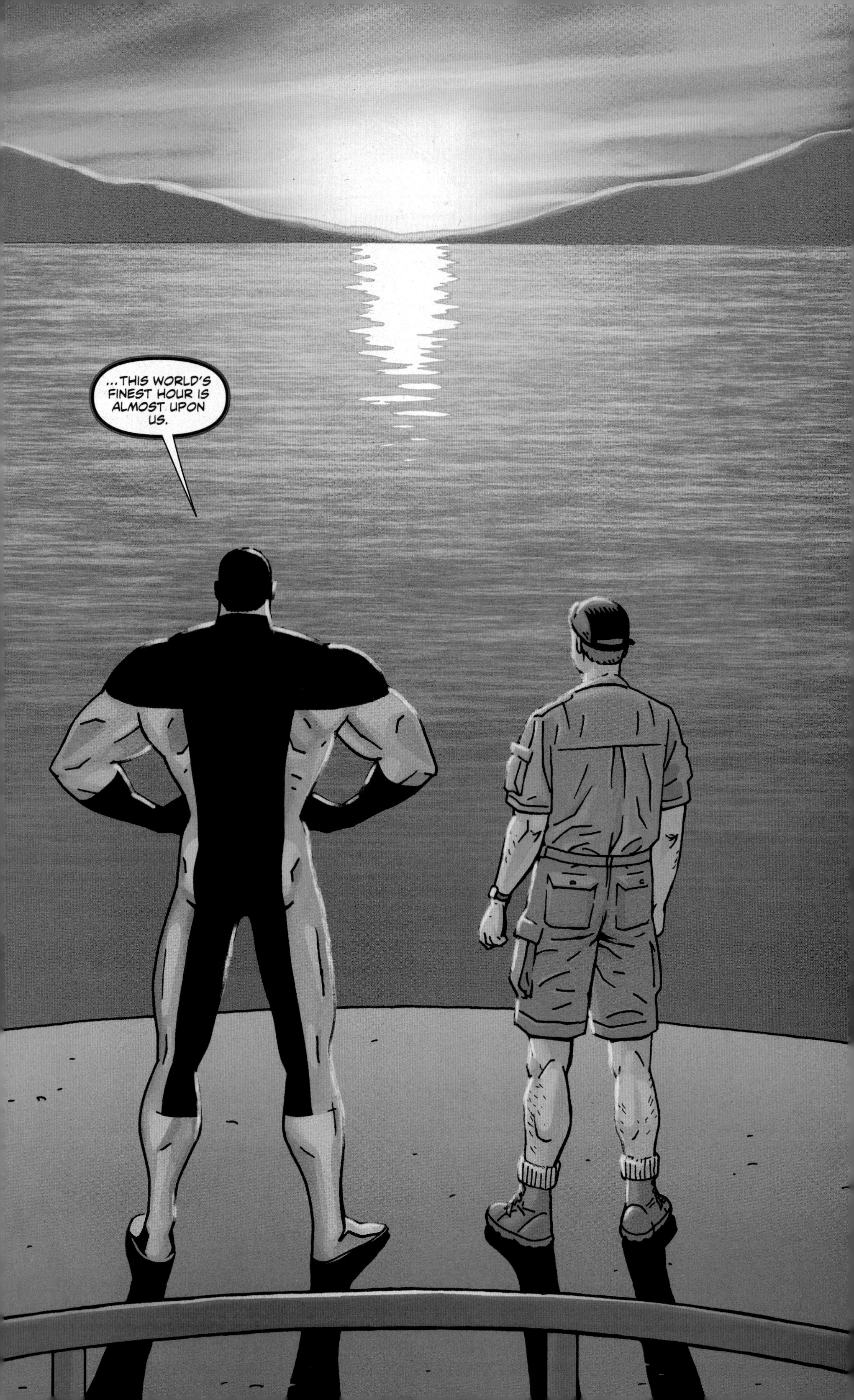
...THIS WORLD'S FINEST HOUR IS ALMOST UPON US.

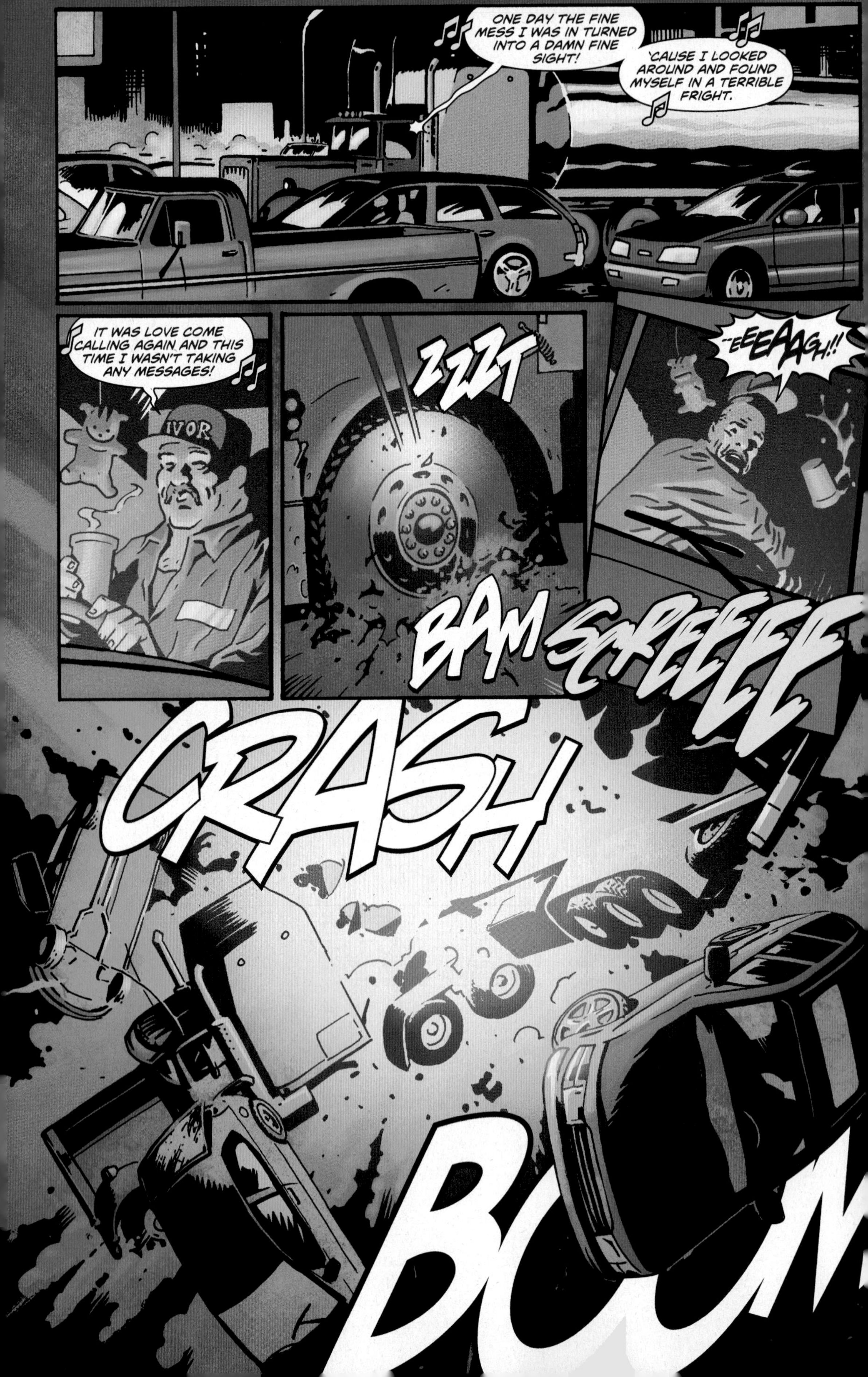
ONE DAY THE FINE MESS I WAS IN TURNED INTO A DAMN FINE SIGHT!
'CAUSE I LOOKED AROUND AND FOUND MYSELF IN A TERRIBLE FRIGHT.
IT WAS LOVE COME CALLING AGAIN AND THIS TIME I WASN'T TAKING ANY MESSAGES!
IVOR
ZZZT
--EEEAAAGH!!
BAM
SCREEEE
CRASH
BOOM

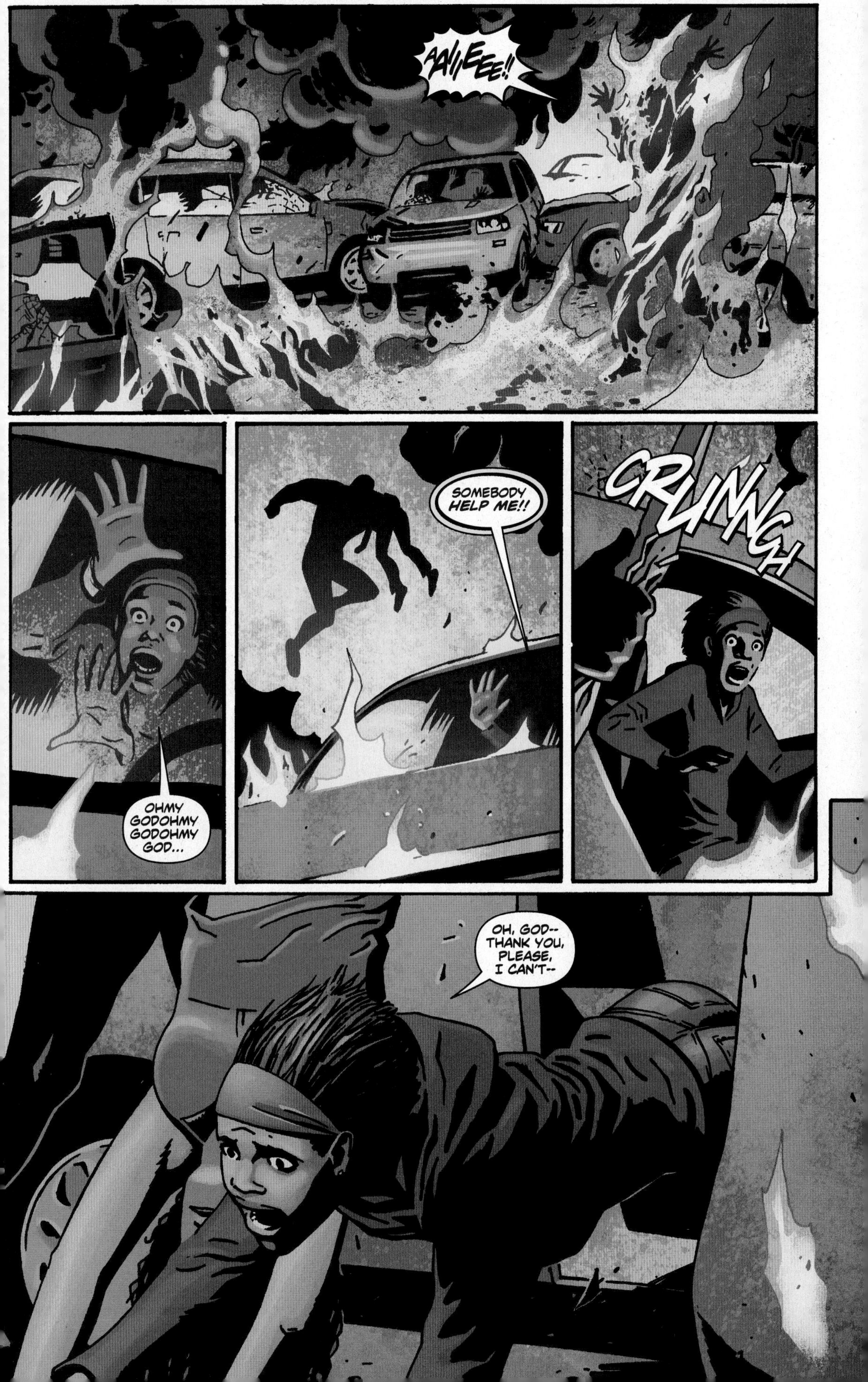
AAIIEEEE!!
OHMY GODOHMY GODOHMY GOD...
SOMEBODY HELP ME!!
CRUNNCH
OH, GOD-- THANK YOU, PLEASE, I CAN'T--

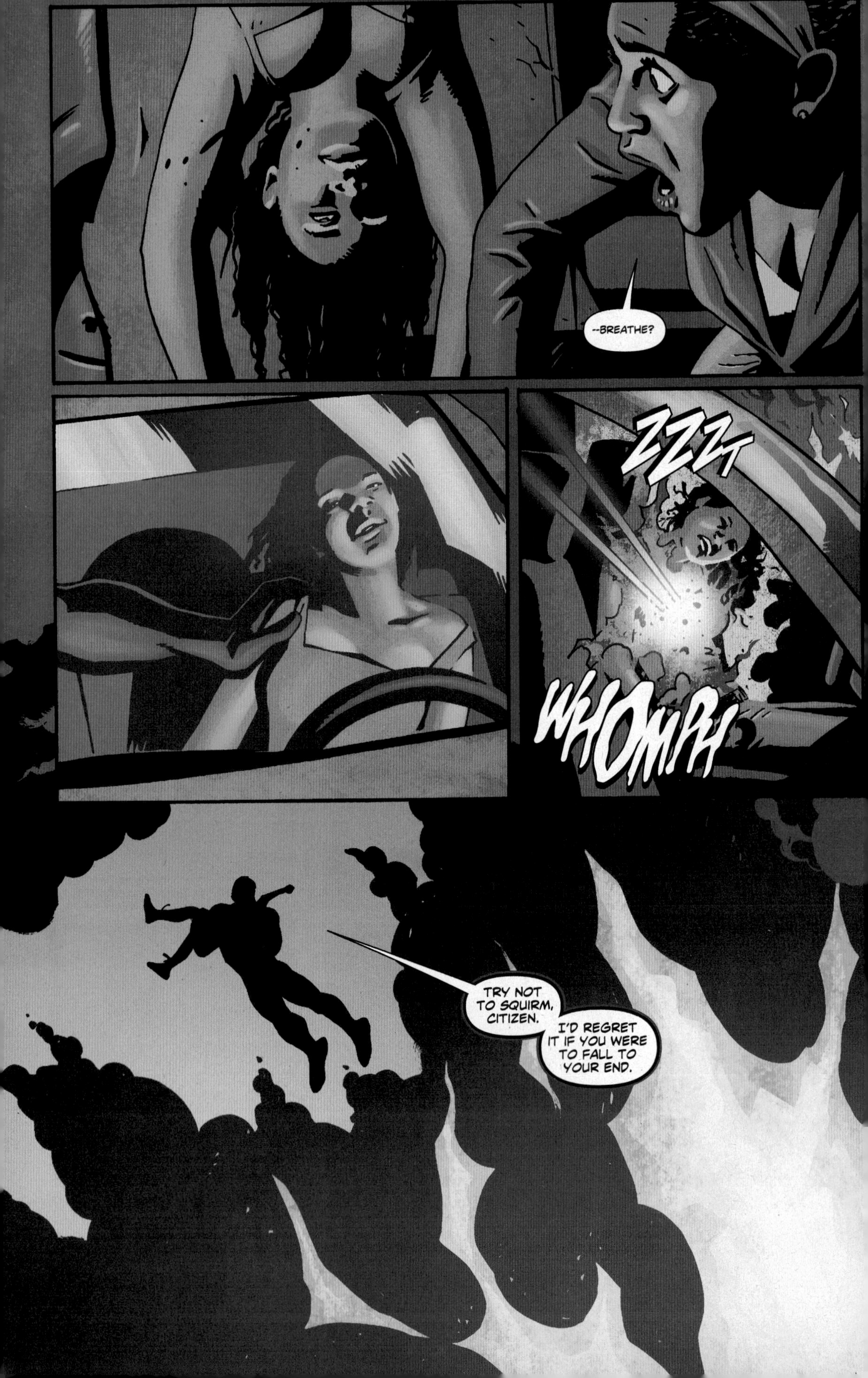
--BREATHE?
ZZZT
WHOMPH
TRY NOT TO SQUIRM, CITIZEN.
I'D REGRET IT IF YOU WERE TO FALL TO YOUR END.

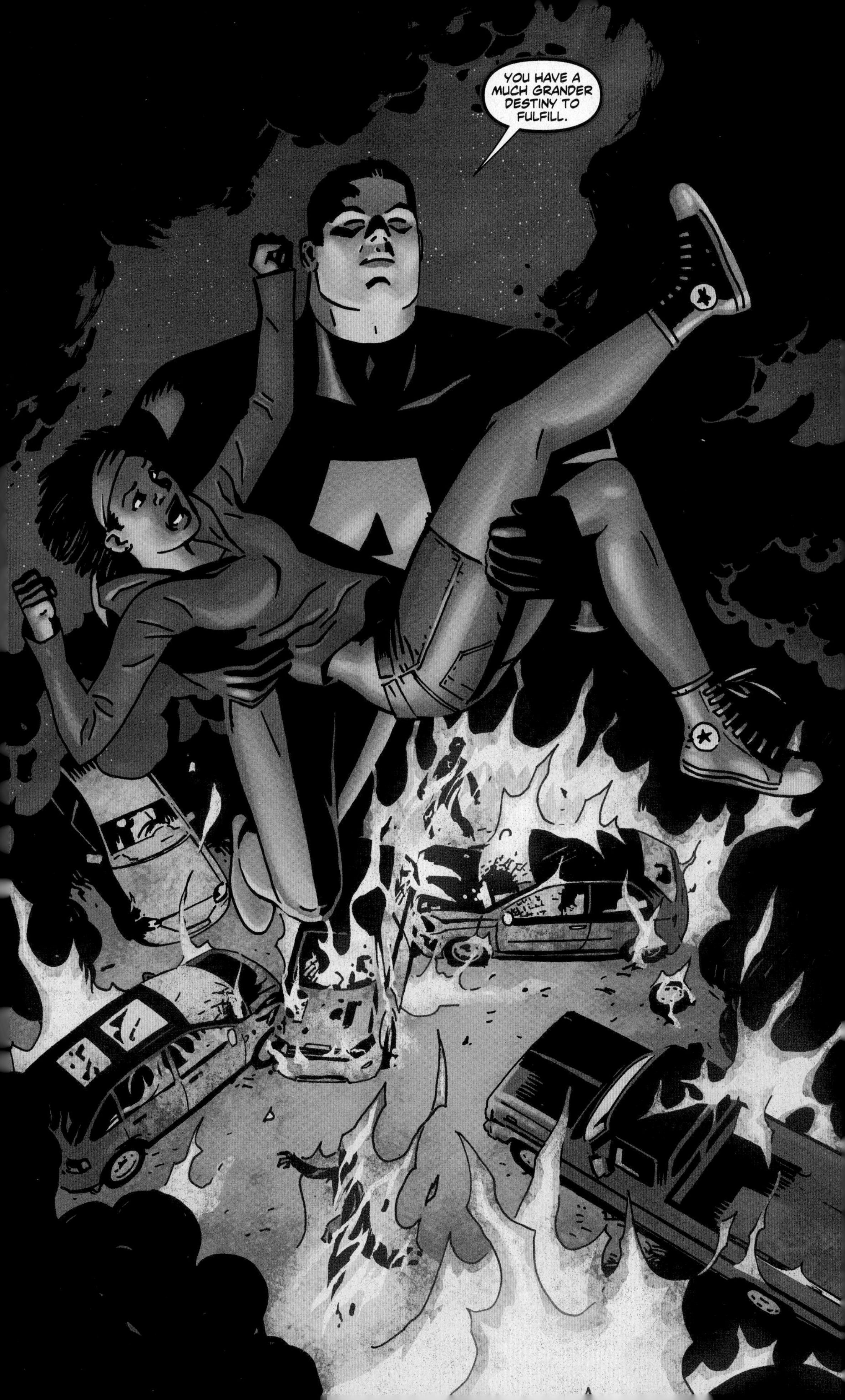
YOU HAVE A MUCH GRANDER DESTINY TO FULFILL.

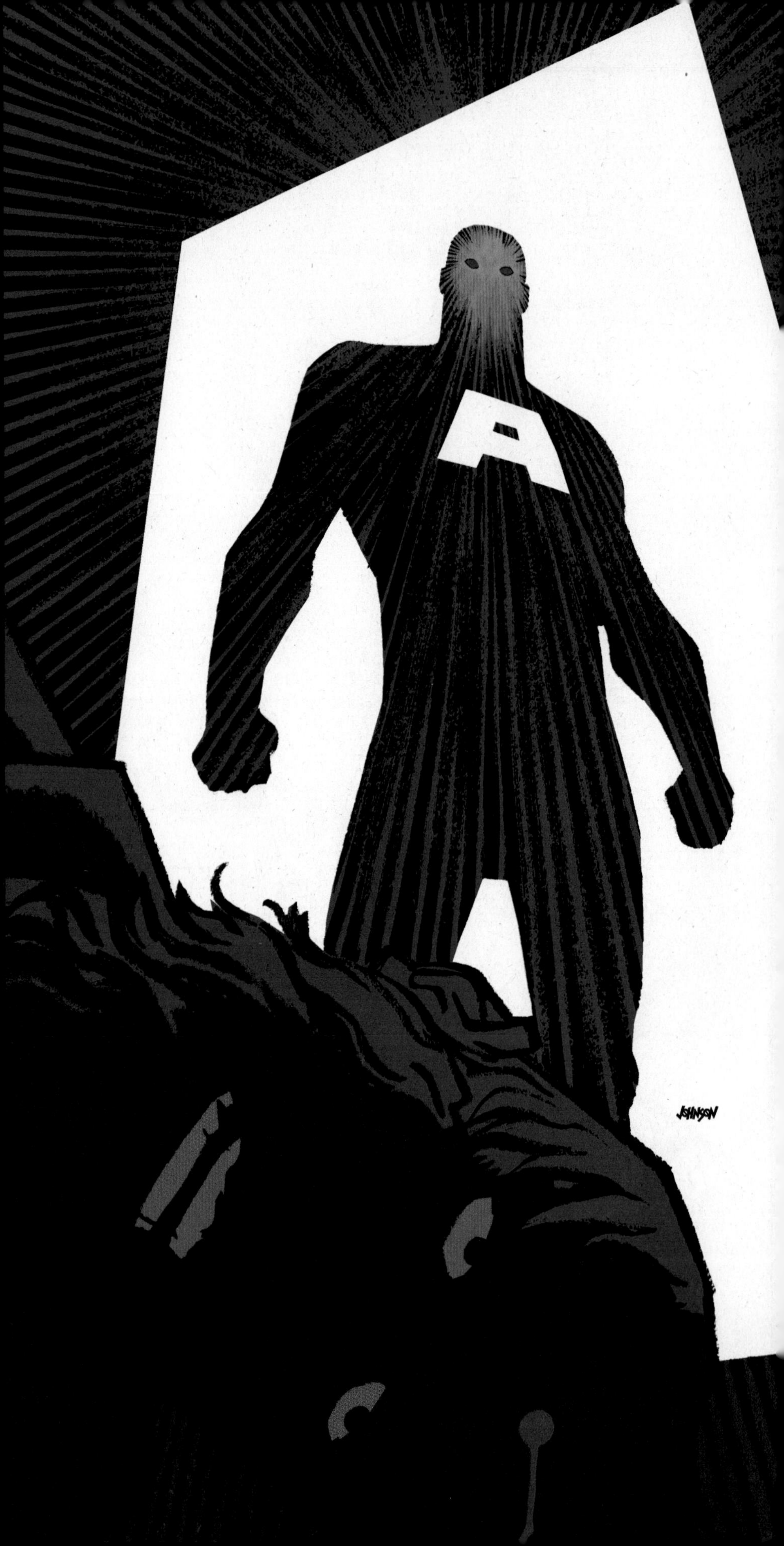
JOHNSON

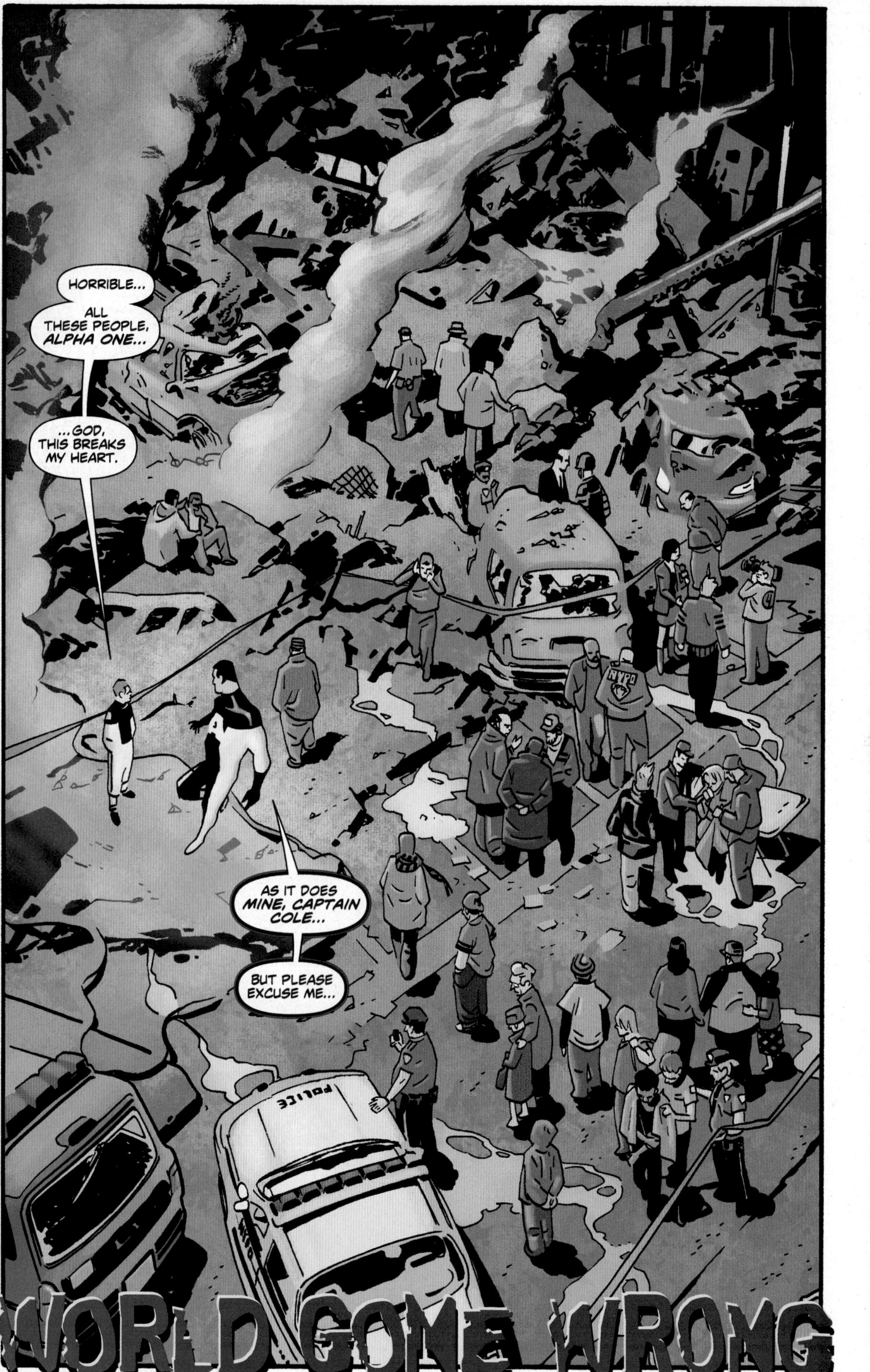
HORRIBLE...
ALL THESE PEOPLE, ALPHA ONE...
...GOD, THIS BREAKS MY HEART.
AS IT DOES MINE, CAPTAIN COLE...
BUT PLEASE EXCUSE ME...
POLICE
WORLD GONE WRONG

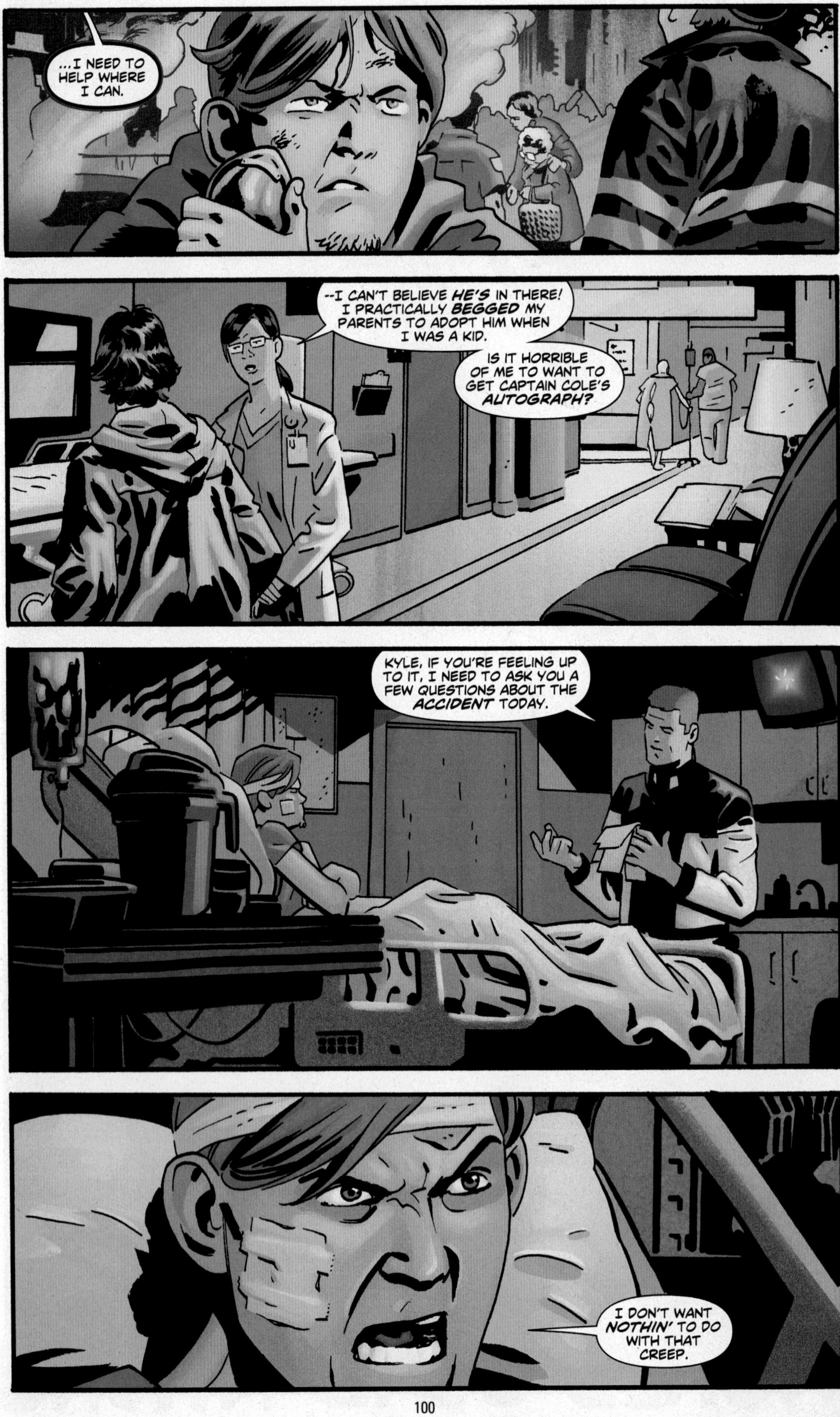
...I NEED TO HELP WHERE I CAN.
--I CAN'T BELIEVE *HE'S* IN THERE! I PRACTICALLY *BEGGED* MY PARENTS TO ADOPT HIM WHEN I WAS A KID.
IS IT HORRIBLE OF ME TO WANT TO GET CAPTAIN COLE'S *AUTOGRAPH?*
KYLE, IF YOU'RE FEELING UP TO IT, I NEED TO ASK YOU A FEW QUESTIONS ABOUT THE *ACCIDENT* TODAY.
I DON'T WANT *NOTHIN'* TO DO WITH THAT CREEP.

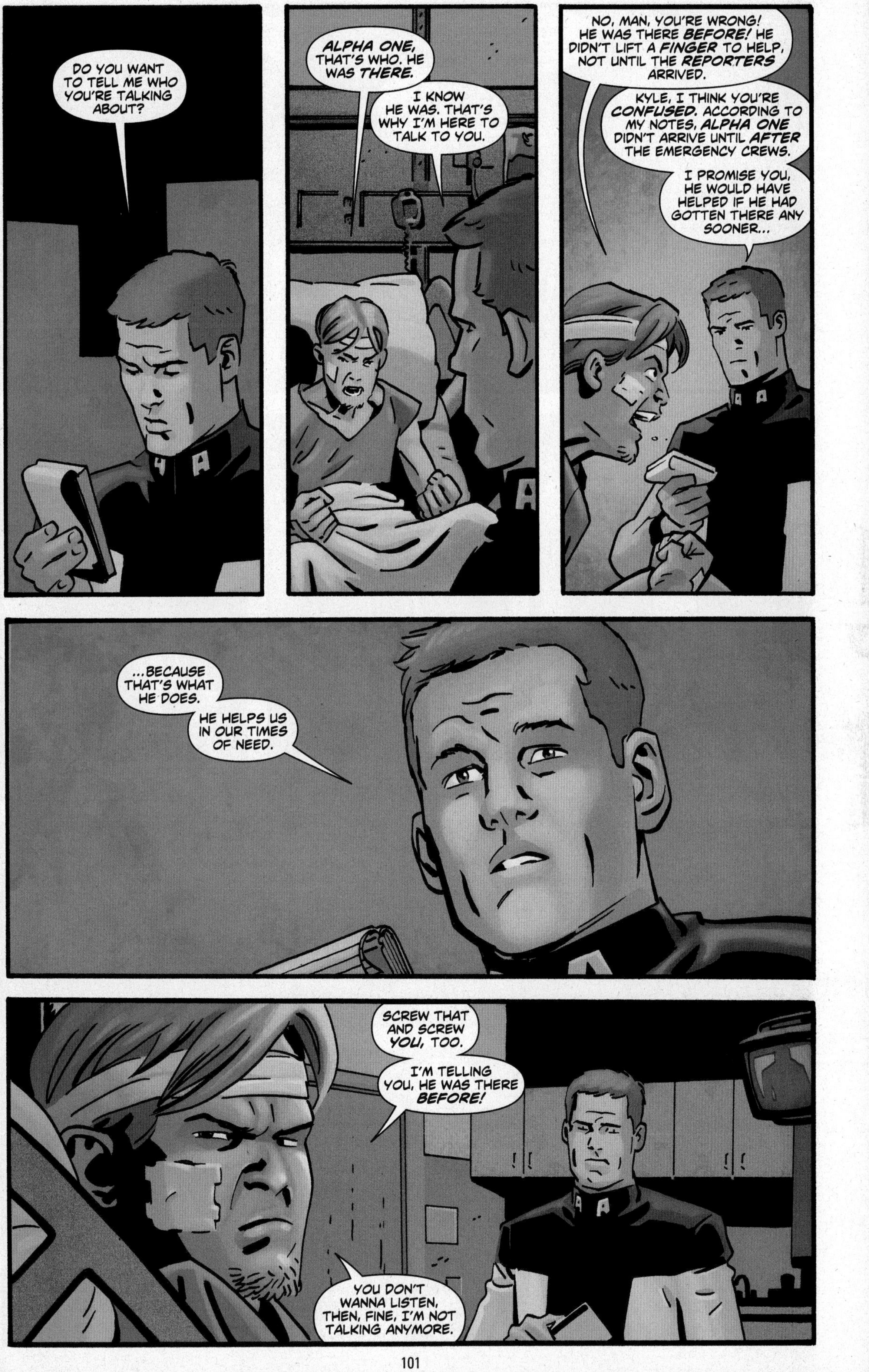
DO YOU WANT TO TELL ME WHO YOU'RE TALKING ABOUT?
ALPHA ONE, THAT'S WHO. HE WAS THERE.
I KNOW HE WAS. THAT'S WHY I'M HERE TO TALK TO YOU.
NO, MAN, YOU'RE WRONG! HE WAS THERE BEFORE! HE DIDN'T LIFT A FINGER TO HELP, NOT UNTIL THE REPORTERS ARRIVED.
KYLE, I THINK YOU'RE CONFUSED. ACCORDING TO MY NOTES, ALPHA ONE DIDN'T ARRIVE UNTIL AFTER THE EMERGENCY CREWS.
I PROMISE YOU, HE WOULD HAVE HELPED IF HE HAD GOTTEN THERE ANY SOONER...
...BECAUSE THAT'S WHAT HE DOES.
HE HELPS US IN OUR TIMES OF NEED.
SCREW THAT AND SCREW YOU, TOO.
I'M TELLING YOU, HE WAS THERE BEFORE!
YOU DON'T WANNA LISTEN, THEN, FINE, I'M NOT TALKING ANYMORE.

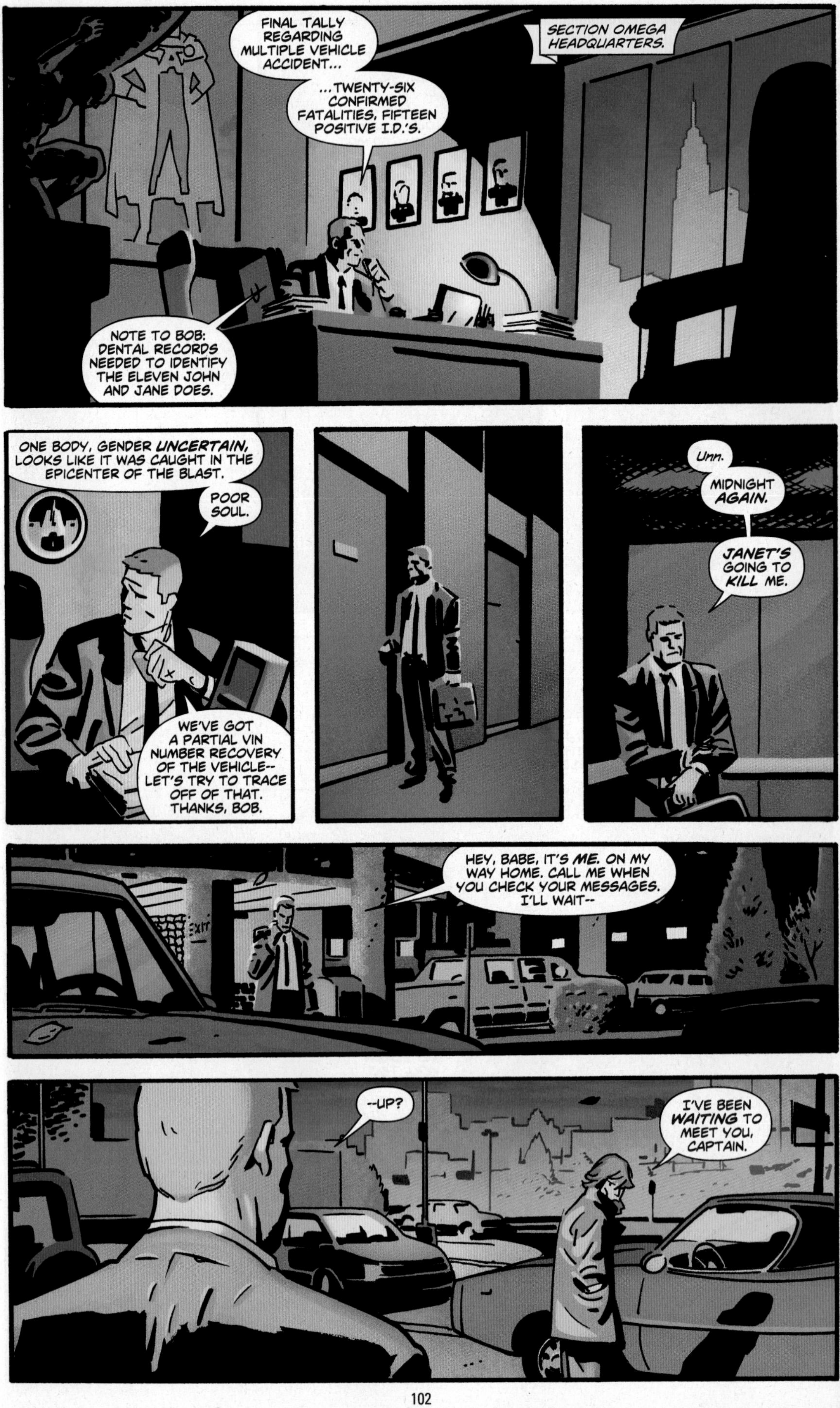

FINAL TALLY REGARDING MULTIPLE VEHICLE ACCIDENT...
SECTION OMEGA HEADQUARTERS.
...TWENTY-SIX CONFIRMED FATALITIES, FIFTEEN POSITIVE I.D.'S.
NOTE TO BOB: DENTAL RECORDS NEEDED TO IDENTIFY THE ELEVEN JOHN AND JANE DOES.
ONE BODY, GENDER UNCERTAIN, LOOKS LIKE IT WAS CAUGHT IN THE EPICENTER OF THE BLAST.
POOR SOUL.
WE'VE GOT A PARTIAL VIN NUMBER RECOVERY OF THE VEHICLE-- LET'S TRY TO TRACE OFF OF THAT. THANKS, BOB.
Unn.
MIDNIGHT AGAIN.
JANET'S GOING TO KILL ME.
HEY, BABE, IT'S ME. ON MY WAY HOME. CALL ME WHEN YOU CHECK YOUR MESSAGES. I'LL WAIT--
EXIT
--UP?
I'VE BEEN WAITING TO MEET YOU, CAPTAIN.

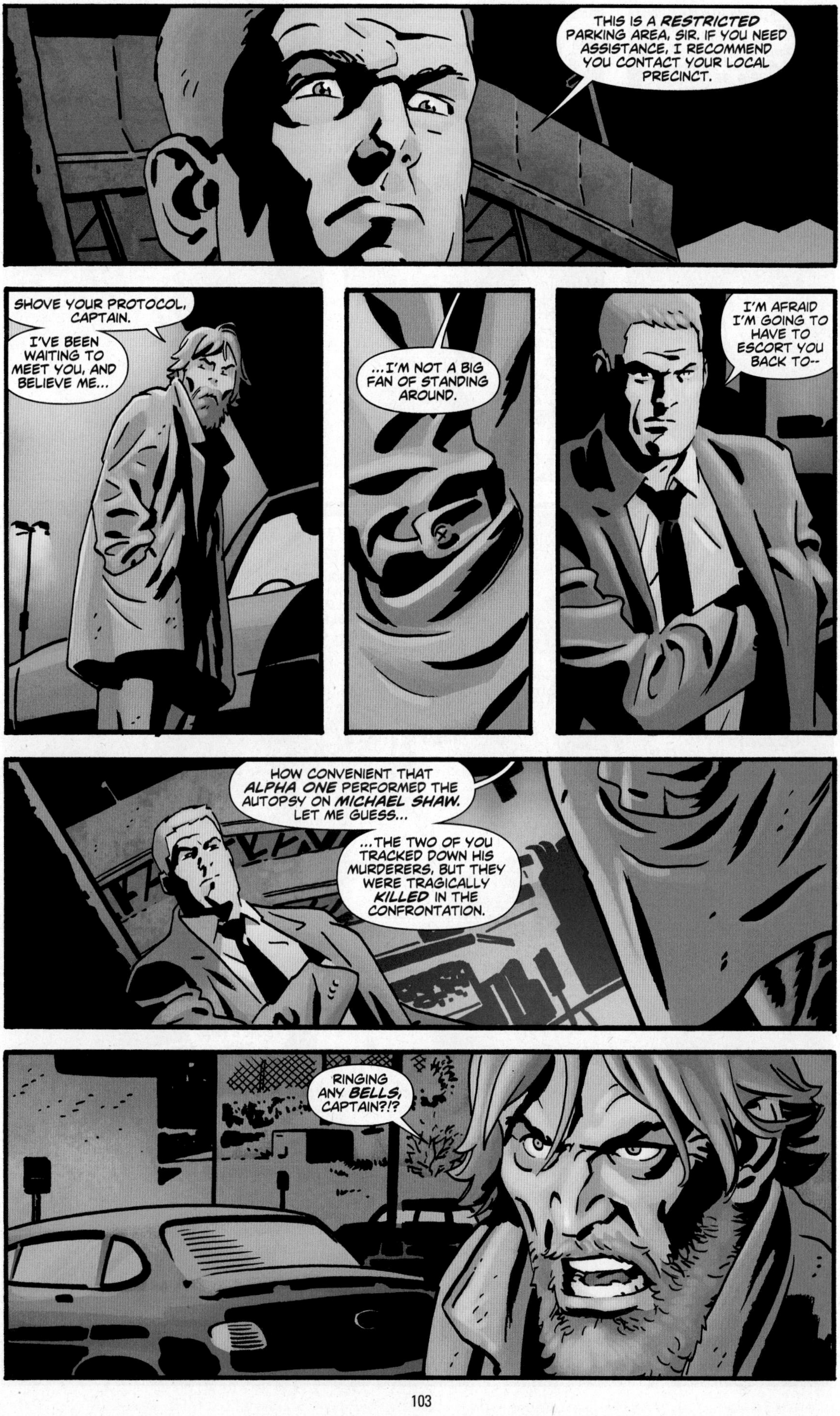
THIS IS A RESTRICTED PARKING AREA, SIR. IF YOU NEED ASSISTANCE, I RECOMMEND YOU CONTACT YOUR LOCAL PRECINCT.
SHOVE YOUR PROTOCOL, CAPTAIN.
I'VE BEEN WAITING TO MEET YOU, AND BELIEVE ME...
...I'M NOT A BIG FAN OF STANDING AROUND.
I'M AFRAID I'M GOING TO HAVE TO ESCORT YOU BACK TO--
HOW CONVENIENT THAT ALPHA ONE PERFORMED THE AUTOPSY ON MICHAEL SHAW. LET ME GUESS...
...THE TWO OF YOU TRACKED DOWN HIS MURDERERS, BUT THEY WERE TRAGICALLY KILLED IN THE CONFRONTATION.
RINGING ANY BELLS, CAPTAIN?!?

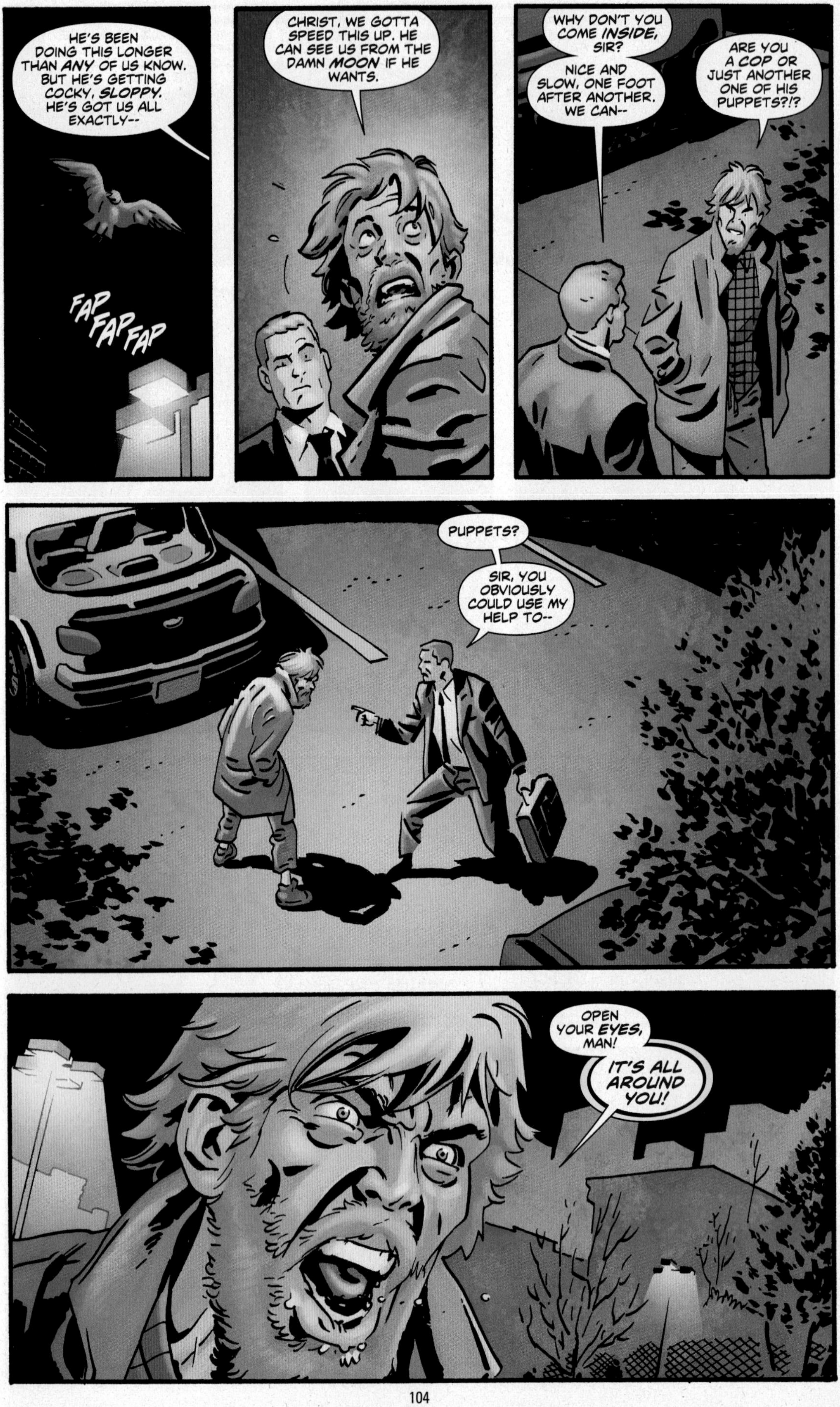
HE'S BEEN DOING THIS LONGER THAN ANY OF US KNOW. BUT HE'S GETTING COCKY, SLOPPY. HE'S GOT US ALL EXACTLY--
FAP FAP FAP
CHRIST, WE GOTTA SPEED THIS UP. HE CAN SEE US FROM THE DAMN MOON IF HE WANTS.
WHY DON'T YOU COME INSIDE, SIR?
NICE AND SLOW, ONE FOOT AFTER ANOTHER. WE CAN--
ARE YOU A COP OR JUST ANOTHER ONE OF HIS PUPPETS?!?
PUPPETS?
SIR, YOU OBVIOUSLY COULD USE MY HELP TO--
OPEN YOUR EYES, MAN!
IT'S ALL AROUND YOU!

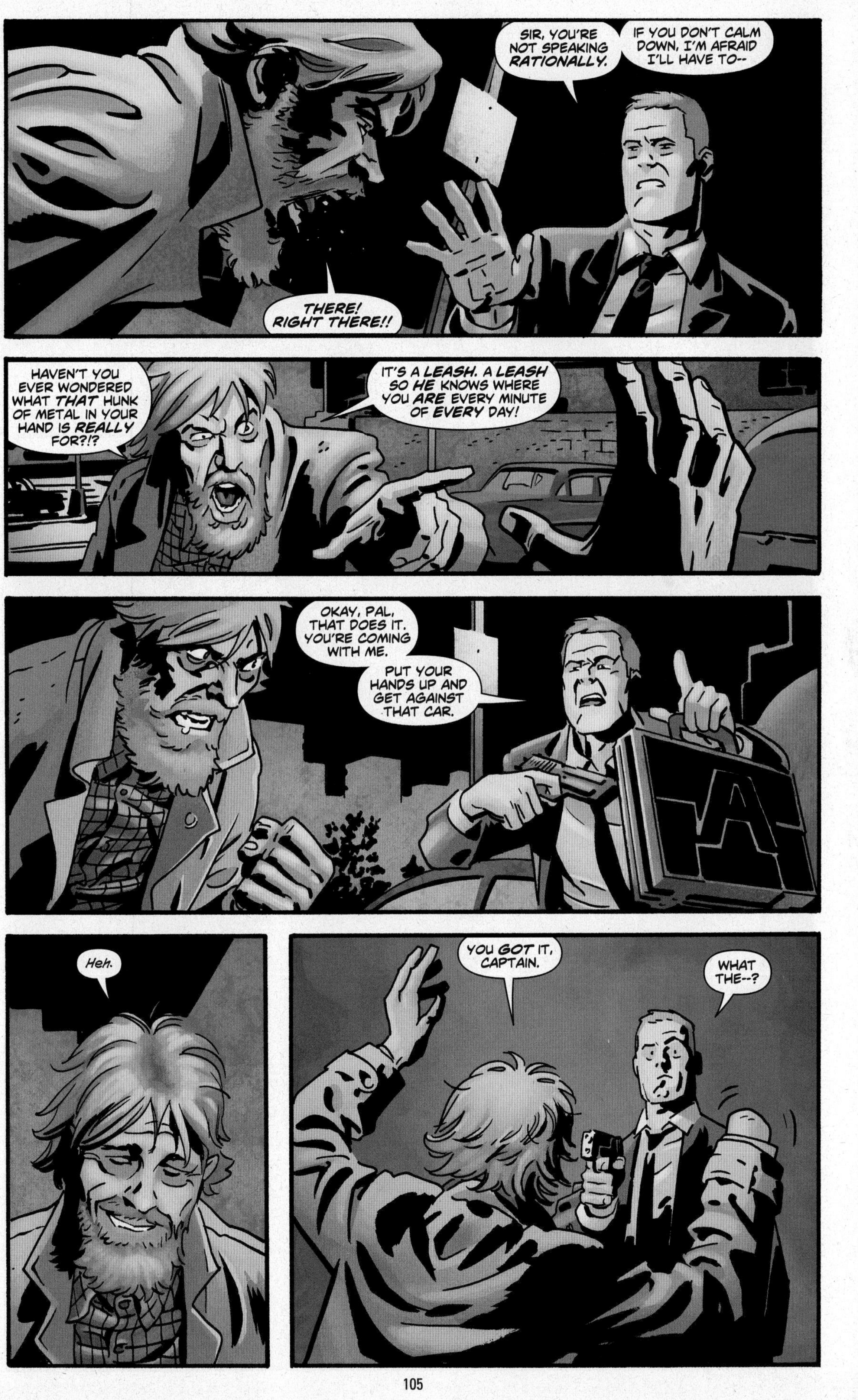
SIR, YOU'RE NOT SPEAKING RATIONALLY.
IF YOU DON'T CALM DOWN, I'M AFRAID I'LL HAVE TO--
THERE! RIGHT THERE!!
HAVEN'T YOU EVER WONDERED WHAT THAT HUNK OF METAL IN YOUR HAND IS REALLY FOR?!?
IT'S A LEASH. A LEASH SO HE KNOWS WHERE YOU ARE EVERY MINUTE OF EVERY DAY!
OKAY, PAL, THAT DOES IT. YOU'RE COMING WITH ME.
PUT YOUR HANDS UP AND GET AGAINST THAT CAR.
Heh.
YOU GOT IT, CAPTAIN.
WHAT THE--?

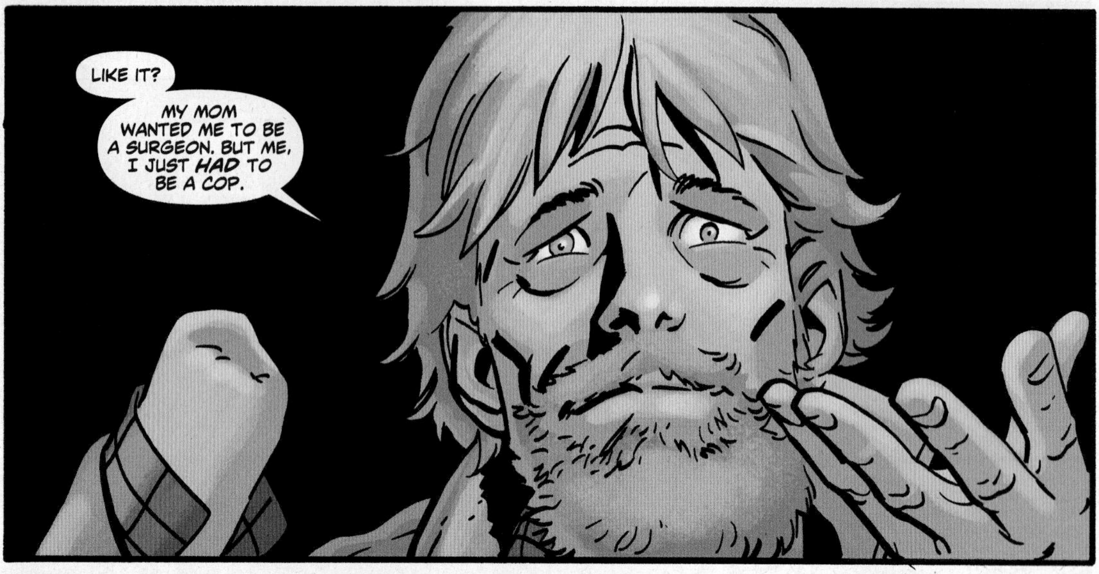
LIKE IT?
MY MOM WANTED ME TO BE A SURGEON. BUT ME, I JUST *HAD* TO BE A COP.

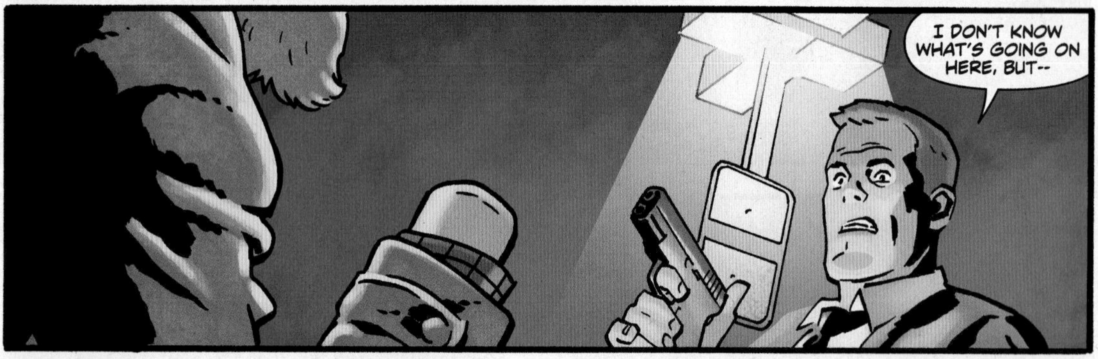
I DON'T KNOW WHAT'S GOING ON HERE, BUT--

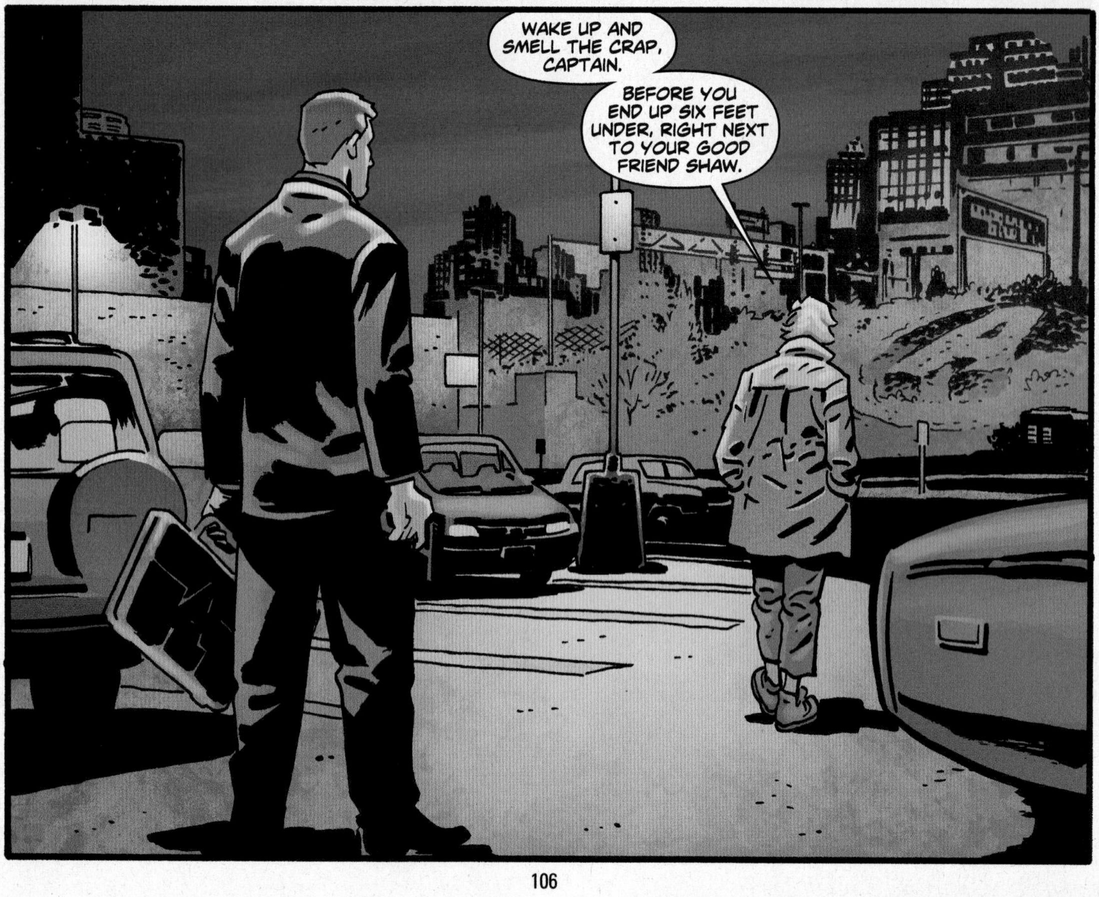
WAKE UP AND SMELL THE CRAP, CAPTAIN.
BEFORE YOU END UP SIX FEET UNDER, RIGHT NEXT TO YOUR GOOD FRIEND SHAW.

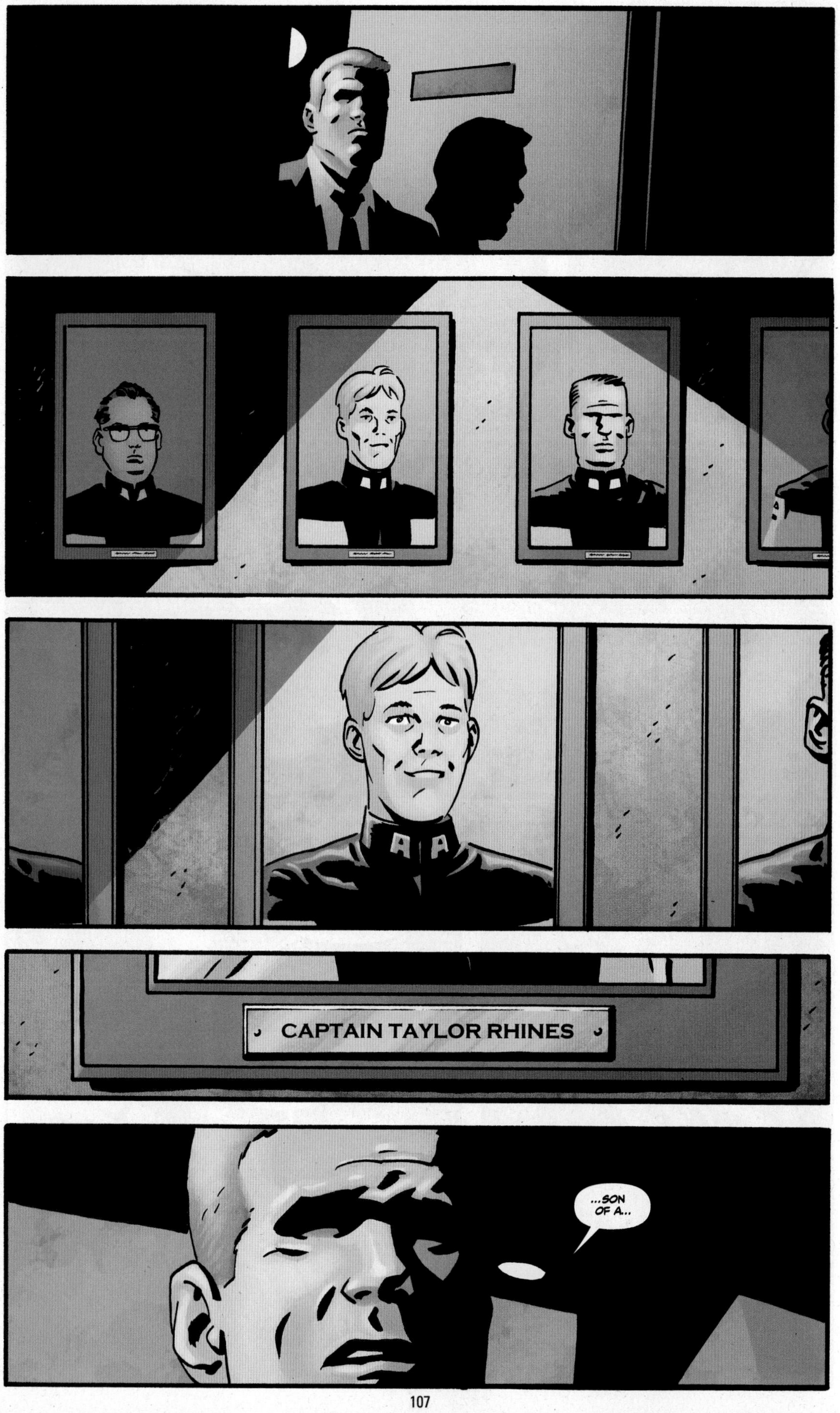
CAPTAIN TAYLOR RHINES
...SON OF A...

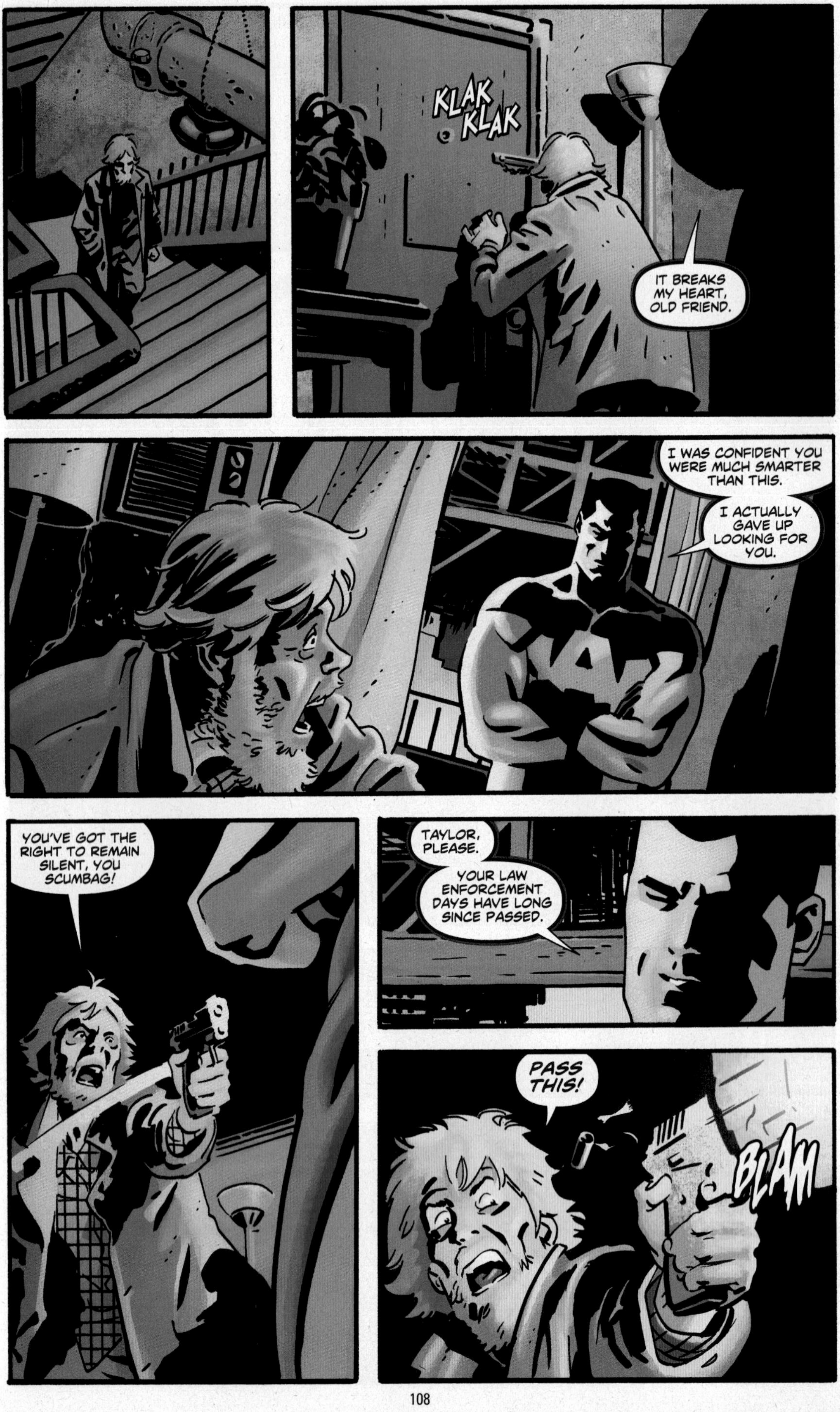
KLAK KLAK
IT BREAKS MY HEART, OLD FRIEND.
I WAS CONFIDENT YOU WERE MUCH SMARTER THAN THIS.
I ACTUALLY GAVE UP LOOKING FOR YOU.
YOU'VE GOT THE RIGHT TO REMAIN SILENT, YOU SCUMBAG!
TAYLOR, PLEASE.
YOUR LAW ENFORCEMENT DAYS HAVE LONG SINCE PASSED.
PASS THIS!
BLAM

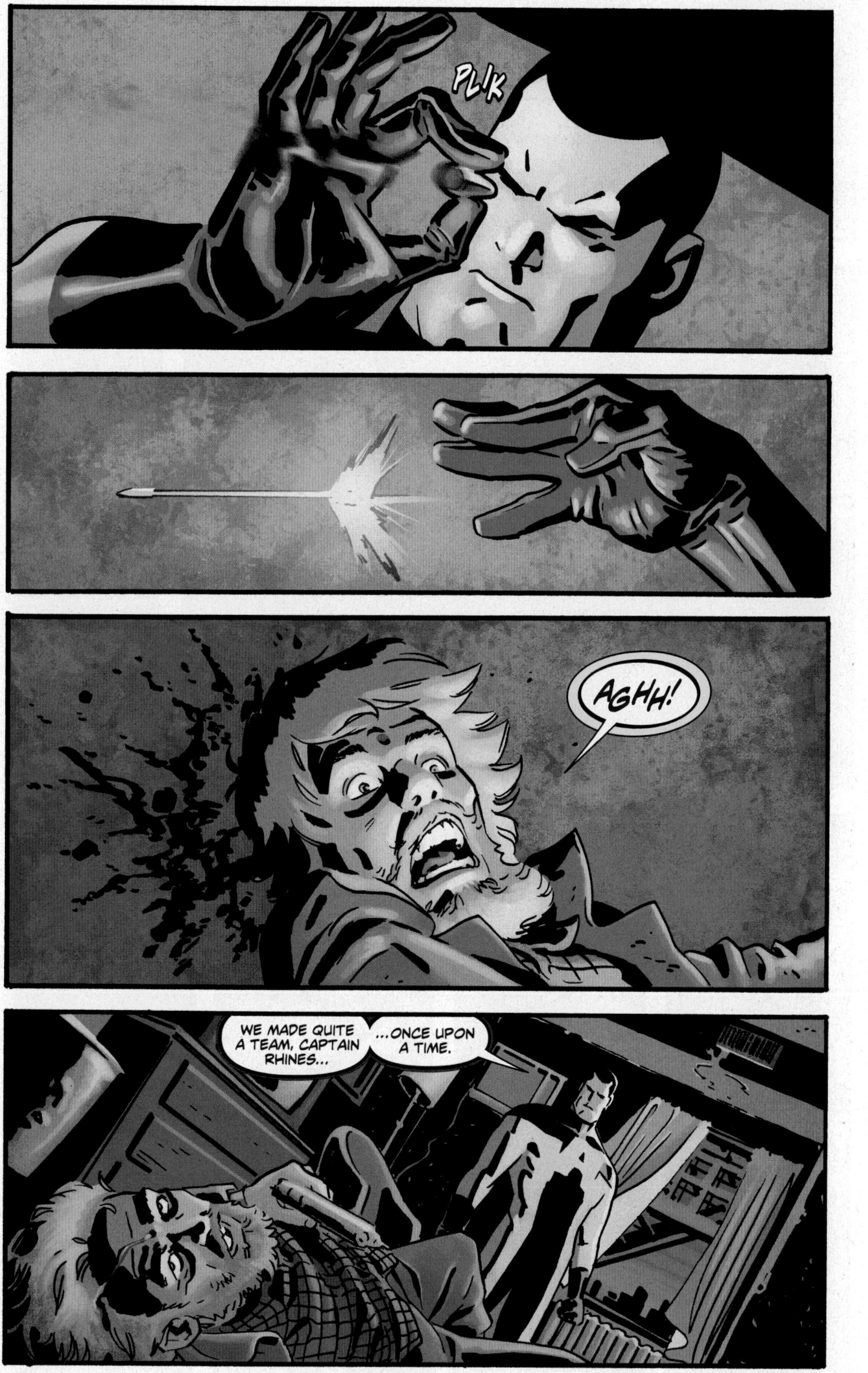
PLIK
AGHH!
WE MADE QUITE A TEAM, CAPTAIN RHINES...
...ONCE UPON A TIME.

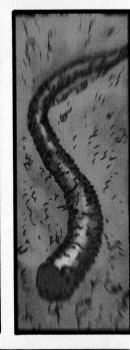

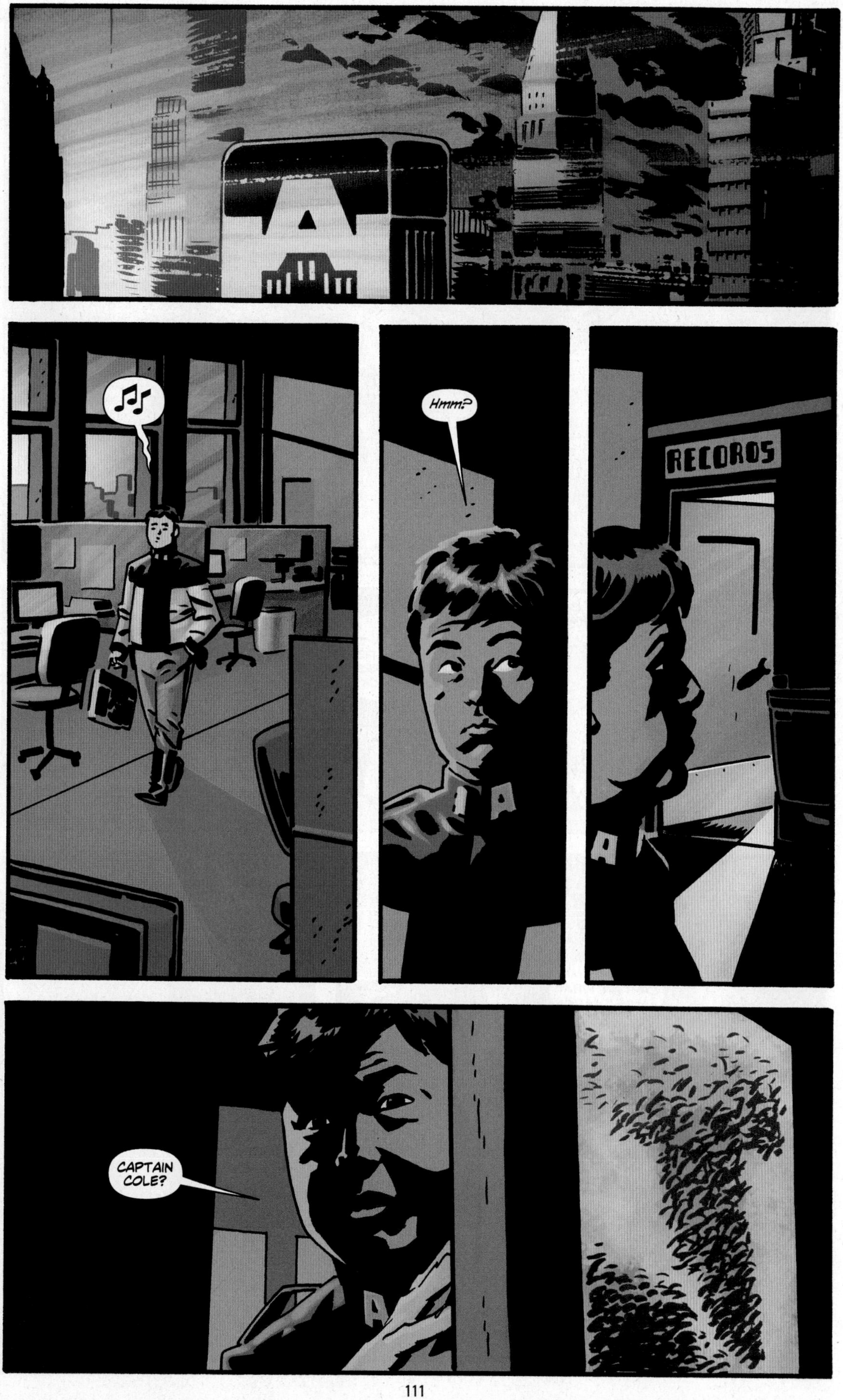
Hmm?
RECORDS
CAPTAIN COLE?

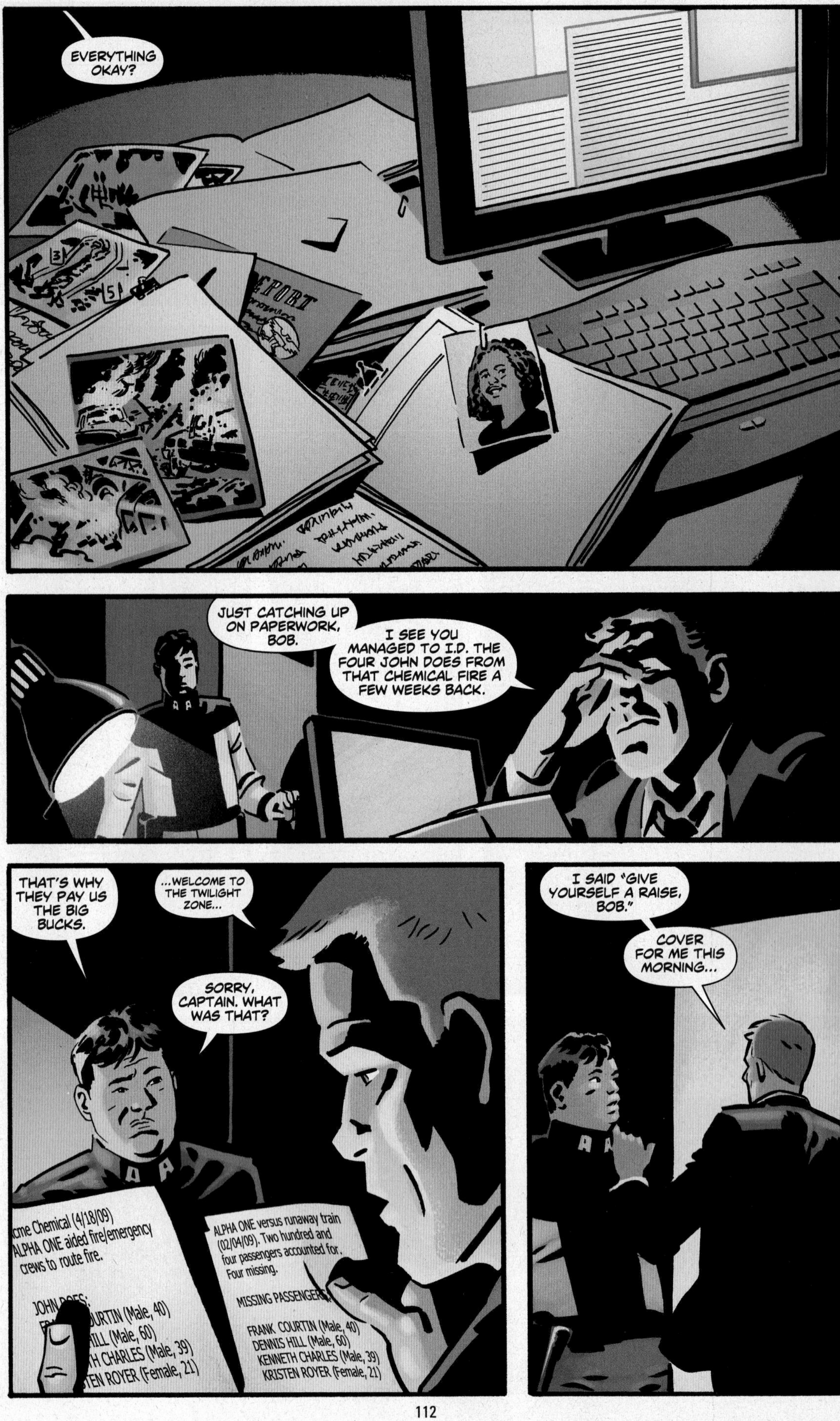
EVERYTHING OKAY?
JUST CATCHING UP ON PAPERWORK, BOB.
I SEE YOU MANAGED TO I.D. THE FOUR JOHN DOES FROM THAT CHEMICAL FIRE A FEW WEEKS BACK.
THAT'S WHY THEY PAY US THE BIG BUCKS.
...WELCOME TO THE TWILIGHT ZONE...
SORRY, CAPTAIN. WHAT WAS THAT?
cme Chemical (4/18/09)
ALPHA ONE aided fire/emergency crews to route fire.
JOHN DOES:
COURTIN (Male, 40)
HILL (Male, 60)
H CHARLES (Male, 39)
STEN ROYER (Female, 21)
ALPHA ONE versus runaway train (02/04/09). Two hundred and four passengers accounted for. Four missing.
MISSING PASSENGERS:
FRANK COURTIN (Male, 40)
DENNIS HILL (Male, 60)
KENNETH CHARLES (Male, 39)
KRISTEN ROYER (Female, 21)
I SAID "GIVE YOURSELF A RAISE, BOB."
COVER FOR ME THIS MORNING...

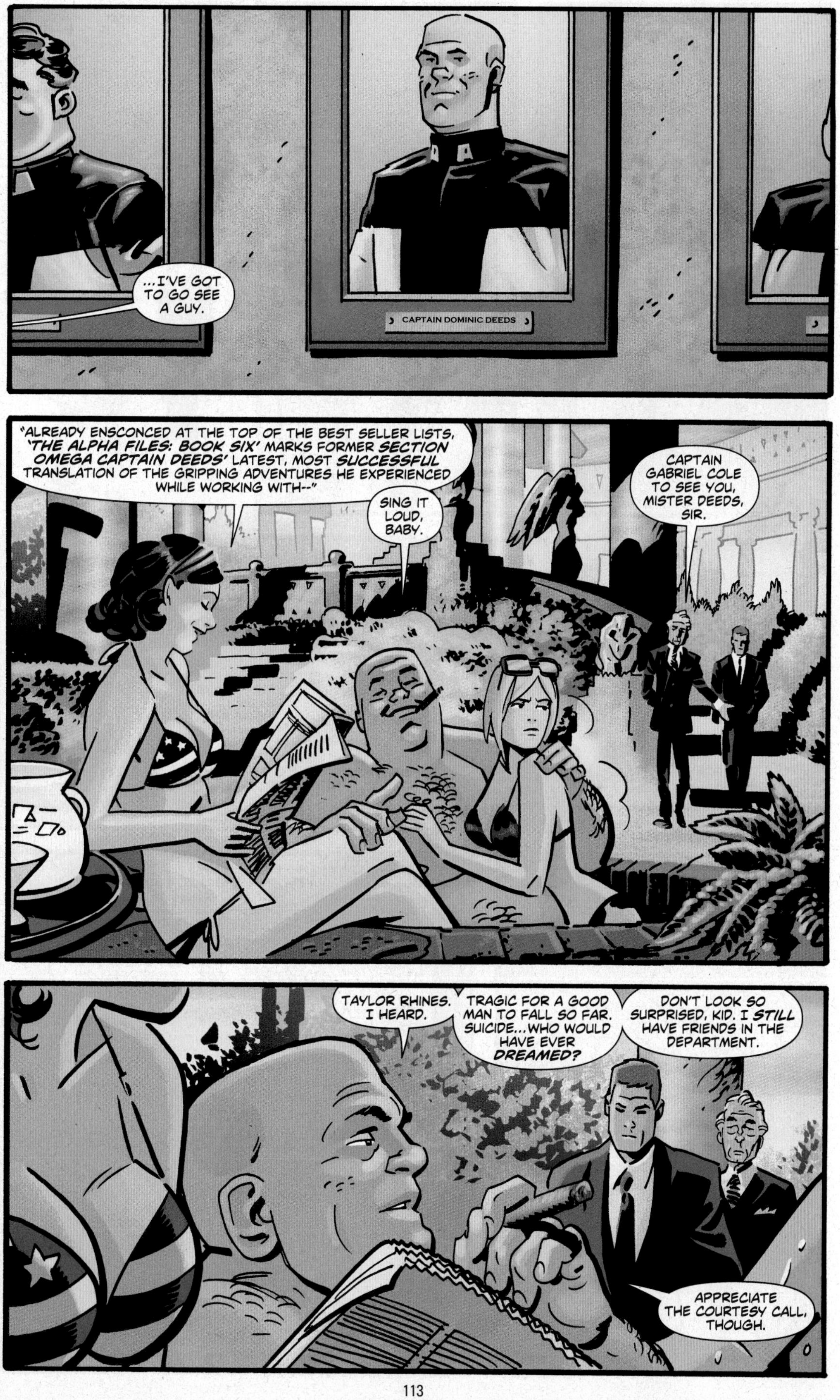
...I'VE GOT TO GO SEE A GUY.
CAPTAIN DOMINIC DEEDS
"ALREADY ENSCONCED AT THE TOP OF THE BEST SELLER LISTS, 'THE ALPHA FILES: BOOK SIX' MARKS FORMER SECTION OMEGA CAPTAIN DEEDS' LATEST, MOST SUCCESSFUL TRANSLATION OF THE GRIPPING ADVENTURES HE EXPERIENCED WHILE WORKING WITH--"
SING IT LOUD, BABY.
CAPTAIN GABRIEL COLE TO SEE YOU, MISTER DEEDS, SIR.
TAYLOR RHINES. I HEARD.
TRAGIC FOR A GOOD MAN TO FALL SO FAR. SUICIDE...WHO WOULD HAVE EVER DREAMED?
DON'T LOOK SO SURPRISED, KID. I STILL HAVE FRIENDS IN THE DEPARTMENT.
APPRECIATE THE COURTESY CALL, THOUGH.

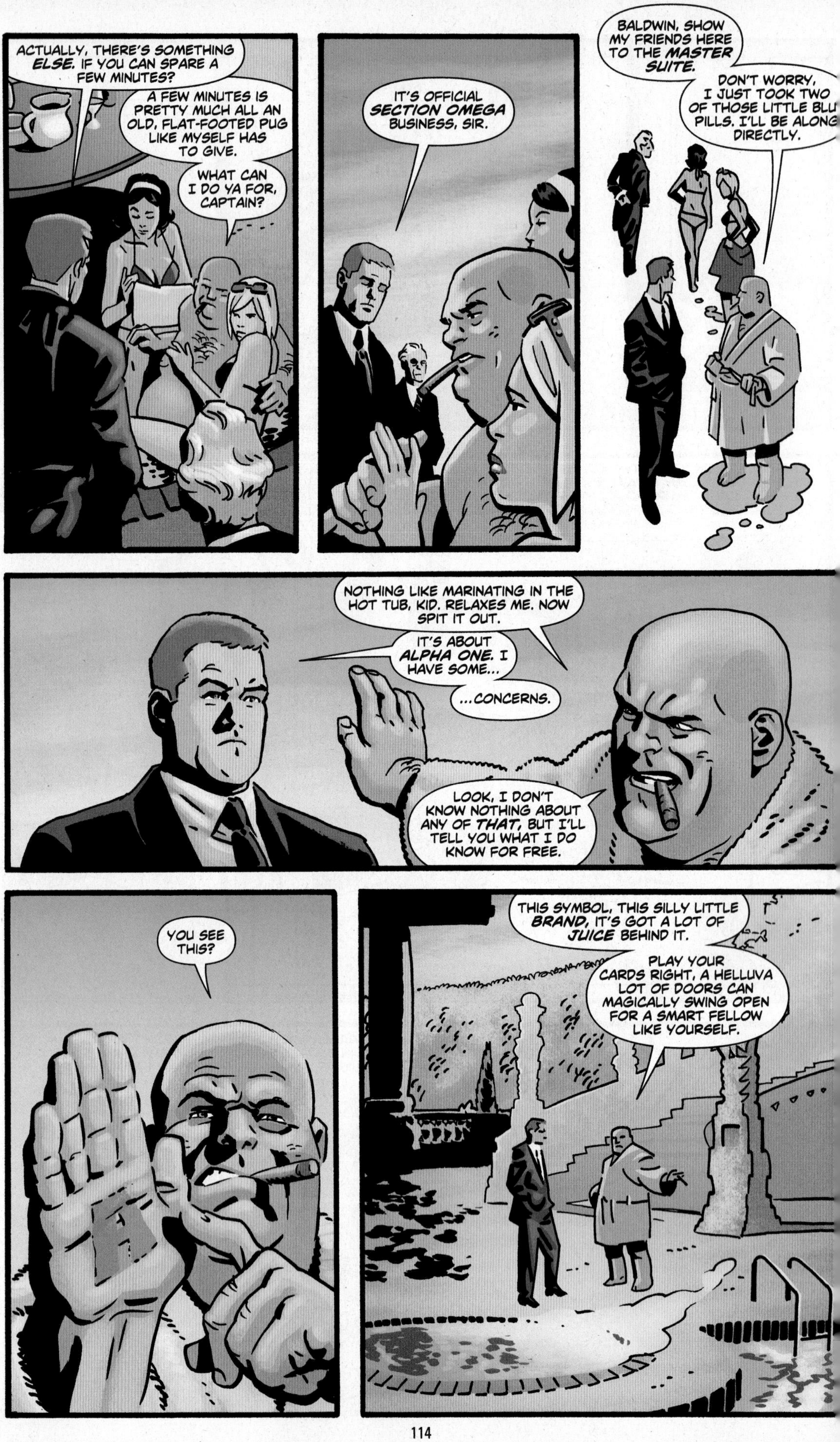

ACTUALLY, THERE'S SOMETHING ELSE. IF YOU CAN SPARE A FEW MINUTES?
A FEW MINUTES IS PRETTY MUCH ALL AN OLD, FLAT-FOOTED PUG LIKE MYSELF HAS TO GIVE.
WHAT CAN I DO YA FOR, CAPTAIN?
IT'S OFFICIAL SECTION OMEGA BUSINESS, SIR.
BALDWIN, SHOW MY FRIENDS HERE TO THE MASTER SUITE.
DON'T WORRY, I JUST TOOK TWO OF THOSE LITTLE BLU PILLS. I'LL BE ALONG DIRECTLY.
NOTHING LIKE MARINATING IN THE HOT TUB, KID. RELAXES ME. NOW SPIT IT OUT.
IT'S ABOUT ALPHA ONE. I HAVE SOME...
...CONCERNS.
LOOK, I DON'T KNOW NOTHING ABOUT ANY OF THAT, BUT I'LL TELL YOU WHAT I DO KNOW FOR FREE.
YOU SEE THIS?
THIS SYMBOL, THIS SILLY LITTLE BRAND, IT'S GOT A LOT OF JUICE BEHIND IT.
PLAY YOUR CARDS RIGHT, A HELLUVA LOT OF DOORS CAN MAGICALLY SWING OPEN FOR A SMART FELLOW LIKE YOURSELF.

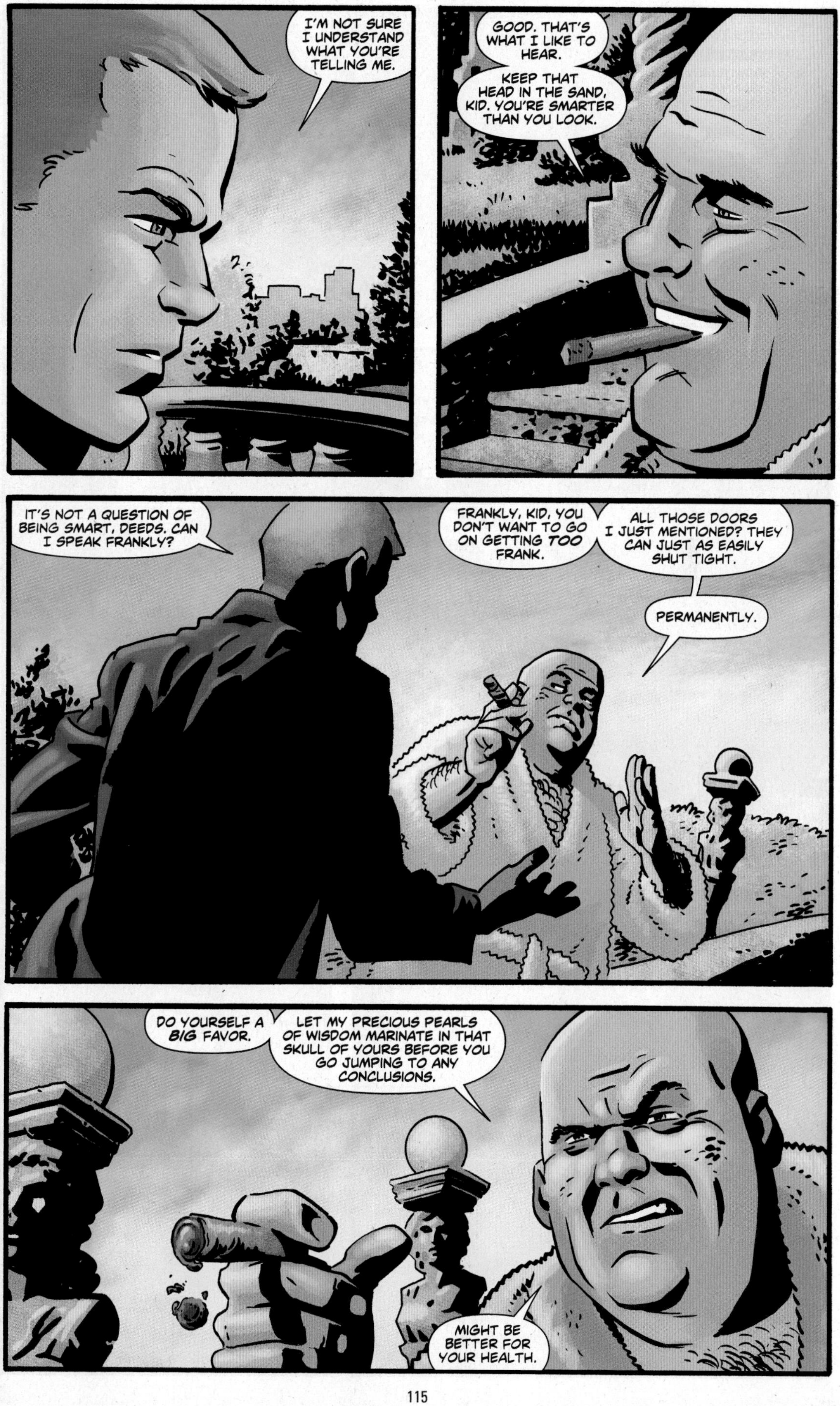
I'M NOT SURE I UNDERSTAND WHAT YOU'RE TELLING ME.
GOOD. THAT'S WHAT I LIKE TO HEAR.
KEEP THAT HEAD IN THE SAND, KID. YOU'RE SMARTER THAN YOU LOOK.
IT'S NOT A QUESTION OF BEING SMART, DEEDS. CAN I SPEAK FRANKLY?
FRANKLY, KID, YOU DON'T WANT TO GO ON GETTING *TOO* FRANK.
ALL THOSE DOORS I JUST MENTIONED? THEY CAN JUST AS EASILY SHUT TIGHT.
PERMANENTLY.
DO YOURSELF A *BIG* FAVOR.
LET MY PRECIOUS PEARLS OF WISDOM MARINATE IN THAT SKULL OF YOURS BEFORE YOU GO JUMPING TO ANY CONCLUSIONS.
MIGHT BE BETTER FOR YOUR HEALTH.

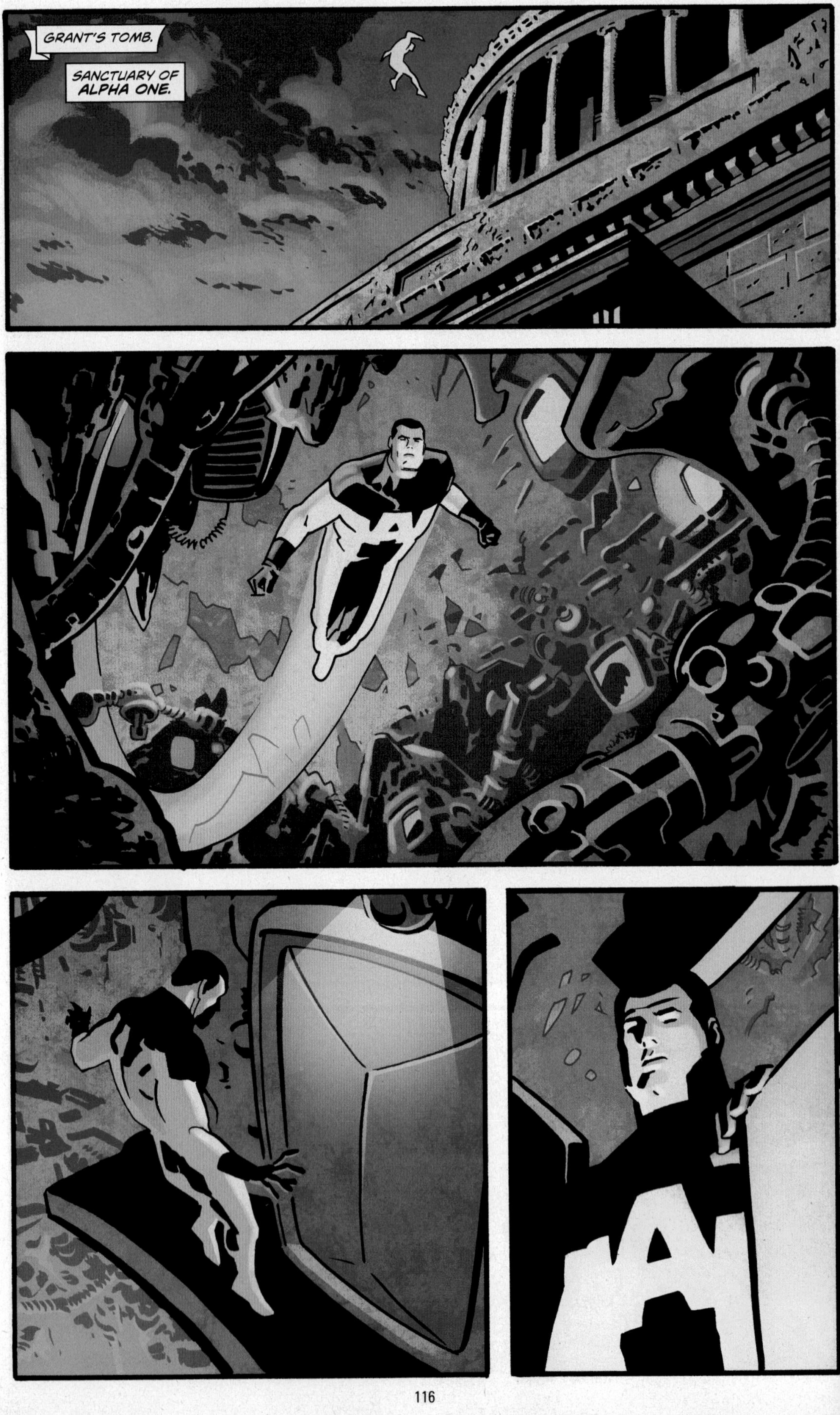
GRANT'S TOMB.
SANCTUARY OF ALPHA ONE.

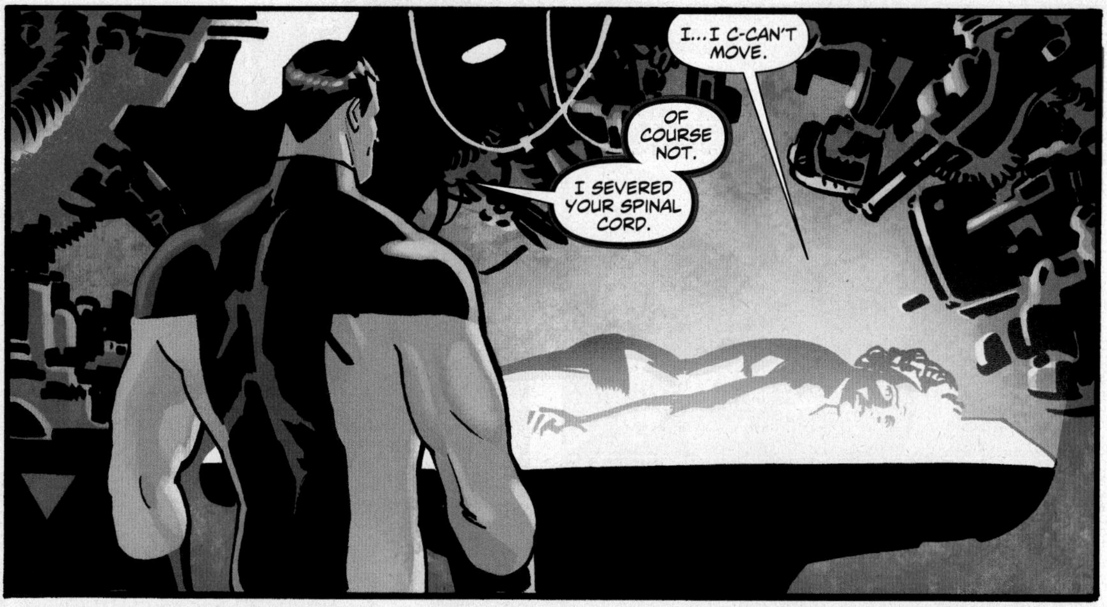
I...I C-CAN'T MOVE.
OF COURSE NOT.
I SEVERED YOUR SPINAL CORD.

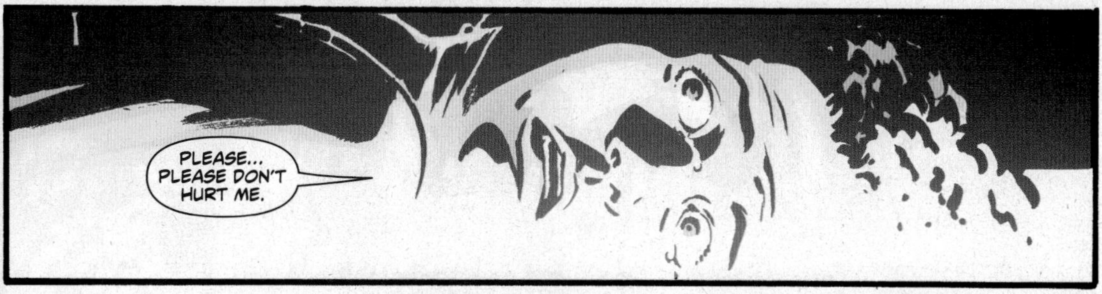
PLEASE... PLEASE DON'T HURT ME.

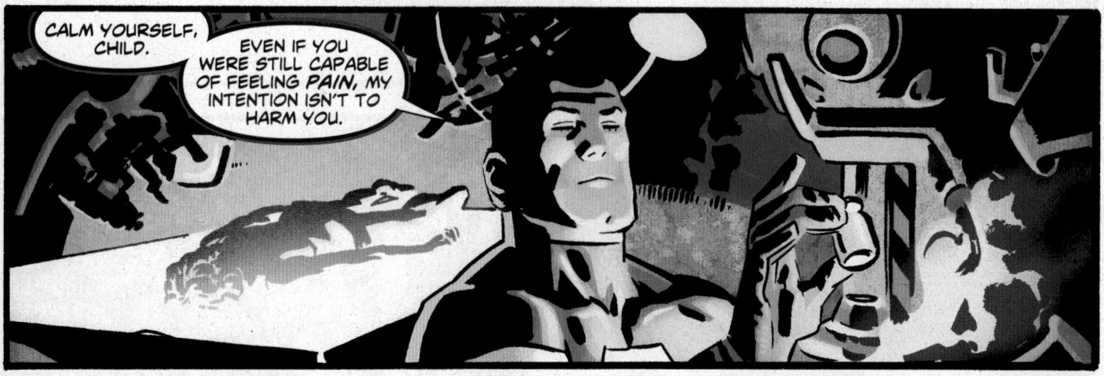
CALM YOURSELF, CHILD.
EVEN IF YOU WERE STILL CAPABLE OF FEELING *PAIN*, MY INTENTION ISN'T TO HARM YOU.

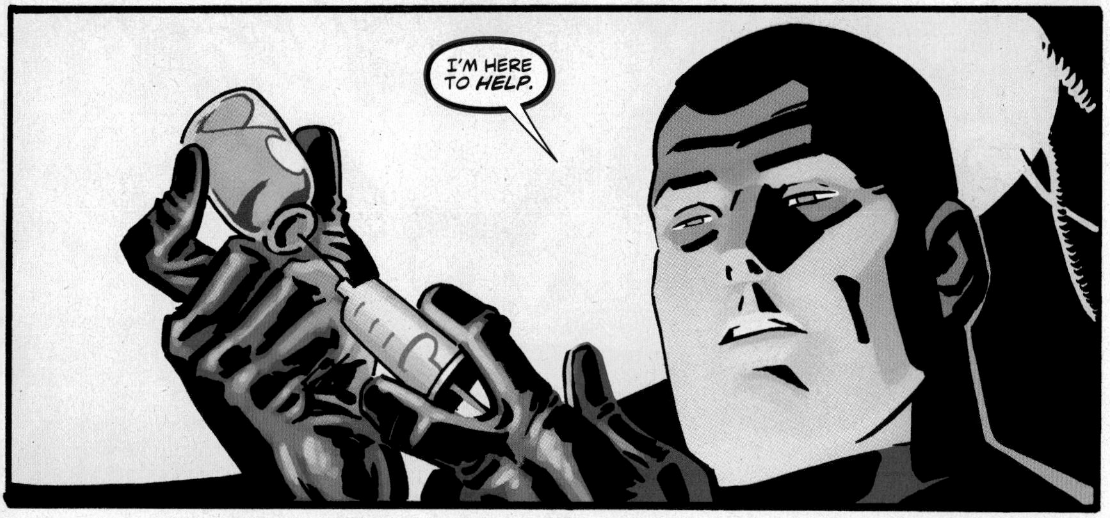
I'M HERE TO *HELP*.

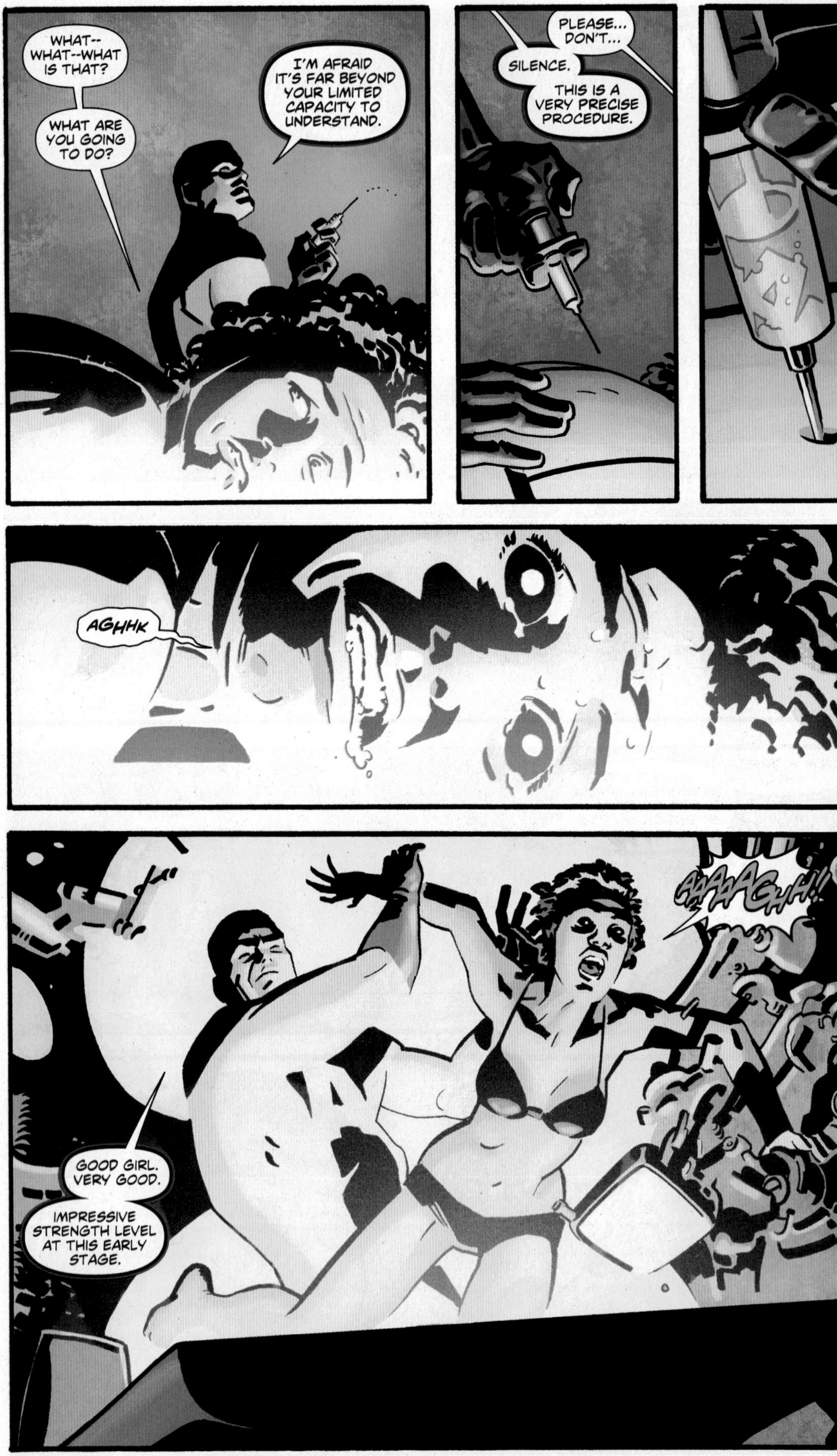
WHAT--
WHAT--WHAT IS THAT?
WHAT ARE YOU GOING TO DO?
I'M AFRAID IT'S FAR BEYOND YOUR LIMITED CAPACITY TO UNDERSTAND.
PLEASE... DON'T...
SILENCE.
THIS IS A VERY PRECISE PROCEDURE.
AGHHK
AAAAAGHHH!!
GOOD GIRL. VERY GOOD.
IMPRESSIVE STRENGTH LEVEL AT THIS EARLY STAGE.

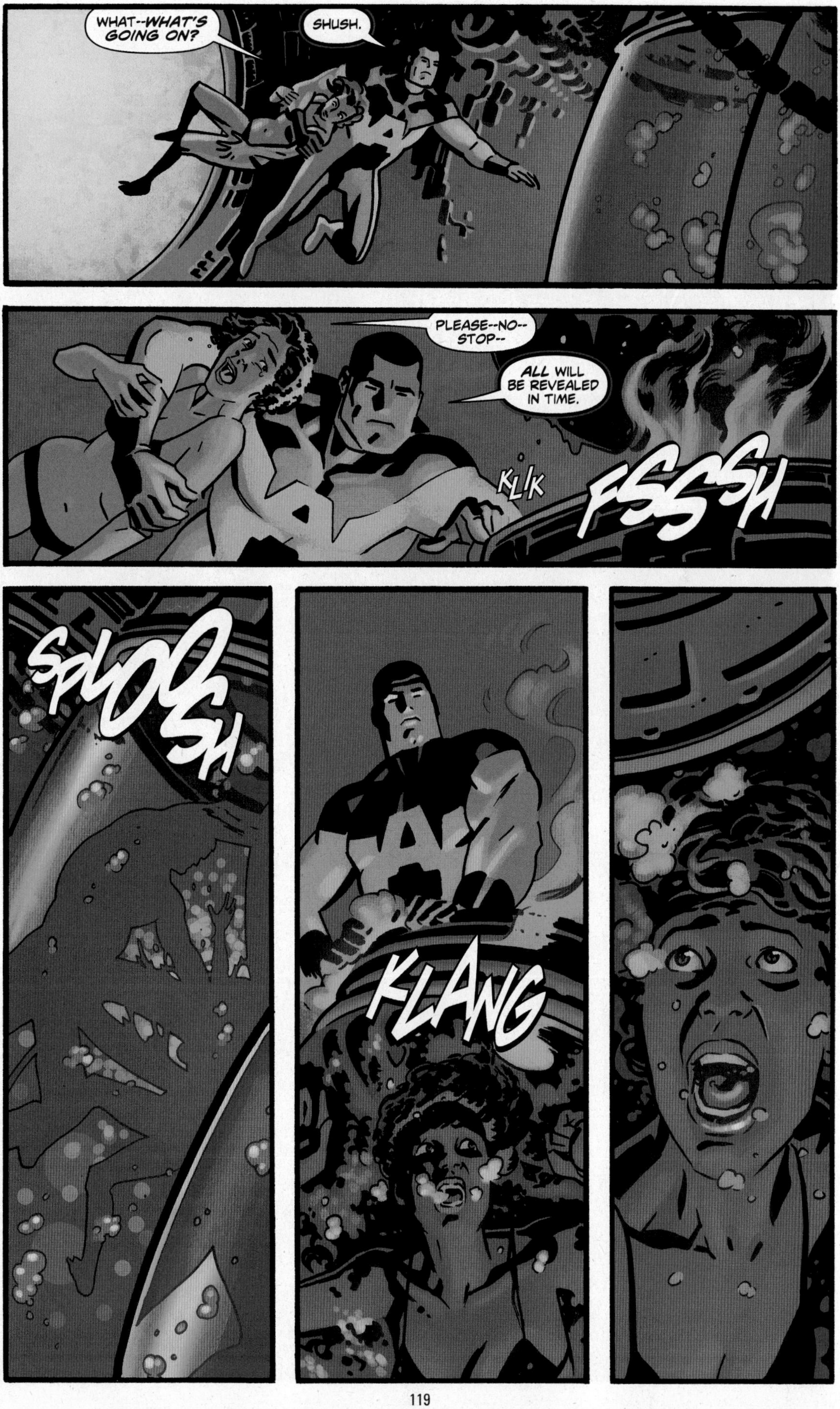
WHAT--WHAT'S GOING ON?
SHUSH.
PLEASE--NO--STOP--
ALL WILL BE REVEALED IN TIME.
KLIK
FSSSH
SPLOOSH
KLANG

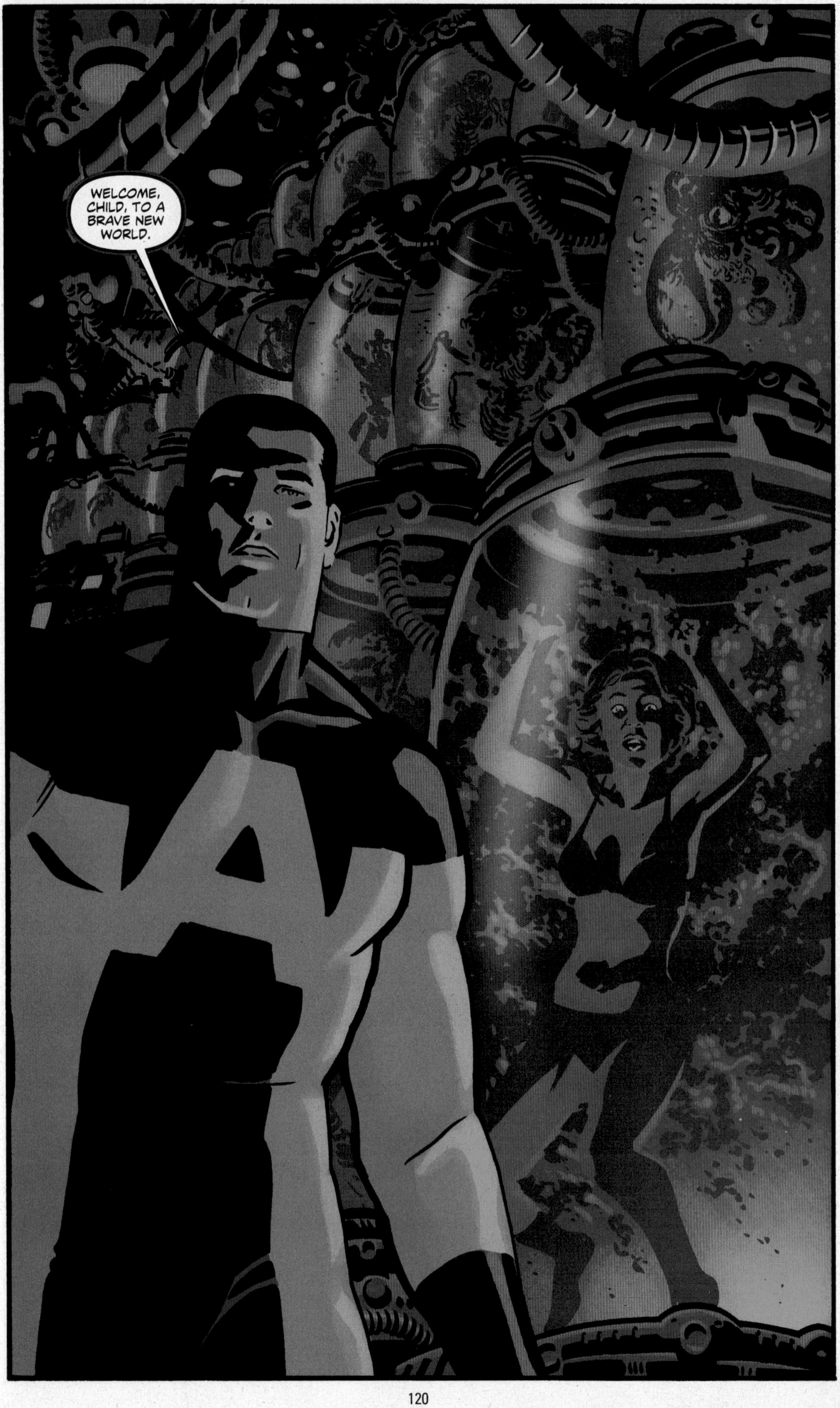
WELCOME, CHILD, TO A BRAVE NEW WORLD.

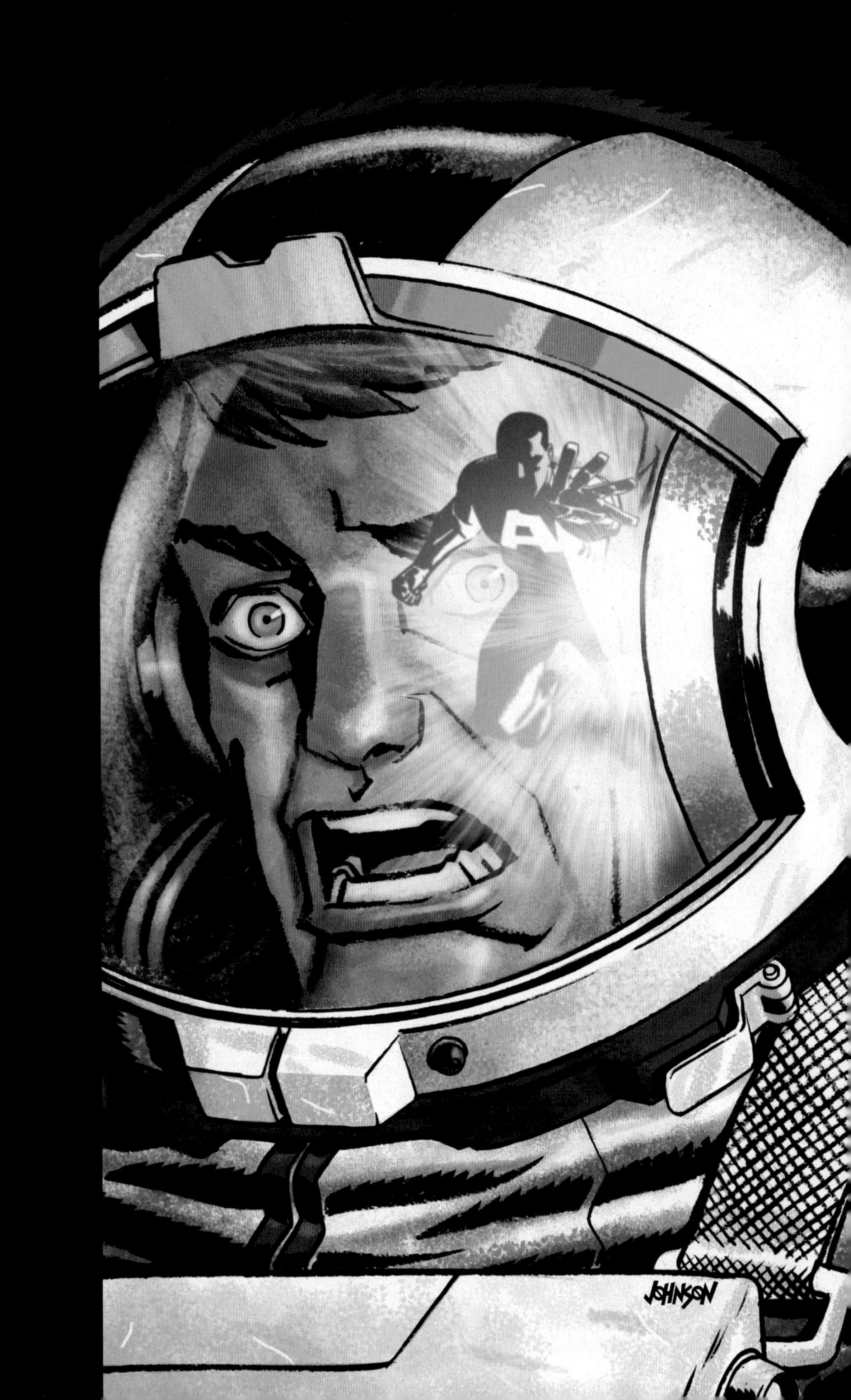
JOHNSON

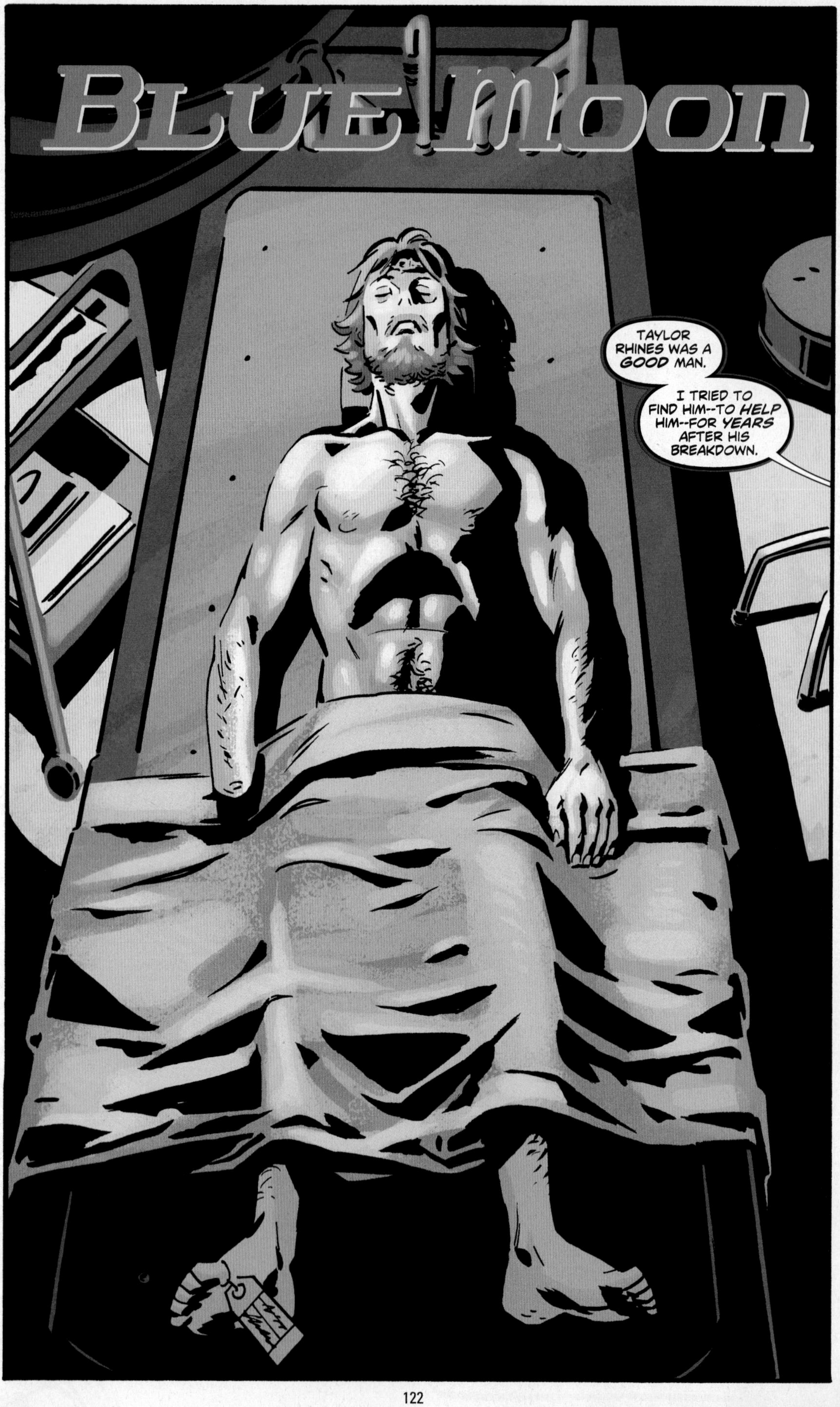
BLUE MOON
TAYLOR RHINES WAS A GOOD MAN.
I TRIED TO FIND HIM--TO HELP HIM--FOR YEARS AFTER HIS BREAKDOWN.

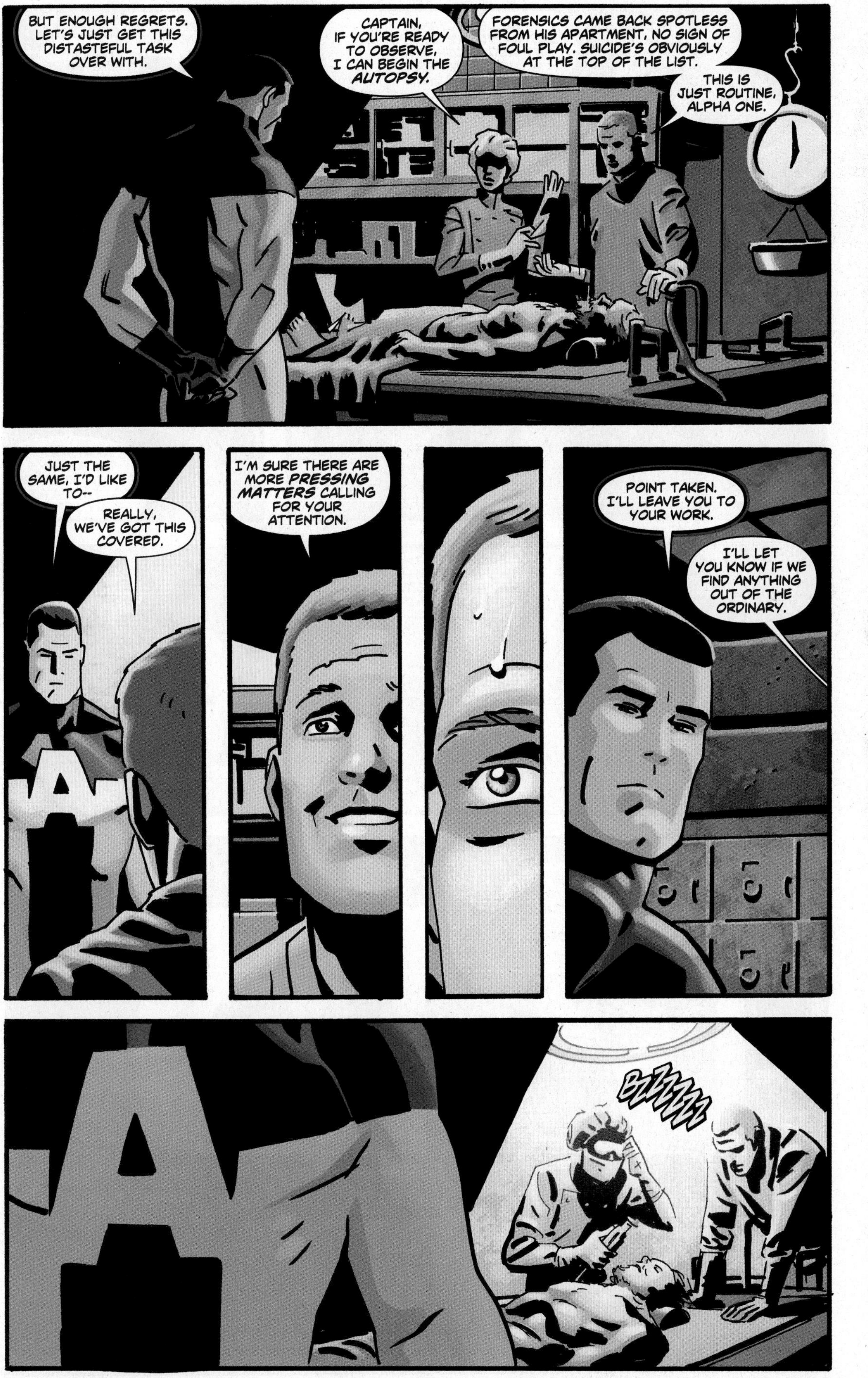

BUT ENOUGH REGRETS. LET'S JUST GET THIS DISTASTEFUL TASK OVER WITH.
CAPTAIN, IF YOU'RE READY TO OBSERVE, I CAN BEGIN THE AUTOPSY.
FORENSICS CAME BACK SPOTLESS FROM HIS APARTMENT, NO SIGN OF FOUL PLAY. SUICIDE'S OBVIOUSLY AT THE TOP OF THE LIST.
THIS IS JUST ROUTINE, ALPHA ONE.
JUST THE SAME, I'D LIKE TO--
REALLY, WE'VE GOT THIS COVERED.
I'M SURE THERE ARE MORE PRESSING MATTERS CALLING FOR YOUR ATTENTION.
POINT TAKEN. I'LL LEAVE YOU TO YOUR WORK.
I'LL LET YOU KNOW IF WE FIND ANYTHING OUT OF THE ORDINARY.
BZZZZZ

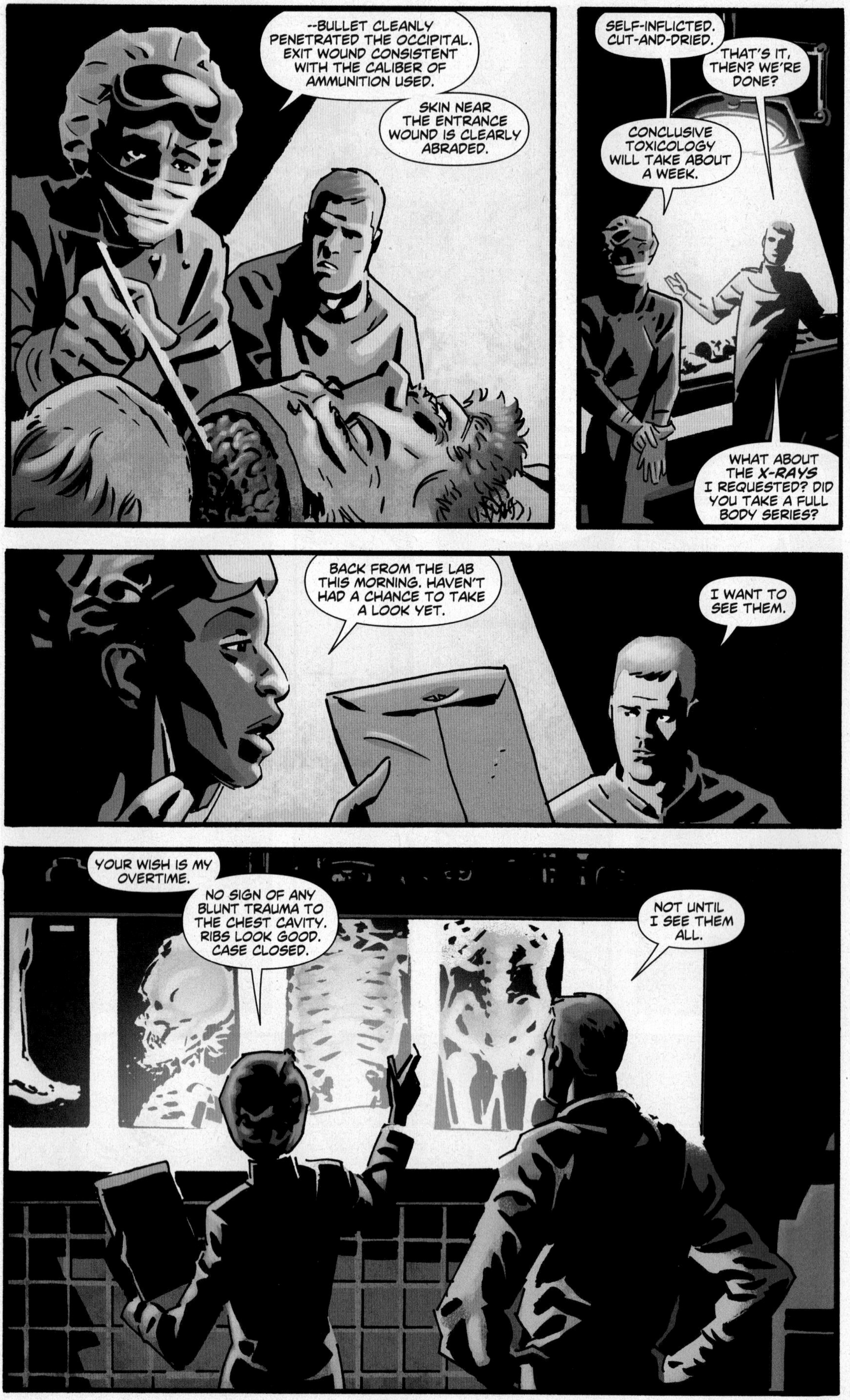
--BULLET CLEANLY PENETRATED THE OCCIPITAL. EXIT WOUND CONSISTENT WITH THE CALIBER OF AMMUNITION USED.
SKIN NEAR THE ENTRANCE WOUND IS CLEARLY ABRADED.
SELF-INFLICTED. CUT-AND-DRIED.
THAT'S IT, THEN? WE'RE DONE?
CONCLUSIVE TOXICOLOGY WILL TAKE ABOUT A WEEK.
WHAT ABOUT THE *X-RAYS* I REQUESTED? DID YOU TAKE A FULL BODY SERIES?
BACK FROM THE LAB THIS MORNING. HAVEN'T HAD A CHANCE TO TAKE A LOOK YET.
I WANT TO SEE THEM.
YOUR WISH IS MY OVERTIME.
NO SIGN OF ANY BLUNT TRAUMA TO THE CHEST CAVITY. RIBS LOOK GOOD. CASE CLOSED.
NOT UNTIL I SEE THEM ALL.

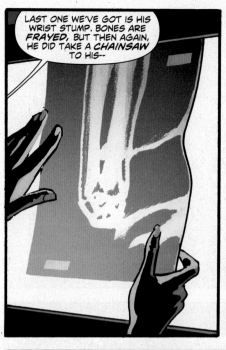

LAST ONE WE'VE GOT IS HIS WRIST STUMP. BONES ARE *FRAYED*, BUT THEN AGAIN, HE DID TAKE A *CHAINSAW* TO HIS--

WHAT IN THE WIDE WORLD OF SPORTS IS THAT?

I'M GOING TO NEED A SCALPEL, HELEN.

AND SOME PRIVACY.

ALL RIGHT, CAPTAIN RHINES. YOU DIED BECAUSE YOU TRIED TO TELL ME *SOMETHING*.

SO HERE I AM.

LISTENING.

SPLUCH

I'LL BE DAMNED.

CLEAR THE ROOM. **NOW!**

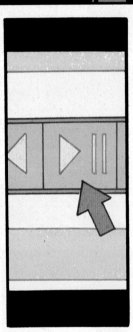

SKRRZZZz

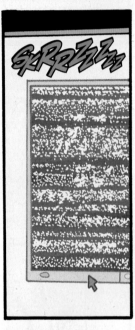

WHAT THE HELL?!

CONGRATS, WHOEVER YOU ARE. IF YOU'RE WATCHING THIS, I'M **DEAD** AND YOU'RE NOT.

HOPE YOU'RE SMART ENOUGH TO WATCH THIS FROM SECTION OMEGA'S SURVEILLANCE CENTER. HAD IT **SOUNDPROOFED** BEFORE I FLEW THE COOP.

OTHERWISE, I TAKE BACK WHAT I SAID ABOUT YOU NOT BEING DEAD.

126

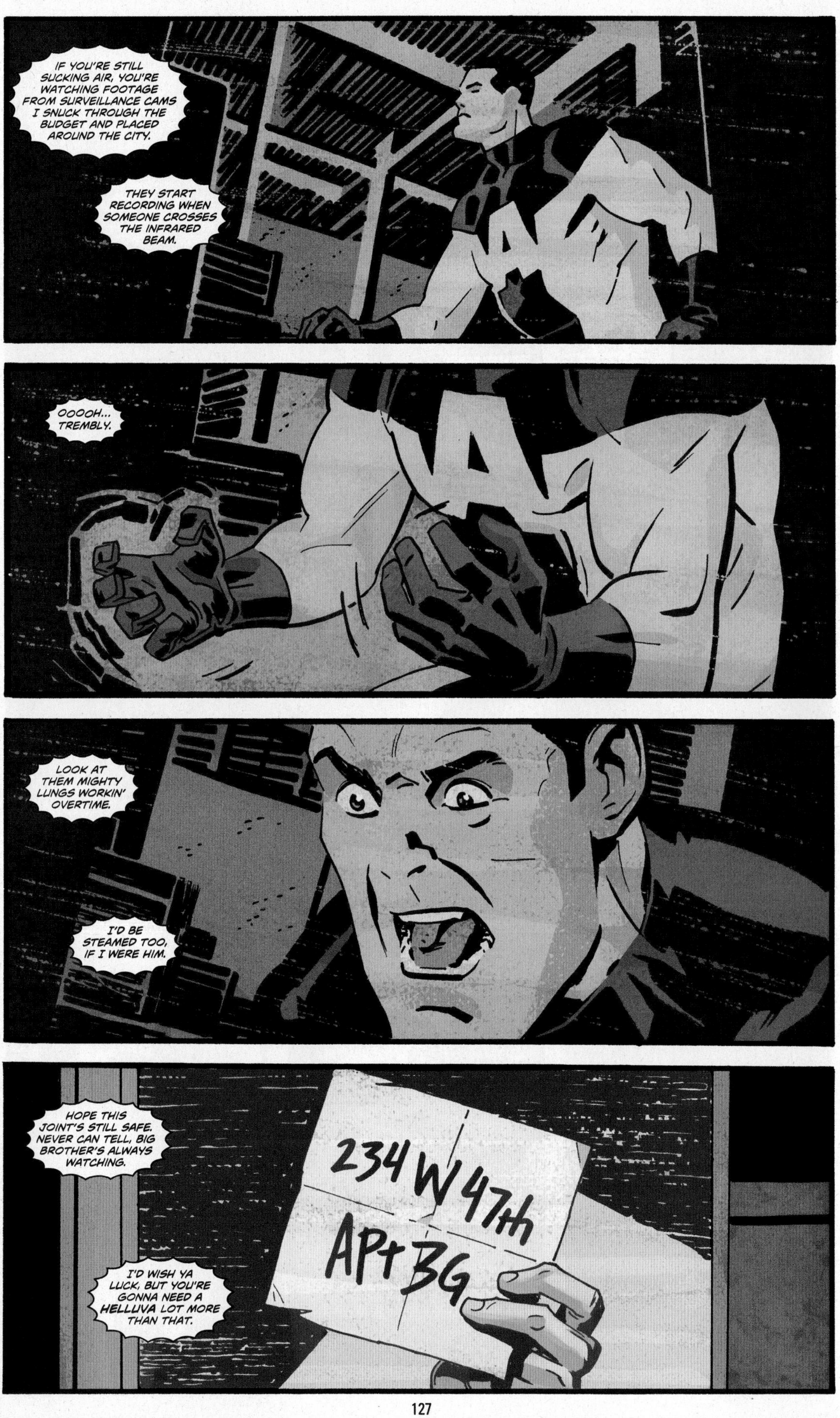
IF YOU'RE STILL SUCKING AIR, YOU'RE WATCHING FOOTAGE FROM SURVEILLANCE CAMS I SNUCK THROUGH THE BUDGET AND PLACED AROUND THE CITY.
THEY START RECORDING WHEN SOMEONE CROSSES THE INFRARED BEAM.
OOOOH... TREMBLY.
LOOK AT THEM MIGHTY LUNGS WORKIN' OVERTIME.
I'D BE STEAMED TOO, IF I WERE HIM.
HOPE THIS JOINT'S STILL SAFE. NEVER CAN TELL, BIG BROTHER'S ALWAYS WATCHING.
234 W 47th
APt 3G
I'D WISH YA LUCK, BUT YOU'RE GONNA NEED A HELLUVA LOT MORE THAN THAT.

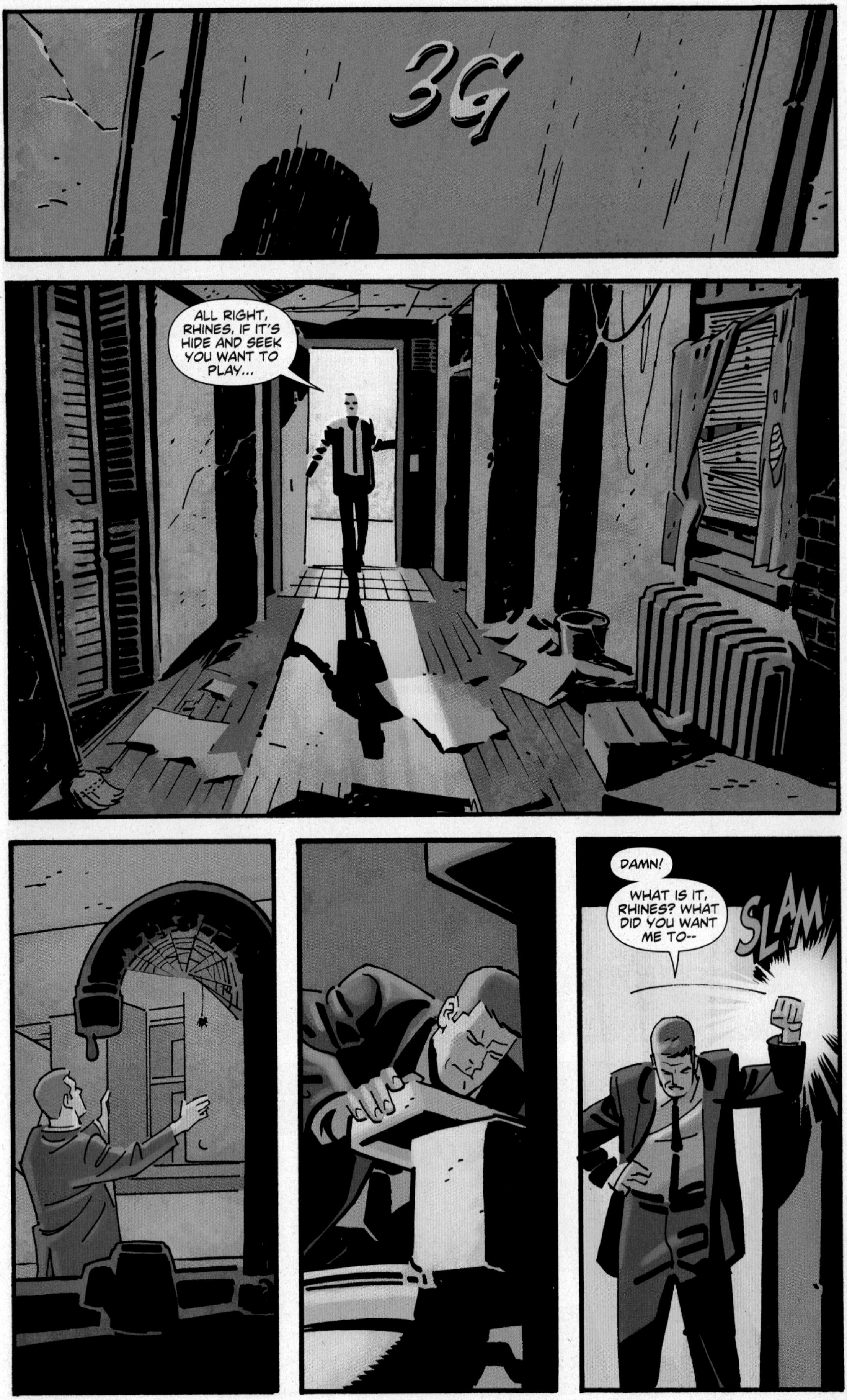
3G
ALL RIGHT, RHINES, IF IT'S HIDE AND SEEK YOU WANT TO PLAY...
DAMN!
WHAT IS IT, RHINES? WHAT DID YOU WANT ME TO--
SLAM

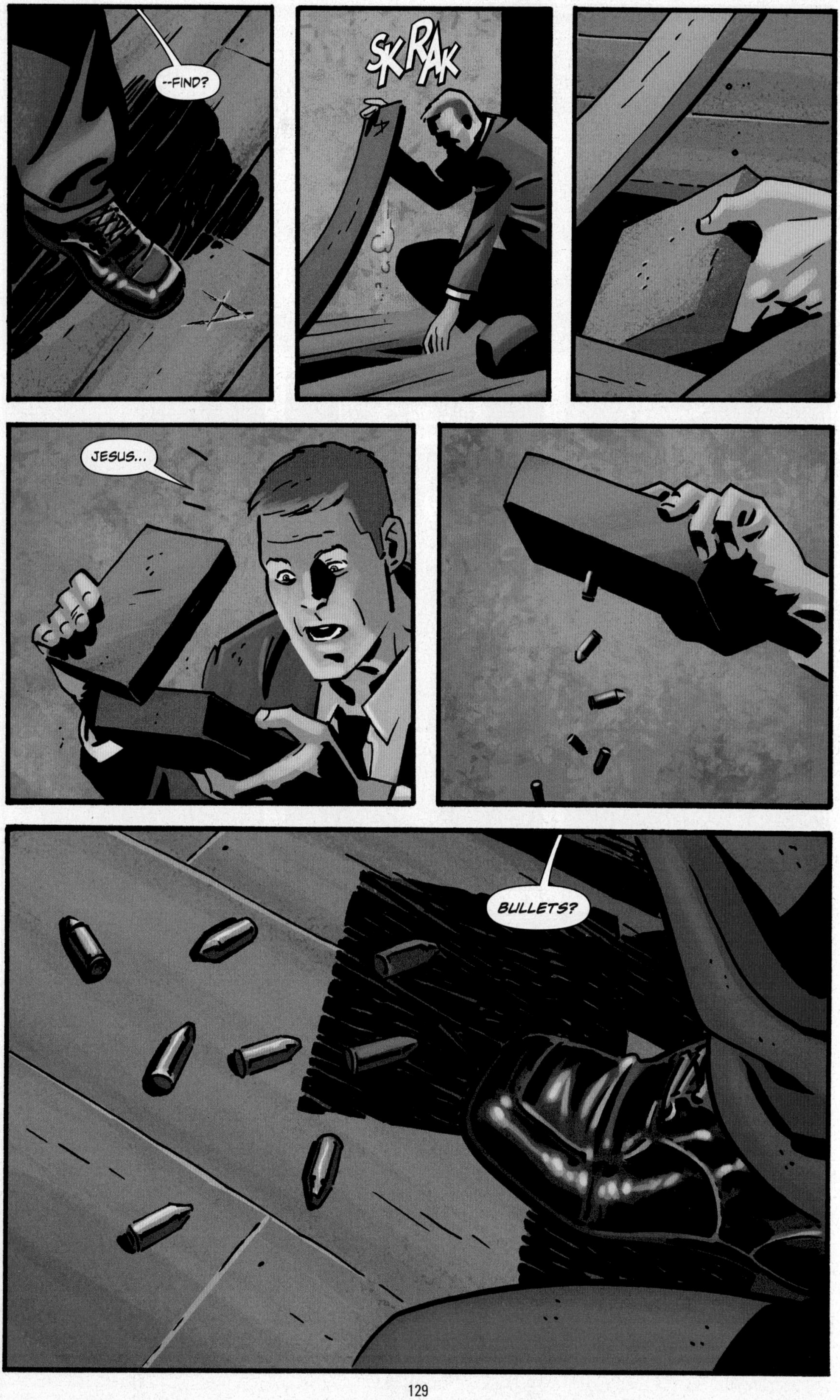

--FIND?
SKRAK
JESUS...
BULLETS?

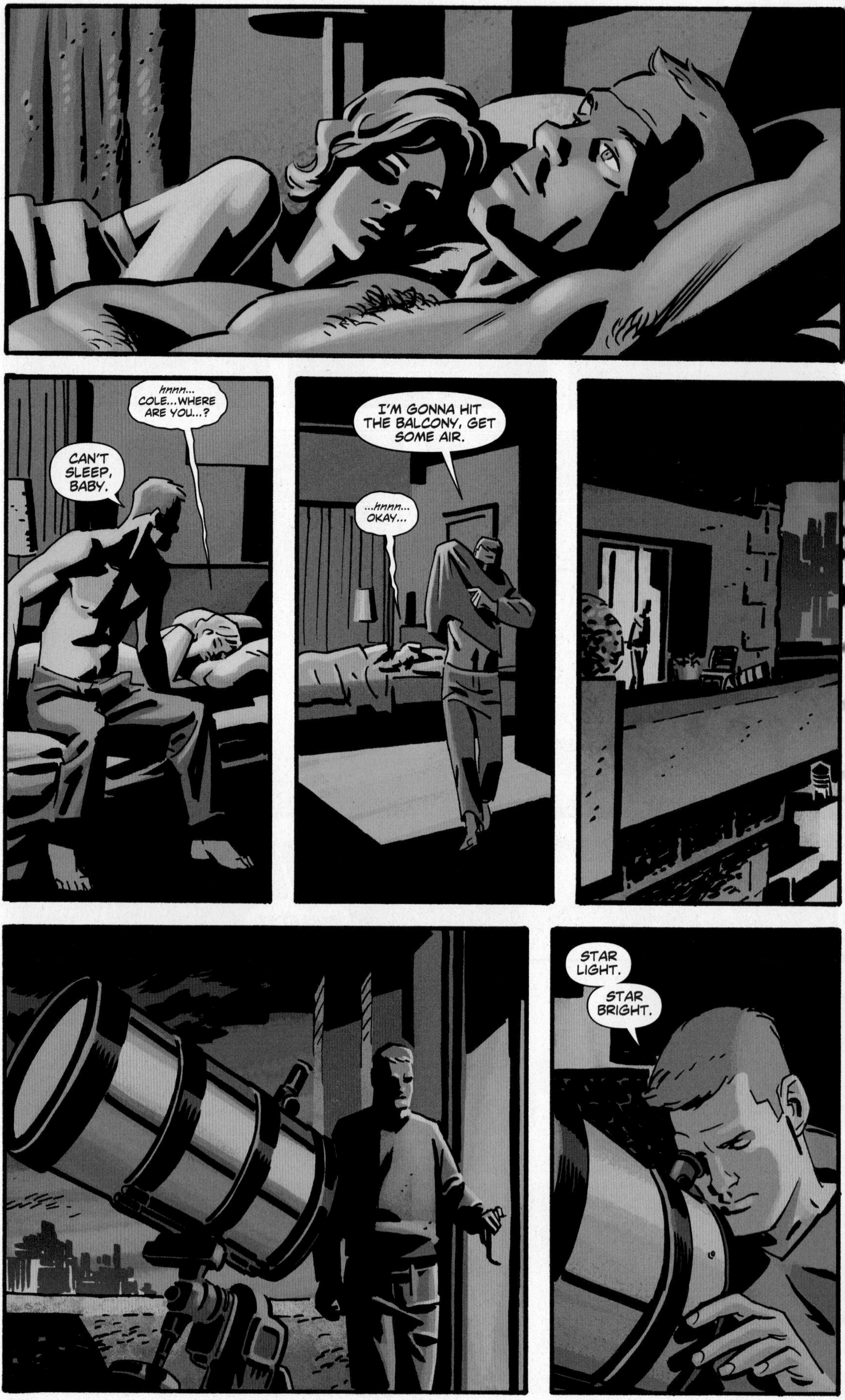
hnnn... COLE...WHERE ARE YOU...?
CAN'T SLEEP, BABY.
I'M GONNA HIT THE BALCONY, GET SOME AIR.
...hnnn... OKAY...
STAR LIGHT.
STAR BRIGHT.

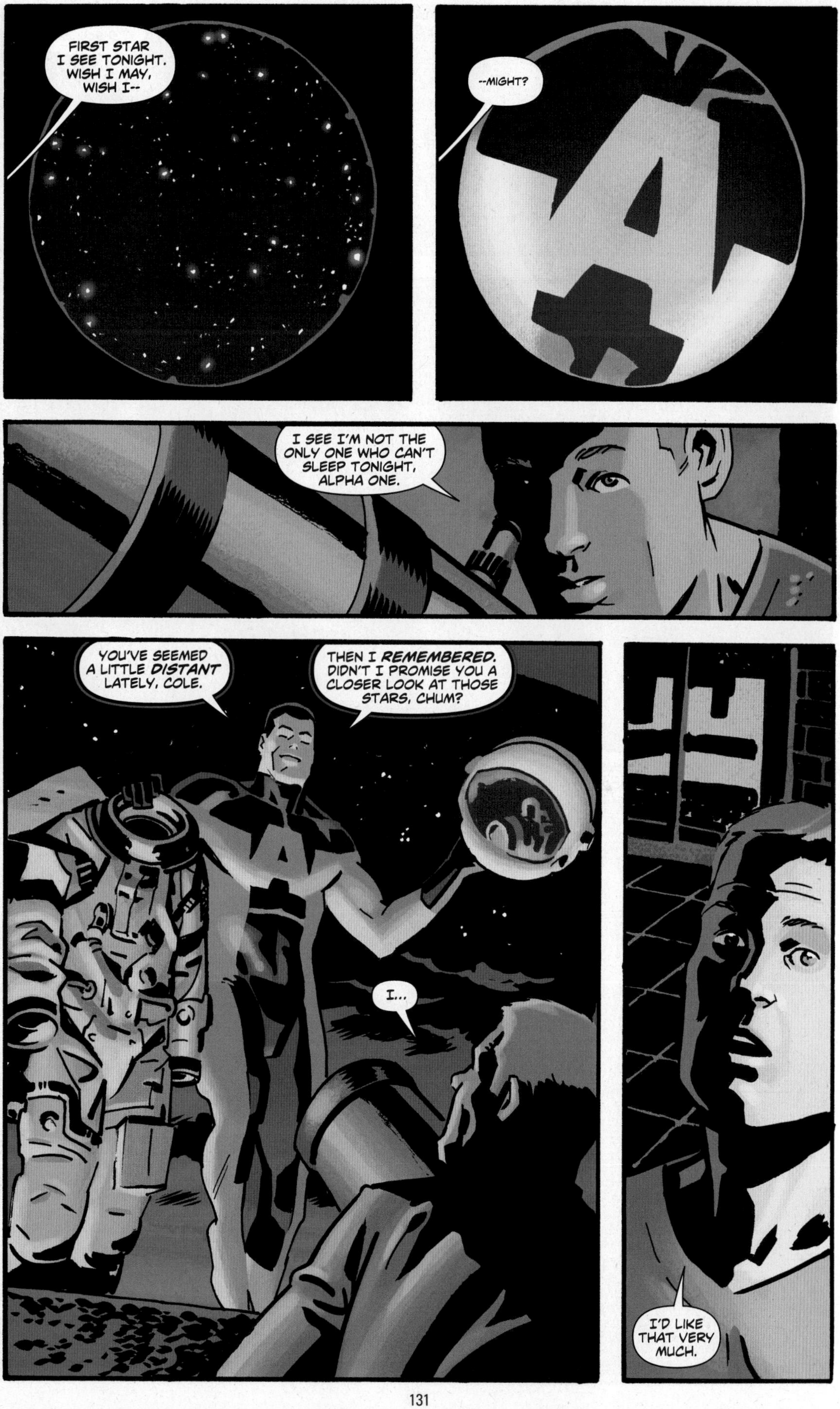
FIRST STAR I SEE TONIGHT. WISH I MAY, WISH I--
--MIGHT?
I SEE I'M NOT THE ONLY ONE WHO CAN'T SLEEP TONIGHT, ALPHA ONE.
YOU'VE SEEMED A LITTLE *DISTANT* LATELY, COLE.
THEN I *REMEMBERED.* DIDN'T I PROMISE YOU A CLOSER LOOK AT THOSE STARS, CHUM?
I...
I'D LIKE THAT VERY MUCH.

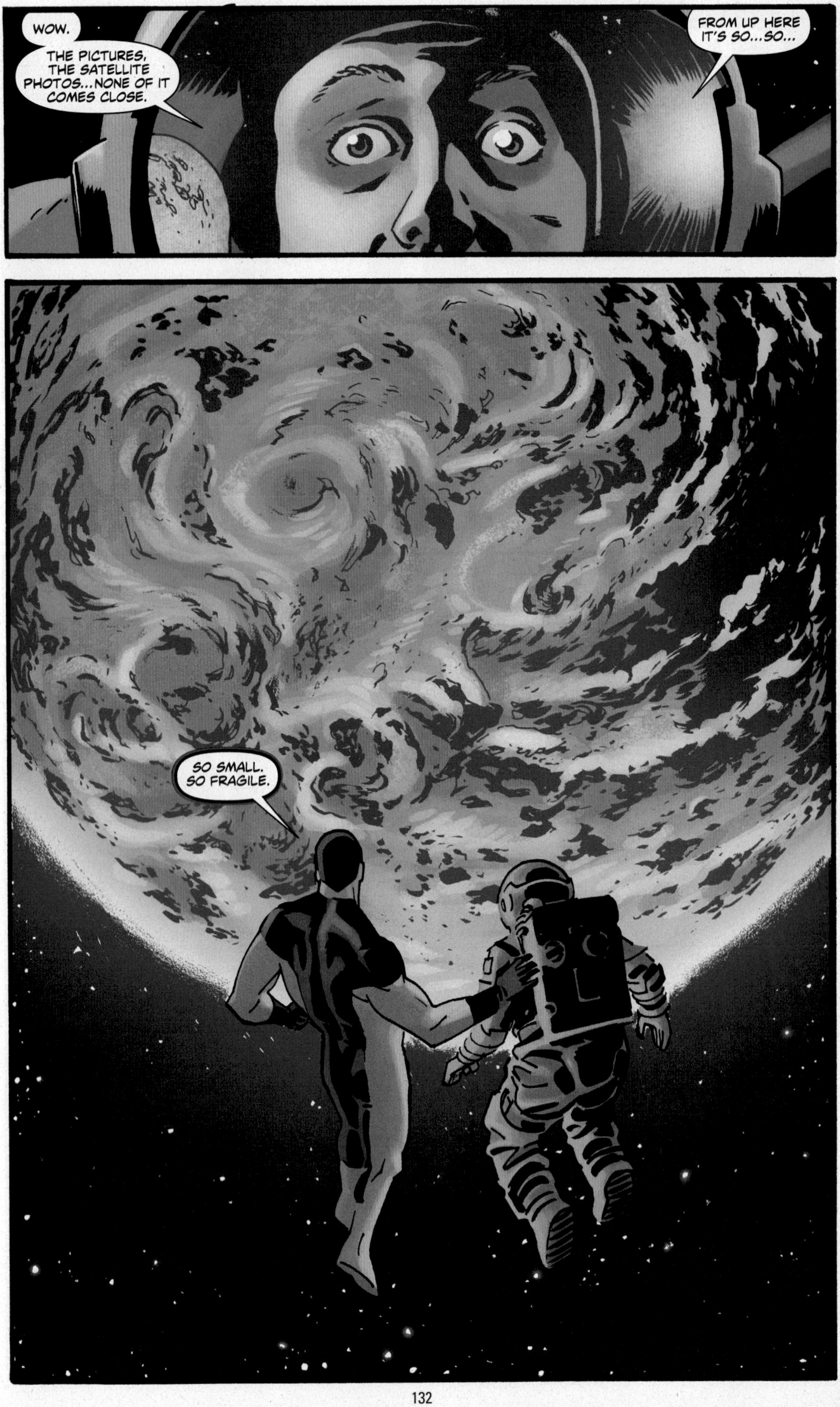
WOW.
THE PICTURES, THE SATELLITE PHOTOS...NONE OF IT COMES CLOSE.
FROM UP HERE IT'S SO...SO...
SO SMALL. SO FRAGILE.

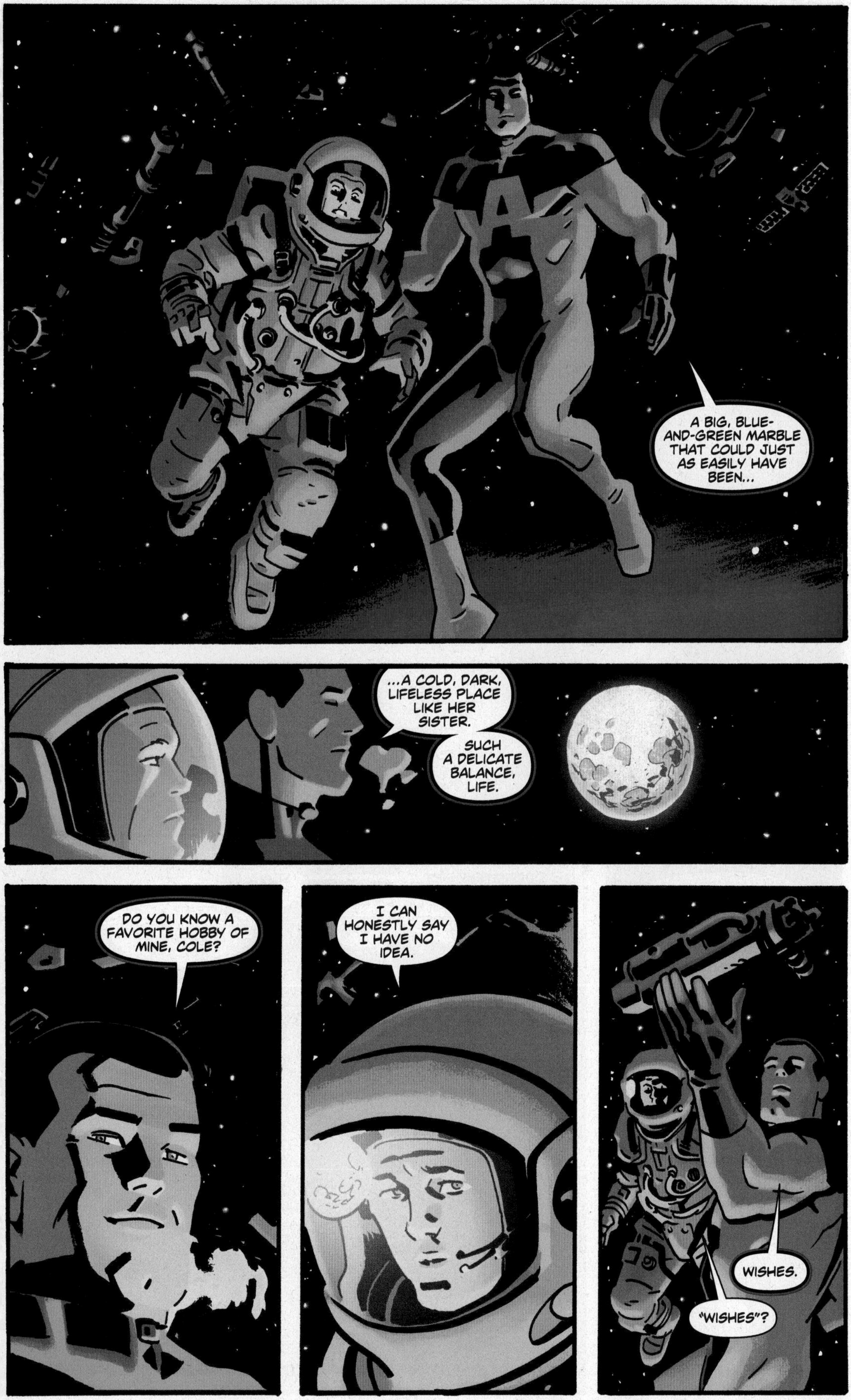
A BIG, BLUE-AND-GREEN MARBLE THAT COULD JUST AS EASILY HAVE BEEN...
...A COLD, DARK, LIFELESS PLACE LIKE HER SISTER.
SUCH A DELICATE BALANCE, LIFE.
DO YOU KNOW A FAVORITE HOBBY OF MINE, COLE?
I CAN HONESTLY SAY I HAVE NO IDEA.
WISHES.
"WISHES"?

SPACE DEBRIS. JUNK.

THERE'S SO MUCH MORE *GARBAGE* UP HERE NOW THAN WHEN I FIRST STARTED ENJOYING THE VIEW.

SOMEONE DOWN BELOW IN NORTH DAKOTA TONIGHT LOOKS UP AND SEES WHAT HE BELIEVES TO BE--

--YEAH, A FALLING STAR SHOOTING ACROSS THE SKY.

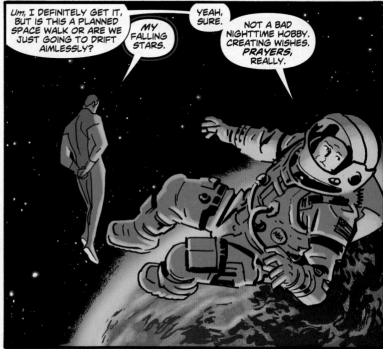

Um, I DEFINITELY GET IT, BUT IS THIS A PLANNED SPACE WALK OR ARE WE JUST GOING TO DRIFT AIMLESSLY?

MY FALLING STARS.

YEAH, SURE.

NOT A BAD NIGHTTIME HOBBY. CREATING WISHES. *PRAYERS,* REALLY.

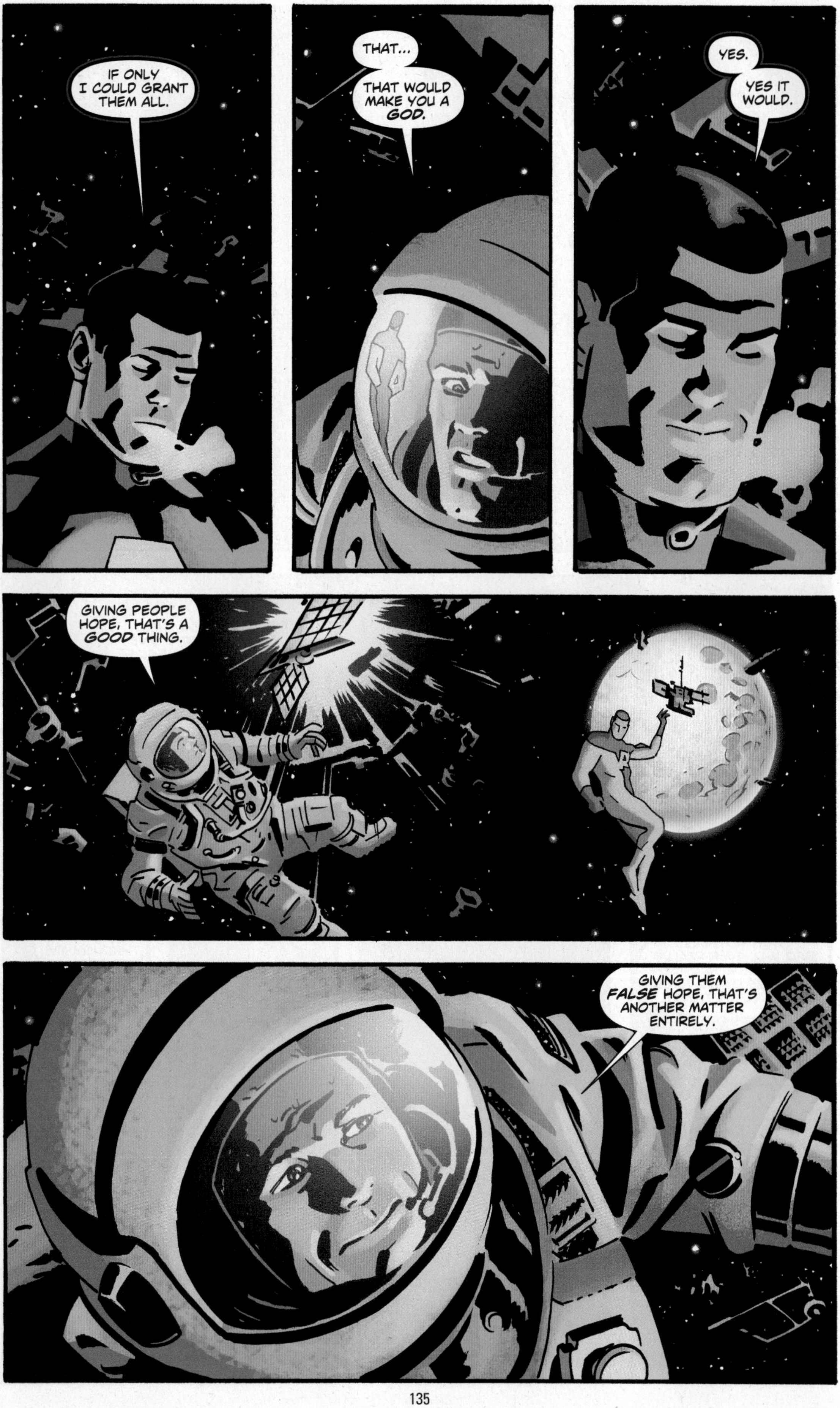
IF ONLY I COULD GRANT THEM ALL.
THAT...
THAT WOULD MAKE YOU A GOD.
YES.
YES IT WOULD.
GIVING PEOPLE HOPE, THAT'S A GOOD THING.
GIVING THEM FALSE HOPE, THAT'S ANOTHER MATTER ENTIRELY.

KRNCH.

IS *THAT* WHAT YOU REALLY THINK OF ME?

YOU THINK THAT I GIVE PEOPLE *FALSE* HOPE?

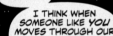

I THINK--

I THINK WHEN SOMEONE LIKE *YOU* MOVES THROUGH OUR WORLD, IT GIVES US A FALSE SENSE OF *SECURITY.*

THAT NOTHING *BAD* WILL EVER REALLY HAPPEN BECAUSE *DADDY* IS ALWAYS GOING TO BE THERE TO FIX THINGS.

A FATHER MUST ALSO *DISCIPLINE* HIS CHILDREN.

TEACH THEM THINGS THAT ONLY THE WISDOM BROUGHT BY PASSING YEARS WILL REVEAL.

I CAN'T EVEN *IMAGINE* THE PRESSURE YOU PUT ON YOURSELF.

EVERY DAY. EVERY MINUTE. WHEN DOES IT EVER *STOP?*

I COME HERE AND WONDER WHO ELSE HAVEN'T I SAVED? WHAT DISASTER DIDN'T I AVERT IN TIME?

ALL THE LIVES THAT HAVE SLIPPED THROUGH MY FINGERS...

AND ALL THE LIVES THAT *HAVEN'T.*

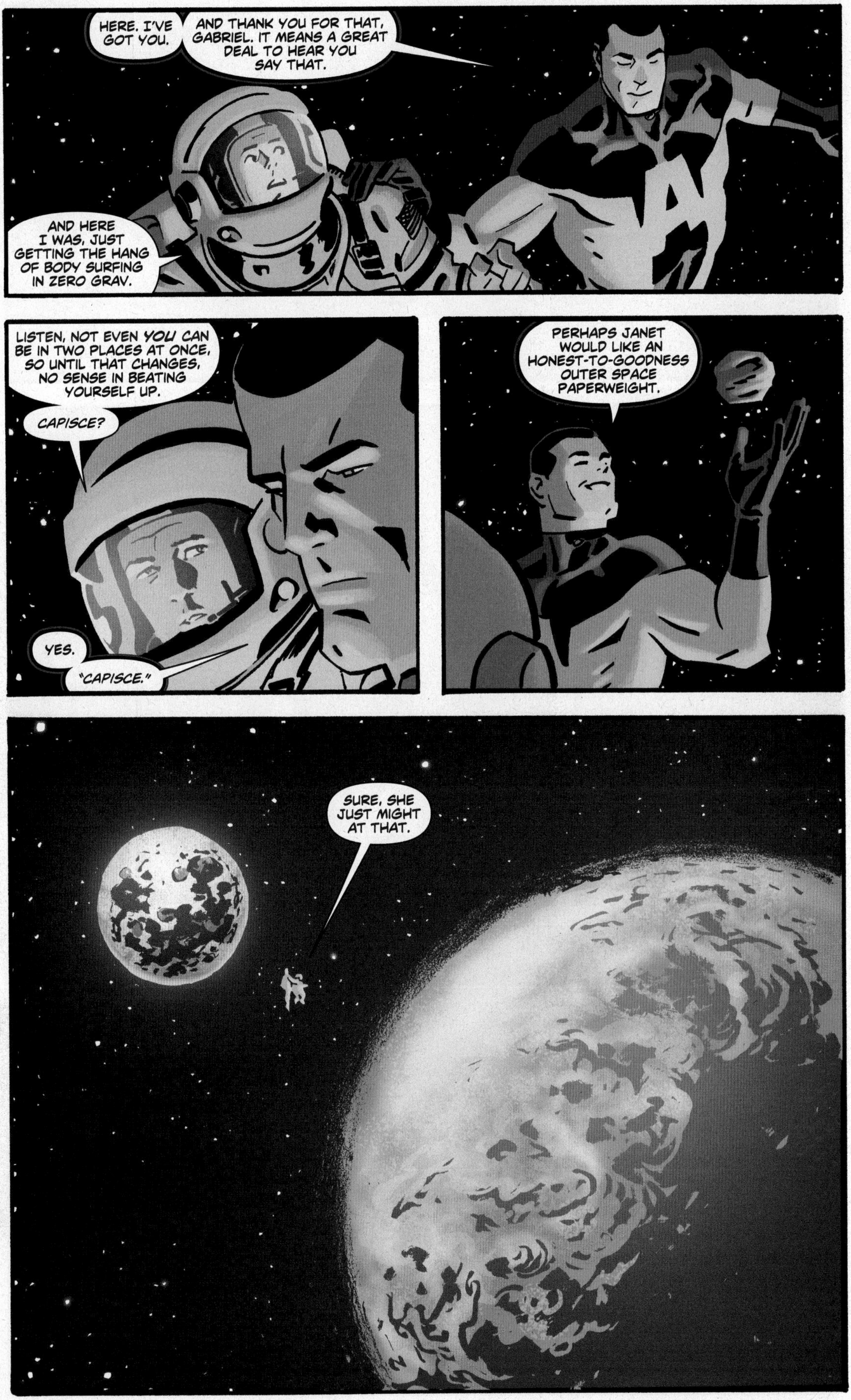
HERE. I'VE GOT YOU.
AND THANK YOU FOR THAT, GABRIEL. IT MEANS A GREAT DEAL TO HEAR YOU SAY THAT.
AND HERE I WAS, JUST GETTING THE HANG OF BODY SURFING IN ZERO GRAV.
LISTEN, NOT EVEN *YOU* CAN BE IN TWO PLACES AT ONCE, SO UNTIL THAT CHANGES, NO SENSE IN BEATING YOURSELF UP.
CAPISCE?
YES.
"CAPISCE."
PERHAPS JANET WOULD LIKE AN HONEST-TO-GOODNESS OUTER SPACE PAPERWEIGHT.
SURE, SHE JUST MIGHT AT THAT.

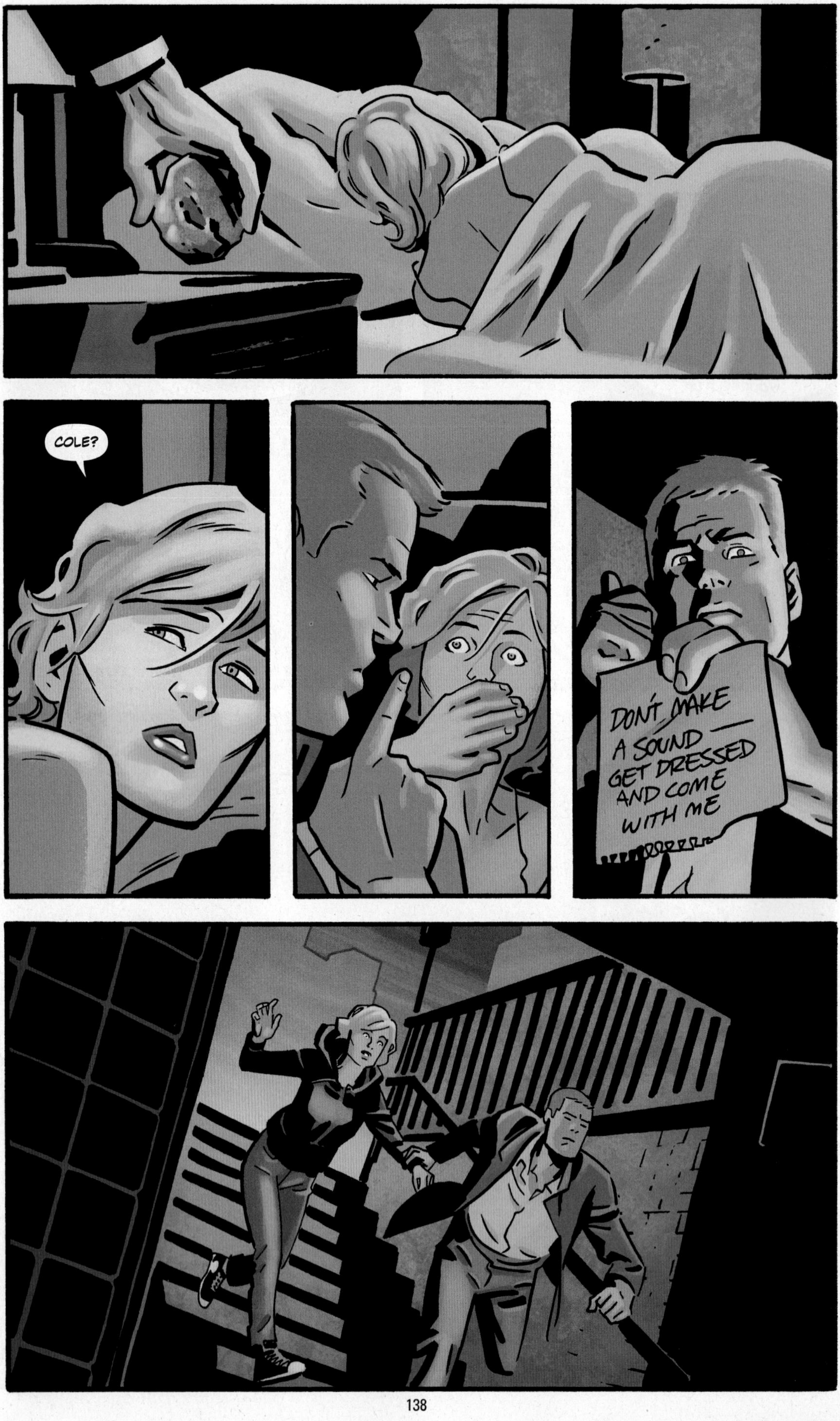
COLE?
DON'T MAKE A SOUND GET DRESSED AND COME WITH ME

NOW BOARDING, 14TH STREET. UNION SQUARE.

'LAKKIAKKLAKKLAKKLAKKLAKKLAKKLA

SORRY FOR DRAGGING YOU DOWN HERE IN THE MIDDLE OF THE NIGHT...

...BUT IT'S LIFE AND DEATH.

'AKKLAKKLAKKLAKKLAKKLAKKLAKKLA

YOU'RE SCARING THE CRAP OUT OF ME, GABE.

WHAT THE HELL IS GOING ON?

AKKIAKKLAKKIAKKIAKKLAKKIAKKI

THE NOISE OF THE TRAIN SHOULD MAKE IT SAFE TO TALK DOWN HERE.

AKKIAKKLAKKLAKKLAKKLAKKIAKKLAI

I HOPE.

AKKIAKKLAKKLAKKLAKKLAKKLAKKLA

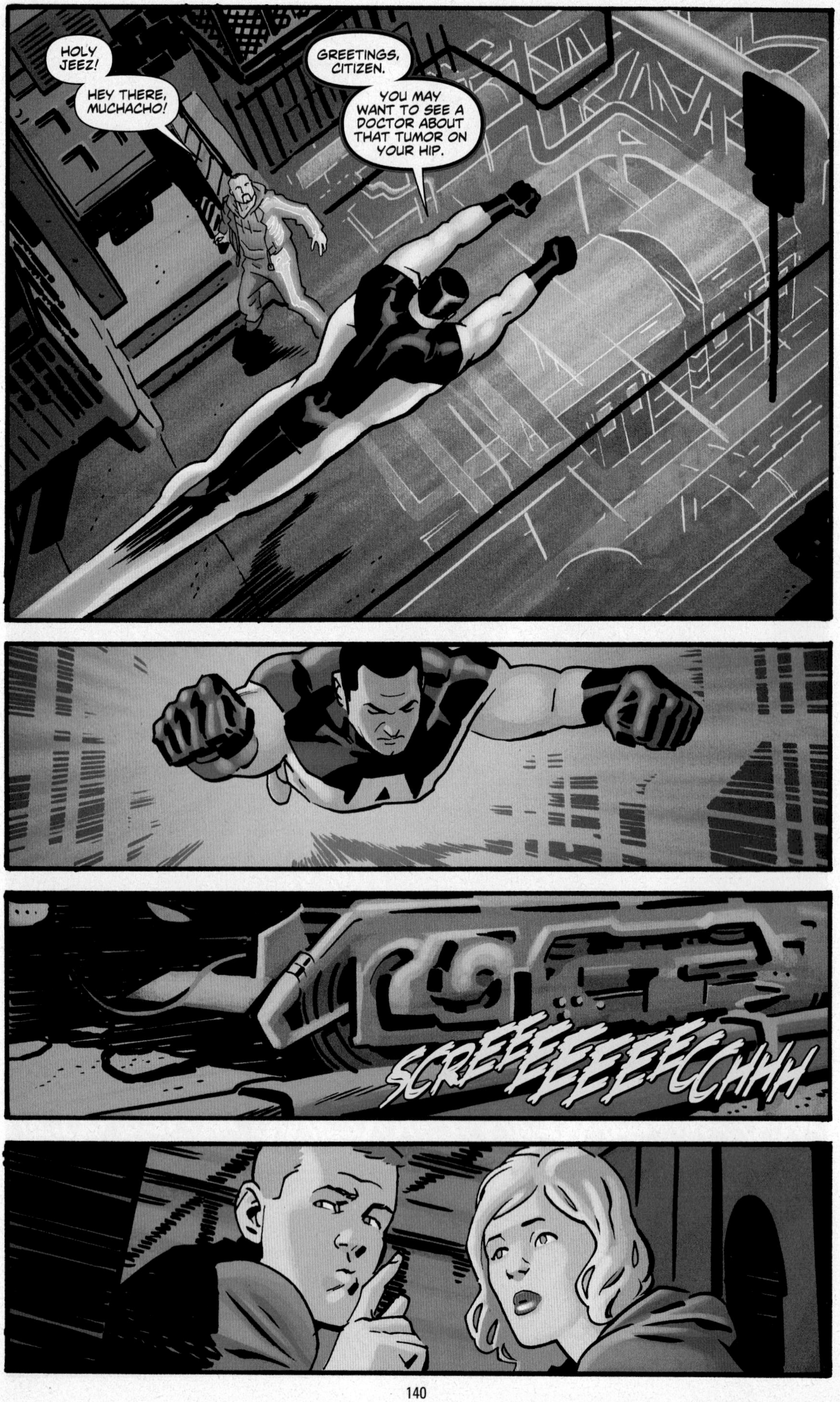
HOLY JEEZ!
HEY THERE, MUCHACHO!
GREETINGS, CITIZEN.
YOU MAY WANT TO SEE A DOCTOR ABOUT THAT TUMOR ON YOUR HIP.
SCREEEEEEEEEECHHH

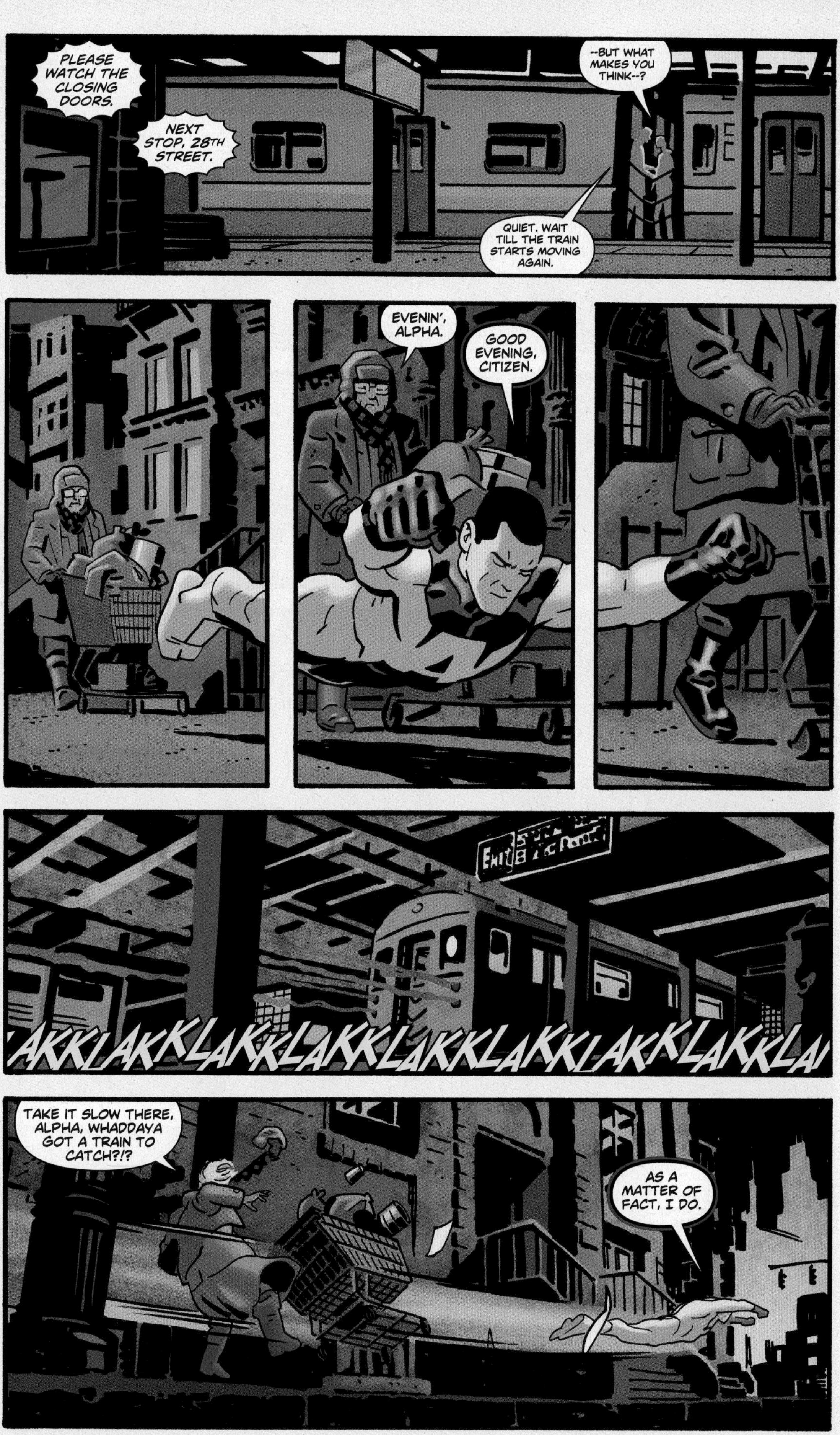
PLEASE WATCH THE CLOSING DOORS.
NEXT STOP, 28TH STREET.
--BUT WHAT MAKES YOU THINK--?
QUIET. WAIT TILL THE TRAIN STARTS MOVING AGAIN.
EVENIN', ALPHA.
GOOD EVENING, CITIZEN.
KLAKKLAKKLAKKLAKKLAKKLAKKLAKKLAKKLAKKLA
TAKE IT SLOW THERE, ALPHA, WHADDAYA GOT A TRAIN TO CATCH?!?
AS A MATTER OF FACT, I DO.

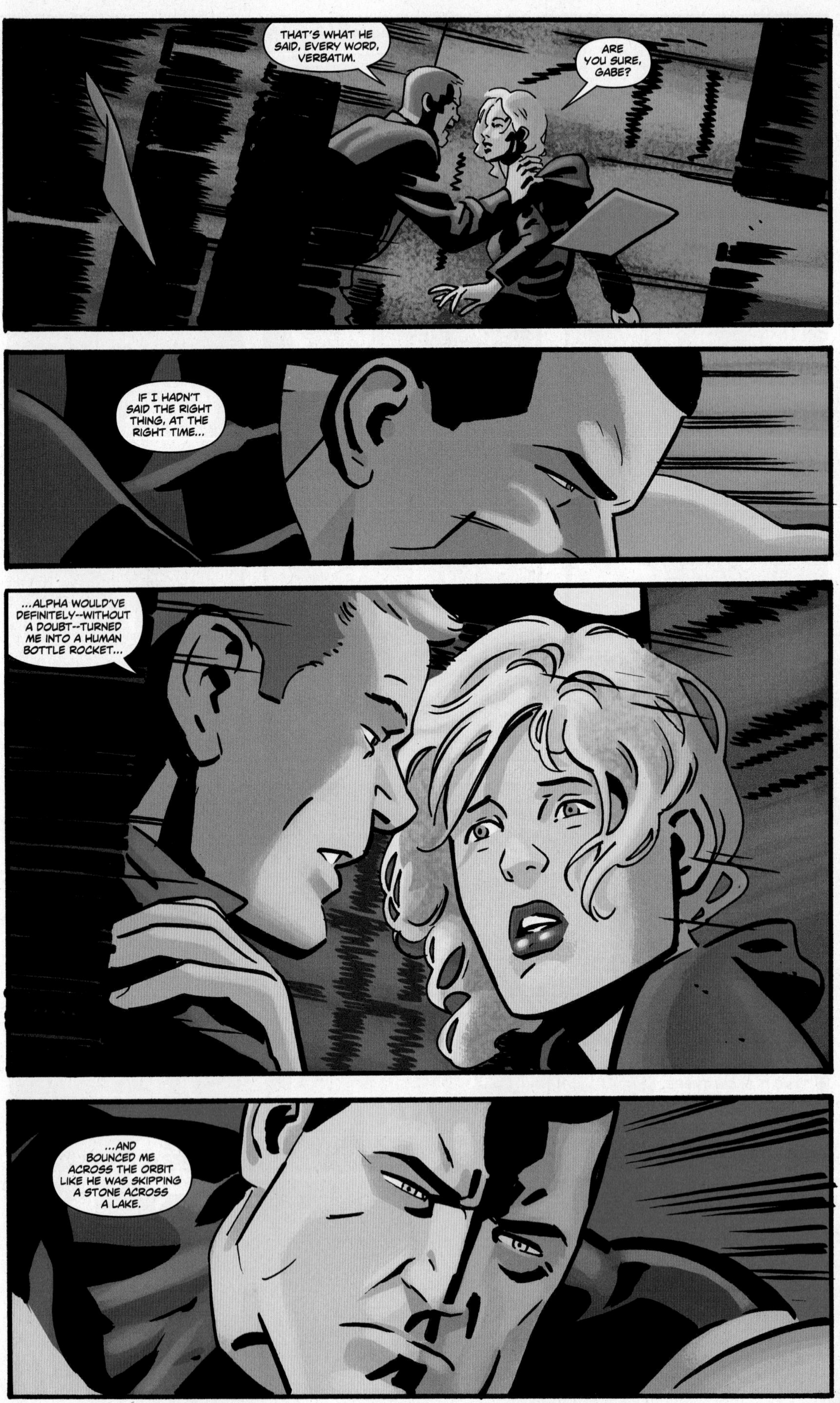
THAT'S WHAT HE SAID, EVERY WORD, VERBATIM.
ARE YOU SURE, GABE?
IF I HADN'T SAID THE RIGHT THING, AT THE RIGHT TIME...
...ALPHA WOULD'VE DEFINITELY--WITHOUT A DOUBT--TURNED ME INTO A HUMAN BOTTLE ROCKET...
...AND BOUNCED ME ACROSS THE ORBIT LIKE HE WAS SKIPPING A STONE ACROSS A LAKE.

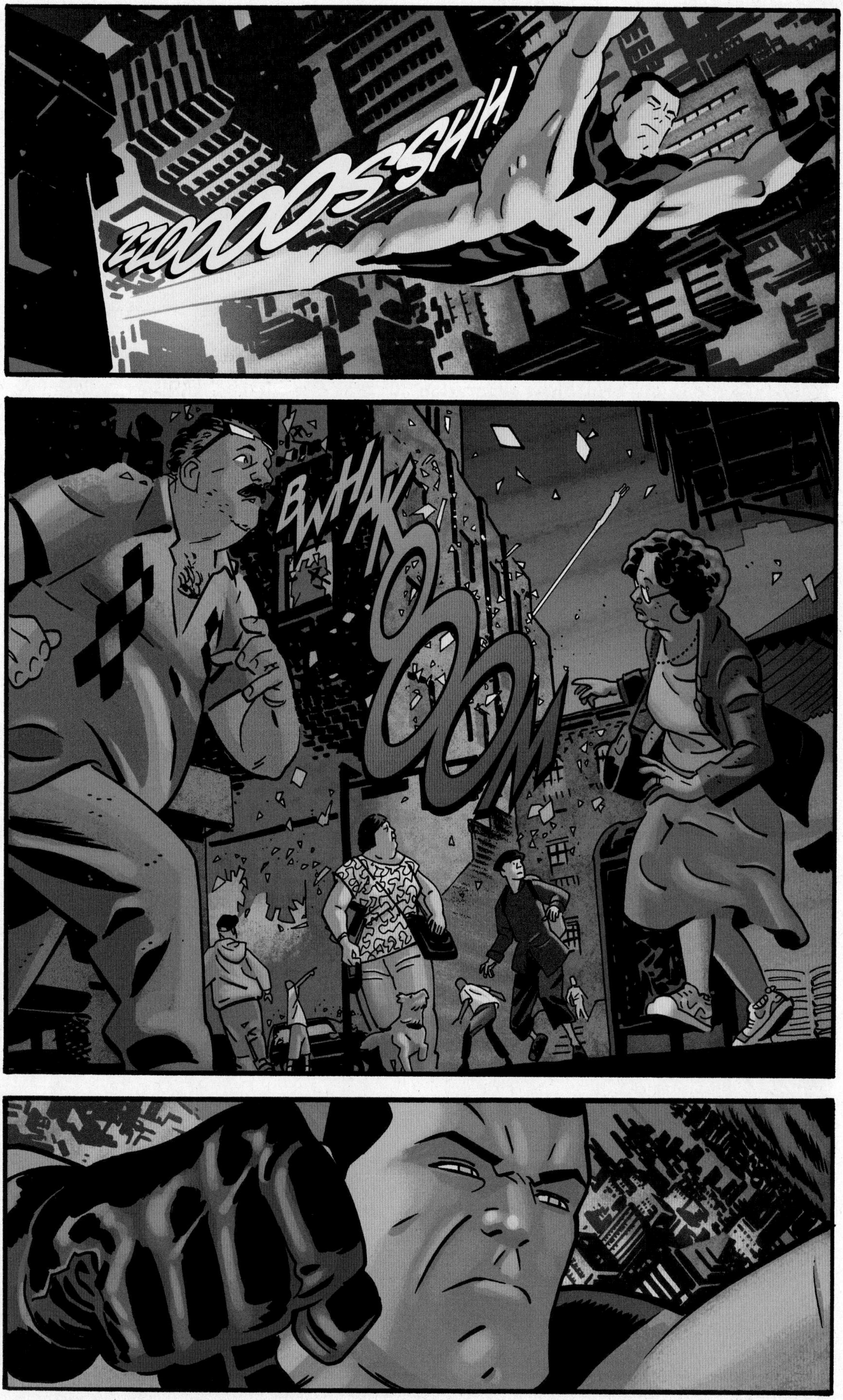
ZZOOOOSSHH
BWHAKOOOM